Vulgar Eloquence

Vulgar Eloquence

On the Renaissance Invention of
English Literature

SEAN KEILEN

Yale University Press   New Haven and London

Set in Minion Roman type by Integrated Publishing Solutions.

Printed in the United States of America.

Library of Congress Cataloging-in-Publication Data

Keilen, Sean.

   Vulgar eloquence : on the Renaissance invention of English literature / Sean Keilen.

      p.   cm.

   Includes bibliographical references and index.

   ISBN-13: 978-0-300-11012-8 (cloth : alk. paper)

   ISBN-10: 0-300-11012-X

   1. English literature—Early modern, 1500-1700—History and criticism. 2. Shakespeare, William, 1564-1616—Knowledge—Ornithology. 3. Whitney, Geffrey, 1548?-1601? Choice of emblemes. 4. English literature—Classical influences. 5. Orpheus (Greek mythology) in literature. 6. Milton, John, 1608-1674. Comus. 7. Mythology, Classical, in literature. 8. Nightingale in literature. 9. Renaissance—England. 10. Birds in literature. I. Title.

   PR428.C48K45 2006

   820.9′003—dc22   2005028850

A catalogue record for this book is available from the British Library.

The paper in this book meets the guidelines for permanence and durability of the Committee on Production Guidelines for Book Longevity of the Council on Library Resources.

10 9 8 7 6 5 4 3 2 1

FOR
The Academy of Tall Ears
docti furor

Nulli sit ingrata, Roma, quae dici non potest aliena, illa eloquentiae fecunda mater, illa virtutum omnium latissimum templum.
[Rome, of which no one can say that she is foreign, should not be unpleasant to anyone. She is the fruitful mother of eloquence, the richest shrine of all the virtues.]
—CASSIODORUS, *Variae* 4.6.3

I shall attempt to heap proof on you that whatever the agency—whether through Wyatt or Spenser, Marlowe or Shakespeare, or Donne, or Milton, or Dryden, or Pope, or Johnson, or even Wordsworth—always our literature has obeyed, however unconsciously, the precept *Antiquam exquirite matrem*, "Seek back to the ancient mother"; always it has recreated itself, has kept itself pure and strong, by harking back to bathe in those native—yes, *native*—Mediterranean springs.
—QUILLER-COUCH, "On the Lineage of English Literature (I)" 198

We can no longer do without the concept of the classical and we need not give it up. But neither will we renounce our right to illuminate our aesthetic categories historically.
—CURTIUS, *European Literature and the Latin Middle Ages* 250

In his or her experience of writing . . . , a writer cannot not be concerned, interested, anxious about the past, that of literature, history, or philosophy, of culture in general. S/he cannot not take account of it in some way and not consider her- or himself a responsible heir, inscribed in a genealogy, whatever the ruptures or denials on this subject may be. And the sharper the rupture is, the more vital the genealogical responsibility.
—DERRIDA, "This Strange Institution Called Literature" 55

Contents

Acknowledgments

I trace the origins of *Vulgar Eloquence* not to my dissertation but to three friends. John Kleiner first inspired me to let my curiosity take my research into strange places. Margreta de Grazia challenged me to find styles of thinking and writing that were adequate to the ideas and material that I discovered there. Paula Blank engaged my work as though she understood it from the inside of my thoughts; the stories about English literature that I tell in this book never seem so ingenious, worthwhile, or conducive to pleasure as when I hear them in her voice. John taught me how to frame this project. Margreta encouraged me to keep working at it patiently. Paula showed me how to finish and enjoy that work. These friends read every word that is printed here, and many more that were written and discarded. From beginning to end, this book is therefore theirs as well as mine.

Smart people generously gave their attention to different sections of *Vulgar Eloquence* as it evolved. I am especially grateful to Martha Rojas who, over the years, has adopted an attitude toward my work that is as consistently skeptical and incisive as her friendship is affirmative and tender. I thank Colin Burrow and Stephen Orgel, bright lights in the firmament of my graduate education, and Stephen Fix and Clara Claiborne Park, whose eloquence and love of literature moved me, at Williams College, to enter my profession. My colleagues at the University of Pennsylvania never failed to provide intellectual, moral, and financial support. For their encouragement and criticism, in a variety of ways, I am grateful to Charles Bernstein, Rebecca Bushnell, Shane Butler, Stuart Curran, Emma Dillon, Jim English, Joe Farrell, Michael Gamer, Anne Hall, Josephine Park, Bob Perelman, John Richetti, Emily Steiner, and Peter Stallybrass. Friends at other institutions also helped to bring my book into being, and for their indispensable contributions to my happiness and work, I thank Leonard Barkan, Colin Bayly, Kent Cartwright, Tess Chakkalakal, Bradin Cormack, Jeff Dolven, Elizabeth Harvey, Elizabeth Hersh, Bob Hornback, Rayna Kalas, Coppélia Kahn, Jeanne McCarthy, David Sedley, Bill Sherman, David Sullivan, Jennifer Waldron, and Sarah Werner. Bettina Smith made the bulk of the exquisite photographs that are reproduced in *Vulgar Eloquence*. There would be no book at all, of course, without the expert editorial guidance of Jonathan Brent and the staff of Yale University Press, especially Otto Bohlmann, and of Willa Rohrer at the University of Pennsylvania.

I was the beneficiary of a spirited and congenial colloquium entitled Literature and the Visual Arts that Leonard Barkan and Nigel Smith convened at the Folger Institute in 2003 and 2004; of the criticism of the members of the Northeast Milton Seminar in 2004; and, at various times since 2000, of conversations about my research at the History of Material Texts Seminar, the Medieval and Renaissance Seminar, and the Penn Humanities Forum at the University of Pennsylvania. While I was thinking and writing *Vulgar Eloquence*, I received fellowship support from the School of Arts and Sciences, the

Penn Humanities Forum, the Penn Research Foundation, and the Weiler Humanities Faculty Research Fellowship at the University of Pennsylvania; from the Huntington and Newberry Libraries; and from the Folger Shakespeare Library. The Folger Institute's colloquium, Literature and the Visual Arts, together with the year that I spent at the Folger Library as an Andrew C. Mellon Foundation Long-Term Post-Doctoral Fellow, decisively influenced the pitch and direction of my arguments in *Vulgar Eloquence.* So I am particularly grateful to Kathleen Lynch, Barbara Mowat, Richard Kuhta, Gail Kern Paster, and Georgianna Ziegler for creating an environment in which my thoughts could flourish; to Betsy Walsh and the staff of the Reading Room for expediting my research and writing; and to the extraordinary people who were fellows and readers at the Folger during a time that was, for me, transformative.

Introduction:
Fables of Literature

Diserto, *wasted, desolate, made a wildernesse, ruined, made desert, spoiled.*
Diserto, *eloquent, well spoken, of good vtternance.*[1]

This book is a reassessment of the terms in which the English Renaissance imagined its poetic activity. It offers a genealogy of English literature, in the sense that it describes the conditions that led to the birth of this concept during the late sixteenth century, and examines the myths through which Renaissance poets like Geffrey Whitney, William Shakespeare, and John Milton invented archaic origins for a new kind of writing. In particular, it examines three classical fables that English writers commonly used in order to articulate the rarity and excellence of their vernacular compositions; to distinguish their writing from Greek and Latin literature, even as they imitated it with conspicuous intensity; and to understand what it meant to fashion their modern texts from ancient materials.

Englishmen always wanted to be Romans, in order to be like their fathers; but at the point where my story begins in the 1580s and 1590s, at the moment when fables about Orpheus, Philomela, and Circe came to prominence as representations of English poetic agency, England's broader relationship to Rome was suffering an unprecedented strain.[2] During this critical time, the idea that Brutus, Aeneas's great-grandson, had sired English culture[3] was entering its final decline, as Reformation antiquaries discovered that the traces of a Roman presence in early Britain told a story that differed sharply from the celebratory legends of Geoffrey of Monmouth: a story in which a foreign empire conquered Britain, enslaved its population, and occupied it as a colony for nearly half a millennium.[4] Newly recovered texts by Roman authors and Roman artifacts taken out of England's soil corroborated this ignominious history of conquest and subjugation. At the very moment that Roman remains were more familiar and desirable than they had ever been, England's claim on them, and on the past that they represented, had never seemed more tenuous, illegitimate, and shameful.

I argue that this crisis precipitated the emergence of English literature. For when history obliged English poets to regard themselves as the victims of the Roman Conquest, rather than the rightful heirs of classical Latin culture, it also required them to redefine their long acquaintance with Roman literature in a radical way.[5] Searching for a new beginning, they paradoxically tacked toward the myths that Antiquity had used in order to express the origins and nature of its own poetic activity. And thus, as they reworked familiar fables about Orpheus, Philomela, and Circe, they not only reaffiliated themselves with

the Mediterranean heritage from which England had lately
been severed by the Reformation. They also invented a new
point of departure for their own poetic history.

Imitation may be a traditional way of thinking about
premodern writing, but by historicizing the activity of Renaissance writing in the way that I do, I show that the practice of
imitation has not been properly understood in its specifically
English context, and I reinstate its centrality as the basis of Renaissance notions of literary creation. In the ancient texts that
made them familiar to the Renaissance, Orpheus, Philomela,
and Circe are figures not only of poetic virtuosity but also of
conquest (Orpheus conquers animals, plants, and stones; Philomela is conquered by Tereus; Circe conquers men), and in each
case, they stand at the threshold between the human and the
animal order, or between civilization and wilderness (Orpheus
makes his music in the woods; Philomela becomes the nightingale; Circe turns men into beasts). In this pivotal situation,
they offered poets like Whitney, Shakespeare, and Milton a
framework for reevaluating the relationship between classical
literature and English writing, at a time when the humiliation
of the Roman Conquest was uppermost in the minds of English writers, and when the English language was ordinarily
distinguished from Greek and Latin in terms of its barbarity,
indecorum, and lack of cultivation.[6] The phrase "vulgar eloquence" in the title of my book points to England's deepening
attachment to Rome and to the widening rift between them in
the sense that it names what may well have been regarded as a
contradiction in terms. I also use this phrase in order to refer
to a matrix of complicated oxymorons that English writers internalized as principles of imitation, and thus to a kind of English writing that Orpheus, Philomela, and Circe came to symbolize for them: a writing that cleaved as much to the vulgarity

and wildness of its linguistic origins as it did to the eloquence and refinement of its classical models; a writing, moreover, that tended to expose the incommensurability of the different categories on which it was conceptually dependent (ancient and modern, foreign and native, classical and vernacular, Roman and English) and then attempted to commensurate them. In this context, I argue that the English literature of this period was distinguished by a lively hybridity; by a willingness to emphasize rather than dissimulate England's subaltern and relationship to ancient Rome; and by a tendency to synthesize antithetical concepts of origin and value in the process of creating the vocabulary of its own literary status.

> Setting aside the consideration of the more solid advantages, . . . the lover of true poetry will ask, what have we gained by this revolution? It may be answered, much good sense, good taste, and good criticism. But, in the mean time, we have lost a set of manners, and a system of machinery, more suitable to the purposes of poetry, than those which have been adopted in their place. We have parted with . . . fictions that are more valuable than reality.[7]

The originality and interest of my claims about English representations of Orpheus, Philomela, and Circe during this period partly arise from the disrepute into which the terms "literature" and "literary" have lately fallen as descriptions of Renaissance writing. In this book, I would reverse a basic shift that has occurred in Renaissance literary studies since Raymond Williams first suggested that it is historically inappropriate to describe vernacular writing in Renaissance England as "literature."[8] I mean the shift of our object of study from "literature" to "discourse," and from a concern with the fictionality of imaginative writing to a more limiting concern with its ideological features.

According to Williams, Renaissance English adopted the "general meaning" of the French word *littérature* when it identified "literature" with the "polite learning" that one could acquire by "reading" authoritative texts in Greek and Latin. "Literature," in this sense, "never primarily" meant "active composition," though it did refer to printed books as the material context through which the educational distinctions of "being able to read and of having read" were signified ("Literature . . . corresponded mainly to the modern meanings of literacy"). When he framed "literature" "[a]s reading rather than writing"—and specifically "as reading in the 'classical' languages"—Williams carefully distinguished it from "poetry" and "poesy" as "a category of a different kind": "a category of use and condition rather than of production," in contrast with "poetry," which the Renaissance reserved, in Williams's estimation, for fictional composition and for "making" generally. For Williams, it was during the eighteenth century, "within the basic assumptions of Romanticism," that "literature" absorbed "poetry" in its early sense, at the same time surrendering its dominion as the totality of human and divine learning. Only then was it "specialized towards *imaginative writing*" and directed to its place in "the modern complex of *literature, art, aesthetic, creative and imaginative.*"[9]

I would argue that Williams's claims about "literature" are governing assumptions of the way that we imagine the literary history of the English Renaissance—a paradoxical history in which the category of literature would appear to have been unavailable to English poets with respect to their own textual productions ("literature" is classical reading rather than vernacular writing) and to have subsumed every other kind of textuality within itself ("literature" is the condition of literacy and the sum of what can, or should, be read).[10] Observing that the concepts "literature and literary have been increasingly challenged, on what is conventionally their own ground, by concepts of *writing and communication*," Williams partly anticipated the turn in our literary criticism from "literature" to "discourse."[11] Arguably, however, even he would be surprised that this critical turn has come full circle, and that "literature" and "discourse" are commonly treated as though they were identical in meaning.

For example: When the editors of the *Cambridge History of Early Modern English Literature* gloss the title of their volume, they defend their use of "literature" on historical grounds, writing that they construe it "in the sense that it had in sixteenth- and seventeenth-century English, as helpfully detailed by Raymond Williams. . . ."[12] In fact, they go well beyond the boundaries of Williams's critical etymology. Where Williams argues that the Renaissance usage of "literature" implied a condition of learning that was inseparable from authoritative Greek and Latin texts, the editors of the *Cambridge History* use it, much more expansively, as a synonym for "the domain of all knowledge that has been preserved and transmitted in written form," including vernacular compositions from "the broad spectrum of what later would be classified as history, household advice, religious and political tracts, and much else."[13] Defining "literature" in this way, as every kind of discourse, they express a widely held conviction that "[a]ny treatment of literary production during either the English Reformation or English Revolution reveals how inclusive we need to be in addressing the full range of writings produced then, yet (until recently) rarely analysed in detail by literary scholars."[14]

The same assumption would appear to justify their preference of "Early Modern" over "Renaissance" as a term of periodization. Whereas "the word 'Renaissance'" restrictively "evokes a world of high or urbane literary culture, . . . humanism and the great revival of antiquity leading to the emulation of classical models for composition," they argue that the phrase "'early modern English literature' allows us to develop a more broadly inclusive perspective on literary history."[15] It would appear that in becoming everything, literature also became nothing in particular.

The impulse to define Renaissance "literature" in terms of the totality of all writing may be traced not only to Raymond Williams but also to the New Historicism. It has always been the theoretical goal of this "newer historical criticism" to address "the essential or historical bases upon which 'literature' is to be distinguished from other discourses," and to refuse "unproblematized distinctions between 'literature' and 'history,' between 'text' and 'context.'"[16] Yet in practice the New Historicism's effort to differentiate itself from older methods of interpretation—methods that it identifies with an attempt "to isolate a transhistorical aesthetic domain from didactic and instrumental categories of culture, [and] to separate a literary canon from historical, political and philosophical discourses"—has meant that it tends to "affirm . . . the *connections* between literary and other discourses," though it would "problematize" them too (italics mine).[17] The dilation of "literature" in the *Cambridge History* into "the domain of all knowledge that has been preserved and transmitted in written form" is only the latest stage in the transformation of our discipline according to the dictates of "a will to construe *all* of culture as the domain of literary criticism" and the premises of "the now-familiar assumption that the definitive contexts of literary interpretation are historical ones."[18] In a seminal article, Louis Montrose characterizes "the dominant mode of interpretation in English Renaissance literary studies"—that is to say, the mode that New Historicists, in the infancy of their movement, first defined themselves against—as a combination of "formalist techniques of close rhetorical analysis with the elaboration of relatively self-contained histories of 'ideas,' or of literary genres and topoi—histories that have been abstracted from their social matrices. . . ."[19] From statements like these, we may glean that though the autonomy of the author and of the work are the most celebrated casualties of the newer historical criticism, by no means are they the only ones. It would also appear that any literary history that does not address the social, political, and ideological bases of literary production is inherently deficient as a historical argument.[20]

In this light, it is not difficult to see that another important change has occurred in the assumptions under which we operate as critics of Renaissance literature. As the attention of our literary history has shifted from "literature" to "discourse," there has been a concomitant shift in our attitude toward the idea of history itself. Jonathan Crewe helpfully remarks upon this change when he defines the fundamental tenet of the New Historicism in these terms: "[N]o special criteria, no proper discourse, and above all no autonomy of the literary work are [to be] acknowledged in historicism, which accordingly seeks to absorb literary texts into the total ensemble of political discourses and/or ideological significations at a particular historical moment."[21]

The diversity and interest of the arguments that we can make about Renaissance texts may have increased as we have come to assume that the history of a particular moment is equivalent to "the total ensemble" of its "political discourses" and "ideological significations." At the same time, the expansion of our critical jurisdiction along these lines, to include all kinds of texts, social and political institutions, and categories of human subjectivity, could also be described as a limitation on the scholarly enterprise that we share; and in that sense, it is a sign of our poverty as well as our wealth.

What concerns me about the notions of literary history that are currently in favor in our discipline is the presumption that nothing (or nothing valuable) is lost when we make a scholarly virtue of "inclusiveness" and surrender to the "will to construe *all* of culture as the domain of literary criticism." Friedrich Nietzsche, commenting on "the historical sensibility" of his own time, remarked that "when we cultivate our virtues we simultaneously cultivate our faults,"[22] and it is in these terms that I would suggest that our literary history has run amok, although it has never been so fleet of foot or enjoyed so wide a range.

I do not think that it necessarily essentializes literature to argue, as I shall in this book, that the English Renaissance regarded the category of literature as distinct from other kinds of discourse and granted it a qualified autonomy; or to argue that the literary history of a given period is not reducible either to the history of literature's social production or to the history of its social productivity (however vast and complex those histories might be). In taking this position, I argue, in sharp contrast to the New Historicism, that the literature of the English Renaissance has integrity as an object of study, apart from the political forces that shaped it.[23] I also suggest, more generally, that it has not been entirely beneficial for the discipline of literary studies that we have taught ourselves to be reflexively suspicious of what Montrose calls an "autonomous aesthetic order that transcends the shifting pressure and particularity of material needs and interests"—even to the point of denigrating scholarship that tries to understand literature's claims to autonomy on their own terms, by characterizing it as "gentle/manly," "benignly patriarchal," and "conceptually alien" to the writing that it addresses.[24]

The word "aesthetics" belongs to modernity, of course, and it is therefore shrewd of Montrose to use it as a term of art for the older approaches to Renaissance literature that the "newer historical criticism" intends to supersede. Deployed in this way, "aesthetic" attaches a certain stigma to any literary criticism that declines to establish the social as the ground for interpretation of texts. In seeking to rehabilitate aesthetics as an object of study—and possibly it would be better for me to say "the imaginary" rather than "aesthetics"—I am not arguing for a less ambitious literary criticism. Nor, indeed, do I withdraw from the field of inquiry that has lately been enlarged by the critical methodologies that I would put in perspective. The account of the Renaissance literary imaginary that I offer here depends on precisely the rich range of non-literary materials that the New Historicism has made available to the discipline, including: historical and antiquarian writing; classical numismatics; mythographies and iconologies; theories of rhetoric, both ancient and modern; humanist pedagogical texts; even zoology. If, however, I ask how we might imagine the distinctive nature, and distinctive value, of literary writing during the English Renaissance, and if in that sense I resist the tendency of current scholarship to extend the literary across the Renaissance arts and sciences or to subsume it under a broader rubric of ideology or culture, it is because the notions of history, ideology, and culture that now inform the ordinary analysis of literary texts strike me as oddly positivist and, in that respect, as restrictions on the freedom and variety of our discipline. Though it goes without saying that this was never the destination that the New Historicism intended to reach, it is not surprising that when new avenues were opened to interpretation, others were foreclosed. Specifically: In creating a sense of the discipline in which a "genuinely historical" approach to literature came to be defined in opposition to "merely aesthetic" or "imaginative" ones, the New Historicism established a set of methodological constraints, and assumptions about the relationship between literature and history, that are (to my mind) as narrow as the ones from which it allowed us to break free.

Stephen Greenblatt's recent argument that "what we call ideology, . . . Renaissance England called poetry"[25] exemplifies the direction in which literary studies has been headed lately, and apparently it assumes that it is neither possible nor worthwhile to sustain any distinction between the human imagination and the social forces that influence its activity. I would suggest that the losses that we incur by adopting these assumptions are at least as significant as the benefits that we reap. The primary claim about the discipline of literary studies that I make in this book—that it is worthwhile for *some* literary critics to try to dislodge literature from the social and political contexts in which it was embedded, and in that way to lay foundations for different kinds of literary history—is an argument that our profession should be heterogeneous in the assumptions, resources, and methods that it brings to bear on its objects of study. It is also an argument for the historical contingency of literature as an artifact of the human imagination. Thus it exactly takes its cue from Jacques Derrida's epoch-making arguments that "the existence of something like a *literary reality in itself* will always remain problematic"; that "[n]o *internal* criterion can guarantee the essential 'literariness' of a text"; and that "even the convention which allows a community to come to an agreement about the literary status of this or that phenomenon remains precarious, unstable and always subject to revision."[26] Or to put it another way: Though I would restore classical literature and the practice of imitation to a central place in the literary history of the English Renaissance, I am interested in the mythology, rather than the truth, about the origins of England's vernacular literature. As a study of the genealogical imagination, this book stands in the same relation to literary history as historiography stands to conventional history, in the sense that it analyzes the efforts that English Renaissance poets made to invent, and reinvent, a literary lineage for their vulgar writing. By emphasizing the imaginative nature of the literary history that the English Renaissance fabled for itself, I try to emancipate literature from its bondage not to history but to a sense of history-making in which the past is nothing more than what our sister disciplines, history and sociology, perceive it to be.

I am, of necessity, equally concerned to liberate history from those same constraints and to fashion a scholarship that is both imaginative and historicizing. For it is noteworthy that in turning to classical fables about Orpheus, Philomela, and Circe in order to create a new past for its incipient vernacular literature, the English Renaissance was evidently capable of believing that the domain of history was defined by the exercise, rather than the absence, of poetic license. A popular emblem by Andrea Alciato held that "Antiquissima quaeque commentitia" (The most ancient things are lies) (see figure 1).

> Pallenaee senex, cui form est histrica, Proteu,
>   Qui modo membra viri fers, modo membra feri:
> Dic age, quae species ratio te vertit in omnes,
>   Nulla sit ut vario certa figura tibi?
> Signa vetustatis, primaevi et praefero secli,
> De quo quisque suo somniat arbitrio.

Antiquiſſima quæque commentitia .

Pellenæe ſenex, cui forma eſt hiſtrica, Proteu,
　　Qui modo membra uiri fers, modo membra feri,
Dic age quæ ſpecies ratio te uertit in omnes,
　　Nulla ſit ut uario certa figura tibi ?
Signa uetuſtatis,primæui & præfero ſecli :
　　De quo quiſque ſuo ſomniat arbitrio .

1. Proteus, from Andrea Alciato's *Emblematum libellus* (Venice, 1546).
By permission of the Folger Shakespeare Library.

["Proteus, old man from Pallene, you have an
actor's form, and now wear the limbs of a man, now
of a beast. Come, tell us: Why do you turn yourself
into all shapes so that, in variation, you have no certain form?" "I am the symbol of antiquity and of
primeval time, of which each man dreams as he
pleases."][27]

Sentiments like these presumably oblige us to see the relationship between literature and history, as it developed during the English Renaissance, in ways that reveal the limitations
of the critical vocabularies that we currently employ, despite
their ambitious scope. I do not mean to say that that the poets
that I examine in this book transcended the social and linguistic horizons of their period. On the contrary, my arguments
attempt to capture the brilliance with which they exploited the
ancient materials to which time and circumstance had bound
them. But if the wings that bear Icarus aloft are invented by his
father, and have a narrow range, it nevertheless belongs to him
to try to imagine a different course. It was in the context of an
attempt like this that English literature, and my arguments
about it, first took flight.

I see the possibility of success and profit in a method
which consists in letting myself be guided by a few
motifs which I have worked out gradually and without specific purpose, and in trying them out on a
series of texts which have become vital and familiar
to me in the course of my philological activity.[28]

When Donald Gordon wrote that it is "probably as dangerous to have too simple ideas about what the 'kinds' were for

the Renaissance poet as it is to forget them and their require-
ments," he was referring, in a general way, to assumptions
about genre and style that the Renaissance had inherited from
Antiquity and the Middle Ages.[29] His comment could be applied more particularly, however, to the late sixteenth and early
seventeenth centuries: the period when English literature first
took shape as a fusion of elements that were both native and
foreign, familiar and strange; and thus as a body of vernacular
writing that was conspicuous for being different from itself. If
questions of distinction and kind were of paramount importance then, it was partly because English poets continued to do
their work within the paradigm of imitation, despite the considerable blow that the Reformation had dealt to the prestige
of Rome and of Roman literature.[30] For these poets, the writing of vernacular texts was tantamount to the reading of classical literature (though the distinction between reading and
writing that Williams attributes to the period makes this feature of Renaissance composition difficult to grasp).[31] As a matter of course, they appear to have embraced an assumption
that Reformers like John Foxe promoted in another context:
"Things which be *first*, are to be preferred before those that be
later."[32]

To the extent that this recursive historical logic informed
even the attempt to differentiate vernacular composition from
its classical models, it pointed the way back to the classics—
where English poets found that Rome not only created a certain predicament for their writing, and for their effort to ele-
vate its status to literature, but also furnished a solution to that
problem. On the one hand, derogatory passages about ancient
Britain were scattered throughout the corpus of Latin literature. The most infamous of these occurred in texts whose authority and value were unimpeachable, like Virgil's *Eclogues*

and Cicero's *Letters*. Virgil remarked, for example, that the Britons lived so far from civilization as to be severed from the whole world ("penitus toto divisos orbe Britannos"); Cicero, upon learning that his brother was going to be stationed there, commiserated that the Britons were so backward that Quintus could expect to enjoy no literature, music, or learning among them ("ex quibus nullos puto te litteris aut musicos eruditos exspectare").[33] By describing the ancient inhabitants of the British Isles in these alienating terms, Roman authors became as inconvenient an obstacle to the desire to trace England's genealogy to Rome as the Reformation itself. But note: It was from classical literature that English poets could also glean the idea that Rome had once regarded itself as the cultural subordinate of Athens and regarded Latin writing as an inferior imitation of Greek literature. Here we arrive at a constitutive paradox of the literary history that the English Renaissance fashioned for itself: Apparently, it was the image of their own primitivism and barbarity that allowed English poets to recognize, ever more clearly, the Roman aspect of their vernacular writing.

Humanists like Richard Mulcaster answered the humiliating account of British antiquity that arose from classical literature by arguing that "eloquence it self is neither limited to language, nor restrained to soil, whose measur the hole world is, whose iudge the wise ear is."[34] Presumably, they took this position in order to imagine that there was a natively English tradition of poetic composition, separate from the venerable Roman literature that Mulcaster elsewhere praises as exemplary. But in the process, they came to depend on the authority of Roman precedent in a different sense. Mulcaster relies heavily on Quintilian's argument that excellence in speaking (as distinguished from the body of knowledge called "rhetoric" or "oratory") is a natural endowment rather than an acquired art—a claim that Quintilian makes, at the risk of contradicting Cicero, in order to defend Latin writing against the charge that it is inferior to Greek literature and inherently incapable of perfection: "Cicero, it is true, attributed the origin of oratory [*initium orandi*] to founders of cities and legislators [cf. *De inventione* 1.2], who must indeed have possessed the power of speech [*vim dicendi*]. But I do not see why he makes this the actual origin [*primam originem*], because there are nomadic peoples [*vagae . . . gentes*] even today who have no cities or laws, and yet people born among them act as ambassadors, prosecute and defend, and, indeed, think that some people are better speakers than others [*alium alio melius loqui credant*]."[35]

I imagine that it was surprising to English Renaissance writers that an author of Quintilian's stature would appear to defend Latin literature on the grounds that it was like the speech of nomads; surprising, too, that during Antiquity it was possible to regard Latin, the language that the English admired so intensely for its classical polish, as a vernacular tongue that was conspicuous for roughness and lack of subtlety. Nevertheless, they were quick to seize upon these ideas in order to establish, on a Roman foundation, the possibility of improving the English language and of transforming English writing into a vernacular literature. Roger Ascham argued, for example, that English writers should be not demoralized but inspired by the fact England now stood in relation to Rome as Rome had once stood in relation to Athens, for therein lay the opportunity to make English perfect, as the Romans had perfected Latin. For "if there be any good in [Latin]," he wrote, "it is either lerned, borrowed, or stolne . . . from some one of those worthie wittes of *Athens*." "*Poetrie*," by the same token, "was neuer perfited in *Latin* vntill by trew *Imitation* of the Grecians, it was at length brought to perfection."[36] Even Mulcaster, who was more critical of linguistic borrowing than Ascham, and who warned English writers against cleaving "to the eldest and not to the best," even he was moved to exploit the analogy that Ascham had framed: "I confesse their [the Romans'] furnitur and wish it were in ours, which was taken from other, to furnish out them. For the tungs we studie, were not the first getters, tho by leerned trauell the[y] proue good kepers, and yet readie to return and discharge their trust, when it shalbe demanded."[37] Mulcaster may lay a foundation for claiming that English and Roman eloquence are as different as the English and Italian ground from which they spring. But as he comes increasingly to rely on the analogy that Ascham draws between English and Roman eloquence, he changes course, allowing that, after all, it may be a Roman plant that grows in England's "natural soil":

> No one tung is more fine than other naturallie, but by industry of the speaker. . . . The use of such a tung, so eloquent for speeche, and so learned for matter, while it keepeth it self within the naturall soil, it both serues the own turn with great admiration, and kindleth in the foren, which com to knowledge of it, a great desire to resemble the like. Hence it came to passe, that the people of *Athens,* both bewtified their speche . . . & enriched their tung with all kindes of knowledge, both bred within *Grece,* and borowed, from without. Hence it came to passe, that peple of *Rome* hauing platted their gouernment, much what like the *Athenian,* for their common pleas, became enamoured of their eloquence, whose vse theie stood in nede of,

and translated their learning, where with theie were
in loue. . . . The *Romane* authoritie first planted the
latin among vs here, by force of their conquest, the
vse thereof for matters of learning, doth cause it to
continew, though the conquest be expired. . . .[38]

In this book, I shall have occasion many times to reflect
upon the relationship that Mulcaster posits between Roman
conquest and English eloquence.[39] For it is my thesis that, in
turning to classical fables about Orpheus, Philomela, and
Circe, English Renaissance poets were trying to come to terms
with the implications of a new historical dispensation for their
vernacular writing—a dispensation under which modern England was not the rightful heir of the Roman Empire, as Geoffrey of Monmouth had claimed, but the victim of a Roman
Conquest, the bastard progeny of a brutal rape. I shall argue
that these fables served English writers as "founding stories,"
linking the practice of poetic composition to the establish-
ment of human civilization; that they are tales told not only *ab
urbe* but also *ab eloquentia condita*.[40] But I shall also argue that
for English poets like Whitney, Shakespeare, and Milton—in
contrast to the French, Italian, and Spanish writers who adapted
them for different purposes—these fables clarified that the
origins of English culture, and of England's poetic excellence,
were tantamount to the experience of devastation. In attempt-
ing to transmute the leaden history of Britain's captivity to
Rome into a Golden Age of English letters, the writers that I
examine framed a paradox that continues to be meaningful in
our language to this day: namely, that ravishment is a condition
of transcendence (eloquence) as well as degradation (rape).

    When English writers began to fix their gaze on the mir-
ror of the classics near the end of the sixteenth century, they

saw a double reflection—double in the sense that they saw an image of English writing and of Roman literature staring back at them. In each case, it was an image not only of barbarity but also of perfection. This multiplication of perspectives on English and Roman kinds, and on their historical relationship, would not have been possible had the monument of Geoffrey of Monmouth's genealogy remained intact. In its fragmentation, however, it proved to be a loamy soil in which new genealogies were able to take root and flourish.[41] I argue that once it was possible to see that England and Rome were fundamentally different (as different, say, as a victim and a victor), it was also possible to see that they were fundamentally the same (different stocks, grafted through conquest into a single plant), albeit "the same" in a way different from what Geoffrey of Monmouth's synthesis had implied. The antiquary William Camden made this kind of argument about the mixed ethnicity of his contemporaries—though in this case he goes to considerable lengths to euphemize the fact of conquest itself. "In writing of these matters," he dilates, "concerning the Romanes government in Britaine, . . . whiles I consider . . . how many Colonies of Romans were in so long a time brought hither from Rome to lie in garrison, . . . who enjoying in marriage with Britans, both planted themselves, and also begat children here . . . I enter oft times into this cogitation, That Britans may . . . truely ingraffe themselves into the Trojans stocke, by these Romanes, who are descended from Trojans. . . . And meet it is we should beleeve, that the Britans and Romans in so many ages by a blessed and joyfull mutuall ingraffing, as it were, have growen into one stock and nation. . . ."[42] Diplomatically rejecting Geoffrey of Monmouth's argument that the first Britons were Romans because they descended from Brutus, Camden subjects history itself to the logic of poetic imitation, according to which the act of composition is preceded by the deconstruction and rearrangement of preexisting materials. In order to be put together in a new relationship, England and Rome first had to be taken apart.

It was in precisely this context that England's vernacular literature first arose as an "Englishe eloquence," the phrase that Richard Tottel used in 1557, crossing two different categories of origin and value in what must have seemed to be a novel way.[43] It is therefore not difficult to understand why the avatars of this new and English kind of eloquence included uncouth but copious shepherds (Tamburlaine, Colin Cloute), rhapsodic savages (Caliban), and aliens whose proficiency in the English tongue seems incommensurate with their evidently foreign origins (Othello, Comus)—to name only a few of the most prominent figures for the crossed kinds that the English Renaissance came to value to an extraordinary degree. Richard Hooker complained that "the mixture of those things . . . which by nature are divided, is the mother of all error," but as I shall argue in this book, mixture was also, evidently, the father of invention.[44] In their striking hybridity, characters like Tamburlaine, Colin Cloute, Caliban, Othello, and Comus were the scions of a new genealogy that English poets invented for their writing, as they meditated upon the fables that Roman authors had used, centuries before, in order to renovate their relationship to more illustrious Greek precursors. This is the genealogy, I mean, of the vulgar eloquence that appeared, in the preface to Thomas Wilson's *Arte of Rhetorique* (1553), in the shape of Hercules Gallicus: a half-divine, half-bestial man in whose brute strength Wilson followed Lucian in finding an image for the civilizing force of eloquence: "Such force hath the tongue, and such is the power of eloquence and reason, that most men are forced to yeld in that which most standeth againste their will. And therefore the poets do feyn that Hercules, being a man of greate wisdome, had all men lincked together by the eares in a chaine, to draw them and leade them euen as he lusted"[45] (see figure 2).

Later, in the pages of Renaissance emblem books and iconolgies, Hercules Gallicus was reborn as Hercules Musagetes (Hercules the Leader of the Muses), assimilating an epithet normally reserved for Apollo. Dressed in animal skins, he wields a lyre rather than a club[46] and represents poetic eloquence in a way that makes it hard to distinguish him from Orpheus, the offspring of Calliope[47] (see figures 3 and 4).

Vilia miretur vulgus mihi flavus Apollo
Pocula Castalia plena ministret aqua.

[Let what is cheap excite the wonder of the crowd;
to me, may golden Apollo minister full cups from
the Castalian fount.][48]

In reworking classical fables about Orpheus, Philomela, and Circe, it was explicitly the program of English poets like Whitney, Shakespeare, and Milton to distinguish their imitative compositions from the other kinds of writing on which they promiscuously drew, and to distinguish them as the *best* kind. If Williams is correct that "literature" is the word that the English Renaissance used in order to distinguish the textual remains of Greek and Latin Antiquity from the mass of modern, vernacular writing, then I would like to propose that "eloquence" is the name that the period particularly gave to the virtuosity of the classical tradition and, through imitation, to its own.[49] More than a synonym for the art of rhetoric, though it was that too, "eloquence" defines what the Renaissance re-

Imagine di Hercole appo Francesi da loro tenuto Dio della e-
loquenza, & dell'essercitio, qual fu da alcuni tenuto anco per
Mercurio & questa imagine dinota la forza della eloquen
za, & disciplina militare, massime in vecchi Capitani, &
consumati, oratori .

2. Hercules Gallicus, from Vincenzo Cartari's *Le vere e nove imagini
de gli dei delli antichi* (Padua, 1615).
By permission of the Folger Shakespeare Library.

cole della voce, e del canto di quelle. Coſi Eumenio, per ſer
uire al ſuo intento, il quale ſi ſerue ancora dell'eſſempio di Fuluio,
che nel circo fabricò il Tempio commune ad Hercole, & alle
Muſe. Ma è neceſſario, che l'Antichità ſi regolaſſe con altro
penſiero, poiche diede in mano ad Hercole la Cithara, & il Plet-
tro, come ſi vede in vn belliſſimo Cameo del gia Patr. d'Aquileia,
& nelle Medaglie della famiglia Pomponia, delle quali ſtà qui
ſotto l'eſtratto.

A car. 309
Lin. 25.   Hercole nelle Medaglie degl'Imperatori Diocletiano, & Maſ-
ſimiano ſi vede armato quaſi di tutte armi, hauendo di più in mano vn Trofeo.

In due

3. Hercules Musagetes, from Vincenzo Cartari's *Le vere e nove imagini de gli dei delli antichi* (Padua, 1615).
By permission of the Folger Shakespeare Library.

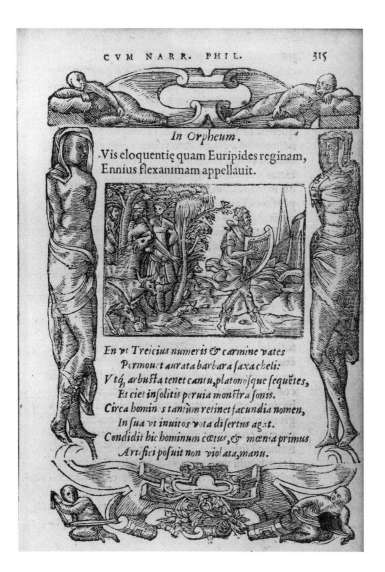

In Orpheum .

Vis eloquentię quam Euripides reginam,
Ennius flexanimam appellauit.

En vt Treicius numeris & carmine vates
Permouet aurata barbara saxa cheli:
Vtq́ arbusta tenet cantu, platonoʃque ʃequētes,
Et ciet inʃolitis peruia monſtra ʃonis.
Circa homines tantùm retinet facundia nomen,
In ʃua vt inuitos vota diʃertus agat.
Condidit hic hominum cœtus, & mœnia primus.
Artifici poʃuit non violata, manu.

4. Orpheus, from Pierre Costau's *Pegma, cum narrationibus philosophicis* (Lyon, 1555).
By permission of the Folger Shakespeare Library.

garded as the literariness of ancient literature, and it thus
evokes the wider vocabulary that the period used in order to
describe the superlativeness and excellence of composition in
general: abundant, rich, graceful, apt, trim, perfect, clean, copious, neat, fine, handsome, polished, exquisite, rare, fluent,
smooth, gallant, easy, choice, judicious, proper, elegant, fresh,
wise, learned, gorgeous, golden, and full of light.[50]

"Eloquence" comes from the Latin verb *eloquor*, meaning
"I speak," and right through the period with which I am concerned it retained a primary association with the utterance of
ancient tongues. In *The Scholemaster* (1570), for example, Ascham observes that "the prouidence of God hath left vnto vs in
no other tong, saue onelie in the *Greke* and *Latin* tong, the trew
preceptes, and perfite examples of eloquence, therefore must
we seeke in the Authors onelie of those two tonges, the trewe
Paterne of Eloquence."[51] In *The Petie Schole* (1587), a book addressed to the youngest pupils in the humanist curriculum,
Francis Clement reinforces this idea when he defines eloquence in terms of the "the gallant, eloquent, and learned
tongue" of Orpheus, a legendary organ that

> surmounted all other, so sweete, so smooth: so
> fayre, so filed: so gallant, so goodly: so passing, so
> pleasant: so leading, so learned. It entised, and pro-
> cured: it delited, and allured: it moued, & *rauished:*
> it pearsed & pleased: it persuaded, and preuayled
> with men, that in those dayes were in maner of
> brute beastes, wildely sparpled, abrode in fieldes,
> forrestes and woody places [italics mine].[52]

On the other hand, though the materiality of eloquence
was often described in acoustical terms—one commonplace
had it that "Eloquence is made by ayre; beaten & framed with

articulate & distinct sound"—eloquence was also, always, a property of writing.[53] As Martin Elsky has shown, it was an article of faith for Renaissance humanists that while eloquence inhered in the *usus loquendi,* or usage, of antique Latin speech, postclassical philologists and poets had to "depend exclusively on classical authors for [their] knowledge of [that] usage": authors who existed no longer as living voices but only as written documents. The humanist inclination to think of classical literature in these terms, as a "transcription of speech," made it easier for English poets, and English theorists of composition, to think of vernacular writing in a similar way.[54] In *A Discourse of Englishe Poetrie* (1586), William Webbe defines "poetry," via the Greek *poiein* and the Latin *facere* as "the arte of making: which word, as it hath alwaies beene especially used of the best of our English Poets, to expresse the very faculty of *speaking or wryting* Poetically."[55] Ben Jonson's precept that "talking and Eloquence are not the same, and to speake, and to speake well, are two things," is animated by the same assumption about poetic composition. Addressed to English poets, it is a distinction that Jonson would have English writers, as well as English orators, bear constantly in mind.[56]

The chapters that follow this introduction make a point of charting the process by which English poets turned *eloquentia* into eloquence, enlarging a category of excellence that pertained to ancient speech so that it included modern writing too. At the same time, each chapter examines the relationship between the conceptual thought of the English Renaissance and its "fabulous thinking," in the sense that I argue that classical fables about Orpheus, Philomela, and Circe provided the context and the texture of the emergent category of vulgar eloquence.[57] I focus on these particular fables because of the sheer propensity of English poets to refer to them. But I also focus on them, rather than the ubiquitous guides to vernacular composition by George Puttenham, Thomas Wilson, and Abraham Fraunce, because I want to acknowledge the contribution that ancient fictions made to the development of Renaissance literary theory and to the taxonomies of writing that the period enthusiastically framed.

Chapter 1, "Choosing Orpheus: The English Eloquence of Whitney's *Emblems,*" concerns Geffrey Whitney, the author of the first printed collection of English emblems. Although he is largely forgotten today, for Shakespeare's generation Whitney was a pioneer in rethinking the relationship between the verbal and the visual arts, and his book was a circuit through which the community of European humanists relayed its classical erudition to Renaissance England. I explain how Whitney came to use Orpheus, the preeminent symbol of classical eloquence, as a symbol for the origins of his vernacular writing. I also suggest that Whitney's poem "Orphei Musica" is a meditation on critical passages about the origins of poetry in Horace's *Ars Poetica*—where Orpheus is the first poet and associated with a time before the advent of human civilization. In this context, I argue that Orpheus presents Whitney's new kind of writing as though it were prior to the ancient literature that it imitates and of a piece with nature.

Chapter 2, "Shakespeare's 'Wild Musick,'" traces the nightingale's line of flight from Homer's *Odyssey* and Ovid's *Metamorphoses* to Shakespeare's *Sonnets* and *Titus Andronicus*. I argue that for Shakespeare and his contemporaries, who believed that eloquence had arrived in England with the Roman Conquest, the tale of Philomela's rape and mutilation served as a metaphor for the process by which the English poet encountered Antiquity's alien literary traditions, finding privilege through abjection and authority in surrender. I also examine the phenomenon of warbling in relation to vernacular writing, claiming that Renaissance poets regarded the natural variety of the nightingale's song as a paradigm of virtuosity for the emergent category of English literature, a kind of writing that characteristically flaunted its identity with, and its difference from, the classical tradition.

Chapter 3, "The Ancient Neighborhood of Milton's *Maske*," argues that John Milton's allusions to Orpheus and Philomela in *A Maske Presented at Ludlow Castle* (1634) constitute a critique of ancient authors like Virgil, Horace, and Ovid, and also of earlier English poets like Whitney and Shakespeare, and of the use that they made of Orpheus and Philomela as fables about their vulgar eloquence. I suggest that Milton uses Circe in order to represent classical literature and late Elizabethan writing as dangerous seductions. I also claim that he uses the trope of the forest (*silva*) in order to identify this literature and that writing with nature itself, framing them as achievements that (like nature) can never be repeated by the poet's art. As I bring my account of English eloquence to a close, I argue that the Lady's refusal to be ravished by Comus constitutes a rejection of the concepts of poetic agency, literary tradition, and textual value that Milton had come to identify with an earlier vernacular reception of classical literature and in particular with Shakespeare. Thus, at the conclusion of the *Maske,* the new and radical distinction that Milton would claim for his writing takes the form not of Orpheus's music, or the nightingale's song, or Circe's magic. Instead, it is expressed as an "aesthetics of silence,"[58] and as a faith in "some superior power" that Milton as yet has no language to describe.

To pose questions like "What kind of discourse is English eloquence?" and "How did it originate?" to classical mythology is to use the very materials and methods that Renaissance writ-

ers, following Ovid, preferred for their own etiological proj-
ects. In *The History of Britain* (1672), in an effort to rehabilitate
fables and myths for the genealogy of English culture that he
would construct, Milton recurred to the distinctions that ancient rhetoricians had drawn among mythical, probable, and
factual narratives (*fabula, argumentum,* and *historia*).[59] Although Milton could find "nothing certain, either by Tradition, History, or Ancient Fame" to establish exactly what happened in England during the period of its origin ("from the
first peopling of the Iland to the coming of *Julius Caesar*"),
"nevertheless," he wrote, "seeing that oft-times Relations here-
tofore accounted Fabulous, have bin after found to contain in
them many footsteps, and reliques of something true, . . . I
have therefore determin'd to bestow the telling over ev'n of
these reputed Tales; be it for nothing else but in favour of our
English Poets, and Rhetoricians, who by thir Art will know,
how to use them judiciously."[60] I have followed Milton's example in this book in order to distinguish my work from the
scholarship that illuminates it: in particular, from efforts to describe the historical distinction of English literature during the
Renaissance in terms of language, dialect, and diction; the literary career; the emergence of the vernacular canon; the history of the material text; ideology, politics, economics, and
"the social"; the Reformation; and premodern theories of epistemology.[61] At the same time, I have wanted to make a point
about the standards of our profession, and about the way that
we currently imagine the legitimacy, or illegitimacy, of certain
kinds of writing as scholarship. One reviewer of an early version of this project remarked that I do not "argue in the nor-
mal sense of the term." Presumably he or she meant that I do
not ordinarily make contemporary professional concerns, or
even contemporary readings of English Renaissance poetry,

the objects of my study. Another reviewer commented that my choice in this regard was "puzzling and a little disturbing." The unusual approach that I take to my materials in *Vulgar Eloquence* is a hypothesis that one way to understand the literature of the English Renaissance is to imitate it—a hypothesis, even, that we ought to aspire in our literary history and criticism to the poetic license that Renaissance writers took with their ancient sources. I hope that my style makes that proposition in a different way, for I would free philology in the way that I write and allow it, in its most basic sense as "love of words," to animate the work of literary studies, raise it up, and let it soar.

I
Choosing Orpheus:
The English Eloquence of
Whitney's *Emblemes*

The Force of Eloquence

The origin of something is the source of its essence.[1]

There is no time since Antiquity that Orpheus has not stood for eloquence. It may therefore be surprising to learn that he came to represent English eloquence only in the late sixteenth century—when vernacular authors first adopted him as an image of a certain kind of writing, different from every other kind by virtue of its relationship to the Greek and Roman classics.[2]

This shift is partly evident in Philip Sidney's *Defence of Poesy* (wr. ?1580, pub. 1595). "Nay, let any history be brought that can say that any writers were there before [Musaeus, Homer, and Hesiod], if they were not men of the same skill, as Orpheus, Linus, and some other are named, who having been

the first of that country that made pens deliverers of their
knowledge to the posterity, may justly challenge to be called
their fathers in learning." Here, Orpheus is a placeholder for a
larger claim about the epistemological value of poetry and eloquence: a way of arguing that poetry is the most authoritative
modality of knowledge, because it is the most ancient form of
communication—older even than Musaeus, Homer, and Hesiod, whose poems the Renaissance regarded as the earliest surviving examples not only of poetry but of all the arts and sciences. In this respect, Sidney invokes the Orphic convention in
an utterly familiar way. Unlike Homer, who belongs to history,
Orpheus is a myth, and so may symbolize the origins of all traditions, English as well as Greek. Sidney, however, also modifies the convention whose flexibility he exploits. Referring to
the material condition of his own art, he identifies the "charm-
ing sweetness" with which Orpheus "draw[s] . . . wild untamed
wits to an admiration of knowledge,"[3] with the pen rather than
the lyre, with *writing* as opposed to *song*. This is to make the
genealogical connection between ancient eloquence and modern textuality more precise than it had been, and in that way to
lay a foundation for using Orpheus, at a later date, as the representation of a privileged kind of English writing.

That day was not long in coming. Orpheus symbolizes
the eloquence of English writing, for the first time, in Geffrey
Whitney's *Choice of Emblemes* (1586), where he appears in the
pictura for the emblem "Orphei Musica"(see figure 5).[4]

The image places Orpheus at its center, surrounding him
with an entourage of beasts; then with a circle; and finally, with
a frame of arabesque ornaments, arranged in a square. Beneath the picture, printed scholia in the lower left margin of
the page echo the quadrilateral frame above. Framing the text
of the *epigramma*, the scholia draw the emblem's title, poem,

Ad eundem.

LO, ORPHEVS with his harpe, that sauage kinde did tame:
The Lions fierce,and Leopardes wilde,and birdes about him came.
For, with his musicke sweete, their natures hee subdu'de:
But if wee thinke his playe so wroughte, our selues wee doe delude.
For why ? besides his skill, hee learned was, and wise:
And coulde with sweetenes of his tonge, all sortes of men suffice.
And those that weare most rude, and knewe no good at all :
And weare of fierce, and cruell mindes, the worlde did brutishe call.
Yet with persuasions sounde, hee made their hartes relente,

Horat. Art. poët.
*Sylueftres humanes sa-
cer interprisfq;deorum,
Cædibus & fœde victu
deterruit Orpheus;
Dictus ob hoc lenire ti-
gres, rapidisfq; leones.*

E. P. Esquier.

Propert. lib. 1. de
Lino.
*Tunc ego sim Inachio
nectiar arte Lino.*
De Amphione Ho-
rat. in Art. poët.
*Dictus & Amphion
Thebane conditor vrbis
Saxa mouere sono te-
studinis, & prece blanda
Ducere quo vellet, &c.*

That meeke,and milde they did become,and followed where he wente.
Lo these, the Lions fierce, these,Beares, and Tigers weare :
The trees, and rockes, that lefte their roomes, his musicke for to heare.
But, you are happie most, who in suche place doe staye :   [playe.
You neede not THRACIA seeke, to heare some impe of ORPHEVS
Since, that so neare your home , Apollos darlinge dwelles;
Who LINVS,& AMPHION staynes,and ORPHEVS farre excelles.
For, hartes like marble harde, his harmonie dothe pierce :
And makes them yeelding passions feele,that are by nature fierce.
But, if his musicke faile: his curtesie is suche,
That none so rude, and base of minde,but hee reclaimes them muche.
Nowe since you, by deserte, for both, commended are :
I choose you, for a Iudge herein , if truthe I doe declare.
And if you finde I doe, then ofte therefore reioyce :
And thinke,I woulde suche neighbour haue,if I might make my choice,
In sta-

5. Orpheus, from Geffrey Whitney's
A choice of emblemes (Leiden, 1586).
By permission of the Folger Shakespeare Library.

and picture into apposition. While the picture shows Orpheus pacifying wild beasts with song, the poem extols him, his modern counterpart "E. P. Esquier," and eloquence itself for taming a "sauage kinde" that "weare of fierce, and cruell mindes, the worlde did brutishe call" (1, 8). Here, Whitney's emblem promotes a distinctively Horatian attitude toward Orpheus and eloquence, and the scholia refer the reader to an appropriate passage in the *Ars Poetica:* "Silvestris homines sacer interpresque deorum | caedibus et victu foedo deterruit Orpheus, | dictus ob hoc lenire tigris rabidosque leones" (In the days when men still wandered in the woods, | Orpheus, holy interpreter of the gods, | Taught us to shun the life of blood and killing. | Therefore there's the story of how his music | Tamed the ravening beasts, the lions and tigers).[5] Whitney's conspicuous reference to Horace is a gloss on the emblem's picture as well as its poem, for it tells us when and where Orpheus is, and it suggests what song he is singing. Finding him within the forest and among these beasts, we apparently find him at the occasion of his first song, the eloquence of which separates men from wild animals and thereby creates human civilization in distinction to the wilderness.[6]

As the emblem turns on this Horatian axis, it displays Whitney's sophistication in several respects. The Latin scholia affiliate his modern, vernacular poem with an ancient literary tradition. In this case, they present the English poem, "Orphei Musica," as the offspring of the *Ars Poetica* and Whitney as the vernacular heir not only of Horace but of Orpheus too. The scholia also commend the anthology to humanist elites in Leiden, where Francis Raphelengius printed the *Choice* at Christopher Plantin's press. In a prefatory letter to the reader, Whitney explains that he added the "sentences in Latin" to the second "edition" of his text (of the first, a single manuscript survives)[7] because they express the relationship between the book's ancient and modern elements as a decorum ("they beste fit the . . . matters I wratte of"). He also remarks that the scholia "helpe and further some of my acquaintaunce wheare this booke was imprinted, who hauinge no taste in the Englishe tonge, yet were earnestly addicted to the vnderstandinge hereof" ("To the Reader"). Addressed to the expectations of this educated, cosmopolitan readership, the scholia awkwardly acknowledge the provincial status of the English language. At the same time, they enrich its prestige considerably, making English poetry the object of a Latin commentary.

Whitney's references to ancient eloquence and to Horace are also references to the modern emblem books that the apparatus invokes more explicitly in other parts of the anthology. Orpheus first enters this genre in the *Pegma cum narrationibus philosophicis* (1555) of Pierre Coustau (Costalius), where he is the image of "Vis eloquentiae" (the force of eloquence) (see figure 4).[8] Orpheus appears in the middle ground of the picture, between a forest (teeming with animals and savages) and a city. He resembles the legendary poet Amphion whom Costalius depicts, three pages earlier, in an emblem titled "Pax" (see figure 6).[9]

Amphion sits beneath a tree, building a city out of song, but Orpheus sings in mid-stride, as he crosses the space of the image. His footsteps are a metaphor for the rhythm of his song, and his motion toward the city therefore makes visible a subtler transition that his eloquence effects in the silence of the picture: the original transition from the bestial to the human and from wilderness to culture. This is Orpheus as Horace describes him, a myth of social order and its foundation. This is also a picture of eloquence as Cicero imagined it—asking what power apart from eloquence could "unite scattered

In Amphionem.

Pax.

Musicus Amphion citharam dum pectine
pulsat,
Septifores Thebas condidit ad numerum:
Præstitit hoc concors modulatæ gratia chordæ,
Mænibus vt populum cingeret ille ferum.
Sic diuina statum concordia continet vrbis,
Et ligat vnanimi barbara corda fide.

6. Amphion, from Pierre Costau's *Pegma, cum narrationibus
philosophicis* (Lyon, 1555).
By permission of the Folger Shakespeare Library.

people in one place or, from the life of savages, bring them to
our pitch of cultivation as men and citizens?"[10] The allusion to
Cicero is more emphatic in the final lines of the emblem's
poem, which credits eloquence with the invention of human
community: "[facundia] Condidit hic hominum coetus, et
moenis primus I Artifici posuit non violata, manu" ([Elo-
quence][11] formed this human congress, and first set down its
walls, untouched by the hand of the workman). In 1564,
Thomas Palmer sought to make the Ciceronian subtext of the
emblem clearer still, pasting Costalius's picture of Orpheus
into a notebook above his own verse translation of *De oratore*
1.8.33: "Men in olde time were housde like beastes . . . I Vntill
the eloquente steppes oute, I and with well spoken sowne, I
Broughte those dispersed soules in one, I and walde them in a
towne."[12]

Costalius's word for human community is "coetus," which
refers to an assembly of people but also to sexual congress. The
verb *condere* means "to establish or found"—as in Livy's mon-
umental history of Rome, *Ab urbe condita*—but it also means
"to compose," particularly in the sense of writing.[13] The resonant conflation of these different meanings, organic and artificial, invokes a commonplace of Renaissance aesthetics, according to which every composition is an imitation, and all
imitations bespeak a family relationship: "We can," observes
Seneca, "choose whose children we would like to be."[14] In this
context, the representation of human beginnings in Costalius's emblem perforce represents the genealogy ("coetus") of
an aesthetic category ("facundia") that the author associates
with the materiality of written composition ("Condidit"), on
the one hand, and with the intangibility of the spoken word
on the other (the city's walls, he insists, were "untouched [un-
hewn] by the maker's hand"). Here, the emblem expresses its

preeminent concern not only with the origins of human civilization but also with the origins of a certain kind of writing and thus with its own status as a text. For Costalius, the power of eloquence inheres in its ability to organize the material world like a well-made composition—or perhaps like a "literature," the word that Henry Bradshaw uses as a synonym for "eloquence" in 1513, complaining that "[t]he comyn people" are "without lytterature and good informacyon" and therefore "[b]en like to Brute beestes."[15] As it distinguishes person from beast, culture from nature, and order from chaos, eloquence ("eloquentia," "facundia," "disertus") comes to signify distinction itself. According to a French version of the Latin poem (1560), it "is the force that enables every heart to know its place."[16]

Creating Orpheus

Orpheus . . . est vestustissimus poetarum, et aequalis ipsorum deorum. [17]

[Orpheus . . . is the most ancient of poets, and a contemporary of the gods themselves.]

In contrast to the ageless poet in Whitney's *Choice of Emblemes*, Costalius's *Pegma* represents Orpheus as an old man. His advanced age seems to contradict the uncanny vigor of his eloquence, but for a Renaissance audience, this picture would likely not have seemed to be "an interlude of age at the wrong time."[18] To the contrary: The beard, slight stoop, and wizened aspect of the figure in this context would have suggested his potency as clearly as the lyre extending from his groin. Orpheus appears to be an elderly man because he is an avatar of eloquence and represents human language and civilization in

an utterly archaic condition. According to the emblem's ge-
nealogistics and its recursive sense of value (the older the better), Orpheus's antiquity is the sign of his eloquence and its
power, and vice versa. The poet can compose a city out of
rocks and a people out of beasts because, in this primeval
scene, time has not yet separated words from things. To compose language is therefore to compose the natural world: Reality is what it is because Orpheus, like Adam, says so.

Or perhaps not like Adam. In this emblem Orpheus is
making the world, rather than *describing* it. Sixteenth-century
readers might have recognized in Orpheus's cap, sash, and
beard a figure of even greater antiquity, creative power, and authority than Adam: God himself. The picture of Orpheus in
the *Pegma* has been attributed to Pierre Vase,[19] who was active
in Lyon in the 1550s and collaborated with the printers Guillaume Rouille and Macé Bonhomme on a variety of illustrated
books, including the *Emblemata omnia* of Andrea Alciato
(1550). Significantly for our purposes, Vase would have known
the series of woodcuts that Bernard Salomon ("Le Petit Bernard") designed for *Les oeuvres de Clement Marot* (1549), published by another Lyonnais printer, Jean de Tournes. This collection includes a translation of the first two books of Ovid's
Metamorphoses. In the illustrations for that text, Jupiter's distinction, as the King of Heaven, is marked by a crown, a sash,
and a beard (see figure 7).

Let us follow the thread of this resemblance and see
where it leads. Jupiter is the youngest child of Kronos and
Rhea, but Salomon's iconography underscores his paradoxical
seniority among the Olympian gods, recasting him as the father that he violently displaced and as the grandfather (Uranus)
who was castrated and displaced by his son before him. In a
less predictable turn, the artist conflates the Jupiter figure with

Et pour garder enseigne de la race
En feit des corps portans humaine face:
Mais ceste gent fut aspre & despiteuse,
Blasmant les Dieux, de meurdres couuoiteuse:
Si qu'à la voir, bien l'eussiez deuinée
Du cruel sang des Geants estre née.

Cecy voyant des hauts cieux Iuppiter,
Crie, gemit, se prend à despiter,
Et sur le champ par luy fut allegué
Vn autre faict, non encor diuulgué,
Des banquets pleins d'horreur espouentable,
Que Lycaon preparoit à sa table:
Dont en son cueur ire va conceuoir
Telle qu' vn Roy, comme luy, peult auoir:
Et son conseil appella hautement,
Dont les mandez vindrent subitement.

7. Jupiter and the Giants, from *Les oeuvres
de Clement Marot* (Lyon, 1551).
By permission of the Folger Shakespeare Library.

the nameless "deus" to whom Ovid attributes the creation of the world. In contrast to Judeo-Christian theology, this creation occurs *ex materia*, from "rudis indigestaque moles" (a shapeless mass of rough, disordered stuff), represented in the second illustration to Marot's translation.[20] From that point, composition unfolds as a process of division and classification: "quisquis fuit ille deorum, I congeriem secuit sectamque in membra redegit" (whoever the god was, he divided that mass and when it was divided, gathered it into parts).[21] When Salomon imposes the sun and moon and the Greek word "ΧΑΟΣ" on this swirling cloud of lines, he preempts the god who arrives in the fifth picture to organize the world by giving distinction to undistinguished matter. In effect, he claims for himself the authority and privilege of making the original composition (see figure 8).

Salomon also uses the image of this pagan god for another text: Claude Paradin's *Quadrins historiques de la Bible* (1553). This book is an anthology of illustrated, verse summaries of episodes from the Old Testament; de Tournes published it simultaneously in an English translation, *The true and lyuely historyke purtreatures of the woll Bible*. Here, the distinctive crown, sash, and beard identify the Judeo-Christian God, Yahweh. The first woodcut in the *Quadrins* opens on the creation of Adam, inscribing the history of the whole world within human history, the cosmos within its microcosm (see figure 9).

This picture is more elaborate than Salomon's earlier, Ovidian image of creation, but it retains some of its most important features. In addition to God's familiar crown, sash, and beard, the sky is divided into day (right) and night (left), while the sea (in the background) is divided from solid earth (in the foreground). By conflating the creation of the universe

A commencer depuis le premier naistre
Du Monde rond, iusqu'au teps de mon estre.

Auãt la Mer, la Terre, & le grãd Oeuure
Du Ciel treshault, qui toutes choses cœuure,
Il y auoit en tout ce Monde enorme
Tant seulement de Nature vne forme,
Ditte Chaos, vn monceau amaßé,
Gros, grand & lourd, nullement compaßé.
Brief, ce n'estoit qu'vne pesanteur vile
Sans aucun art, vne maße immobile,
Là ou gisoient les semences encloses,
Desquelles sont produites toutes choses,
Qui lors estoient ensemble mal couplées,
Et l'vne en l'autre en grand discord troublées.
Aucun Soleil encores au bas Monde
N'eslargißoit lumiere claire & monde:
La Lune außi ne se renouuelloit,
Et ramener ses cornes ne souloit

8. Chaos, from *Les oeuvres de Clement Marot* (Lyon, 1551).
By permission of the Folger Shakespeare Library.

God the heauen mad in the beginning,
The earth and sea withall in perfitnes,
The moone and sonne in the skie bright shining,
Adam after mad to his one licknes.

9. The creation of Adam, from Claude Paradin's *The true and lyvely
historyke purtreatures of the woll Bible* (Lyon, 1553).
By permission of the Folger Shakespeare Library.

(from nothing) with the creation of Adam (from dust), the woodcut articulates, in a biblical context, a characteristically Ovidian argument about composition. In contrast to Ovid's *deus,* the Judeo-Christian God creates ex nihilo and by fiat. Salomon's picture of Chaos is therefore not reused for this sequence. But in its place, the new woodcut suggests that all composition still fundamentally depends on matter: Yahweh looks like Ovid's *deus,* and like him, he composes the world by dividing it into different parts.[22]

Salomon's willingness to blend pagan and Judeo-Christian mythologies of origin was more overt by the late 1550s. In 1557 and 1559, he reused his Ovidian image of creation for two translations of the *Metamorphoses: La Métamorphose d'Ovide figurée* and Gabriele Symeoni's *La Vita et Metamorfoseo d'Ovidio* (see figures 10 and 11).

These books increase the number of woodcuts in *Les oeuvres de Clement Marot* fourfold, giving them new titles, verse texts, and ornamental frames.[23] The image of Chaos is conspicuously absent from *La Métamorphose . . . figurée,* and this absence may indicate a continuing effort to reconcile Ovid to Genesis, and vice versa. The same thing can be said of the second picture in the sequence, "La creacion de l'Homme," which is copied not from Marot's translation of *Metamorphoses* 1 but from Paradin's *True and lyuely historyke purtreatures* (see figures 12 and 13).

On the other hand, it could also be argued that "La creacion du Monde" depicts Chaos by other means. Here, the distortion of grotesque figures in the new frame implies the primordial confusion of matter whose picture has vanished from the sequence. The discomposure of these bodies also serves to emphasize, in the negative, the excellence of the composition that is taking place within the picture. When Salomon used

La creacion du Monde.

Eſtant premier tout ce grand vniuers
En un chaos, confus, lourd & ſans forme,
Les Elemens l'un à l'autre diuers
N'auoient quùm lieu en repugnance enorme:
Mais ce diſcord Dieu promptement reforme,
Les ſeparant en diſtance locale:
Puis d'un moyen à ſa grandeur conforme
Les lia tous en paix concordiale.

a 3

10. The creation of the world, from *Métamorphose d'Ovide figurée*
(Lyon, 1557). By permission of the Douglas H. Gordon Collection of
French Books, Special Collections, University of Virginia Library.

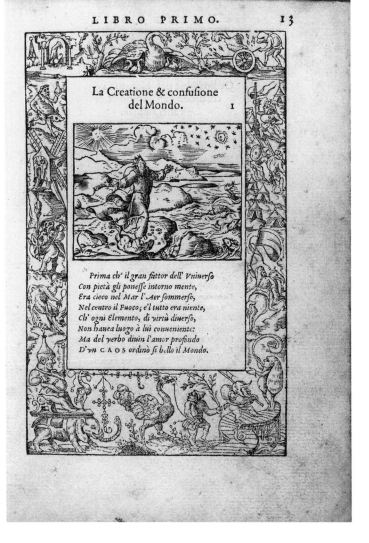

La Creatione & confusione
del Mondo.   1

Prima ch' il gran fattor dell' Vniuerſo
Con pietà gli poneſſe intorno mente,
Era cieco nel Mar l'Aer ſommerſo,
Nel centro il Fuoco; e'l tutto era niente,
Ch' ogni Elemento, di virtù diuerſo,
Non hauea luogo à lui conueniente:
Ma del verbo diuin l'amor profondo
D'vn CAOS ordinò ſi bello il Mondo.

11. The creation and confusion of the world, from Gabriele Simeoni's *La vita et Metamorfoseo d'Ovidio* (Lyon, 1559).
By permission of the Folger Shakespeare Library.

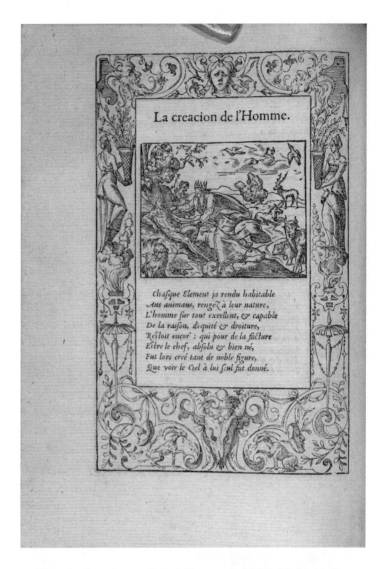

12. The creation of man, from *Métamorphose d'Ovide figurée* (Lyon, 1557). By permission of the Douglas H. Gordon Collection of French Books, Special Collections, University of Virginia Library.

With liuing ghoaſt god mad Adam to liue,
Permitting him to maintain in his breath:
To eate of all except the frute of liue,
Wiche did forbid vnder the pain of death.

13. God breathes life into Adam, from Claude Paradin's *The true
and lyvely historyke purtreatures of the woll Bible* (Lyon, 1553).
By permission of the Folger Shakespeare Library.

this frame again in 1559, for Symeoni's translation of Ovid, he placed a new picture of Chaos on the previous page, as the book's first image (see figure 14).

Falling between "Chaos" and "La creacion du Monde," the frame marks the transition from a totally disordered matter to the orderly world that God composes from it. At the same time, in this new situation, the frame insists on the relationship between matter and the artist: It presents God as the reflection of Chaos and so anticipates Milton's tendency, in *Paradise Lost* (1667), to associate God's infinitude with the indeterminacy of Chaos: "Boundless the Deep, because I am who fill I Infinitude."[24]

It makes sense that Salomon would choose to identify his work with God's. Like Virgil Solis after him, he engages the *Metamorphoses* and Genesis as though they were meditations on his own art. The lines and shapes that Salomon cuts out of wood trace their origins to the creation of the world, where composition is a process of increasingly refined delineations: day from night, land from sky and water, human beings from animals, women from men, and—in Ovid's case—age from age (Gold, Silver, Bronze, and Iron). The fact that this account of creation descended from two ancient sources would have made it doubly prestigious as a story about the origins of Salomon's practice as an illustrator (the conflict of those sources notwithstanding).[25]

It was the achievement of Costalius and Vase, however, to extend Salomon's analogy between the creation of the world and woodcut lines to verbal composition and lines of verse. While Orpheus appears in Salomon only as a young man, in *Pegma* he is an old man and an image of eloquence in order to translate rhetoric's preeminent term for excellence (*eloquentia*) from speech to written poetry and, in the process, to affili-

14. Chaos, from Gabriele Simeoni's *La vita et Metamorfoseo d'Ovidio* (Lyon, 1559).
By permission of the Folger Shakespeare Library.

ate that distinctive kind of writing with the textual authority of the Bible and *Metamorphoses,* as with the ageless authority and value of God's original creation (see figure 15).

Looking again at the picture of "Vis eloquentiae" we find the elements of Salomon's meditation on visual composition and its origins applied specifically to verbal art (see figure 4). Here, but for his lyre, Orpheus resembles God. The city at the right side of the picture is an ordered composition. Where, however, has that city come from? Not from nothing, nor from speech alone: In this respect, Costalius's image of poetry and eloquence differs radically from Sidney's *Defence,* which—in its most audacious move—associates them with God's unique ability to create ex nihilo. "Only the poet, disdaining to be tied to any such subjection [to the natural world], lifted by the vigour of his own invention, doth grow in effect another nature, in making things either better than nature bringeth forth, or quite anew, forms such as never were in nature."[26] Orpheus's song in *Pegma,* which separates the civil from the savage, resembles Yahweh's fiat that distinguishes light from darkness and the greater from the lesser lights, but in a critical turn toward Ovid's account of creation, Orpheus calls those discriminations out of matter. On the left side of the picture stands a forest that we now may recognize as a *silva:* the Latin word not only for "woods" but also for unrefined material, tangible stuff, and the subject matter of a text.[27] Earlier I described the inhabitants of this place as savage beasts and wild men. On closer inspection, they could also be herdsmen with their flocks or an aristocratic hunting party. This ambiguity is an important determinant of the emblem's meaning. For the forest represents matter in its raw potentiality, matter waiting for Orpheus to partition it with his potent words. In an effort to trace modern writing back to ancient speech, Costalius asks us to imagine

15. Orpheus, from *Métamorphose d'Ovide figurée* (Lyon, 1557).
By permission of the Douglas H. Gordon Collection of French
Books, Special Collections, University of Virginia Library.

that these words are uttered as fiat. But he expects that we shall think of them as written too. His own text takes the place of Orphic song and makes a claim to the category of value (eloquence) that the emblem reifies as the city's buildings and the poet's lyre—as the material things and graphic signs through which Orpheus can be said not only to sing but also *to write* the story of eloquent composition.

Eloquent Coinage

Should we not make new for ourselves what is old and find ourselves in it?[28]

Using Horace as its guide, Costalius's picture of Orpheus in old age traces the genealogy of eloquence—as a distinctive kind of composition—backward from modern writing to ancient speech and finally to the foundation of the world itself.[29] In the process, it irrigates the modern emblem book with the reservoir of antique value that Whitney's Latin scholia divert into the pages of the *Choice*. The *Pegma* does not, however, supply the image of Orpheus that Whitney chose for "Orphei Musica." For that picture, he turned to another book.

Orpheus appears twice in an influential text called *Emblemata* (1564), which was written by János Zsámboky, a Hungarian writer known as "Sambucus,"[30] and printed by Christopher Plantin, whose press later published Whitney's *Choice*. The poet appears for the first time in the emblem "In secundis consistere laudabile quoque" (It is also praiseworthy to be in second place). There, he faces Homer across a column that is decorated with four shields, each one emblazoned with the image of a bird (see figure 16).

In fecundis confiftere laudabile quoque.

ORPHEVS *lyra valebat,*
Olor facerque femper
Fuit, fuaue cantans.
Poft hunc bonusque Homerus,
Philomela cui dicata eft,
Tanquam loco fecundo.
Sed rectius fecundum
Illi locum dediffent:
Nam vt Pfittacus meretur
Primas, loquax fecundas

Pica,

16. Orpheus and Homer, from Johannes Sambucus's *Emblemata,
cum aliquot nummis* (Antwerp, 1564).
By permission of the Folger Shakespeare Library.

On the left side, above Orpheus, hang a swan and a nightingale; on the right side, above Homer, a parrot and a magpie. Orpheus, who is young and cleanshaven, sings and plays the harp and wears a laurel crown, while Homer, who is old and bearded and wears a cap, is relieved of his legendary blindness and illiteracy[31] so that he can write in the book that he balances on his lap. The picture is displayed in a quadrilateral frame, beneath which a gnomic poem, written in Latin, glosses the equally gnomic title and image:

> Orpheus lyra valebat,
> Olor sacerque semper
> Fuit, suave cantans.
> Post hunc bonusque Homerus,
> Philomela cui dicata est,
> Tanquam loco secundo.
> Sed rectius secundum
> Illi locum dedissent:
> Nam vt Psittacus meretur
> Primas, loquax secundas
> Pica, iste vincit illum.
> Hoc Symbolum referri
> Ad eos potest, gradum que
> Laudemque non tenere
> Primam queunt: sed inde
> Virtute mox sequentem.

[Orpheus was good with the lyre and always was a sacred swan, singing sweetly. After him, Homer, who was a good man, was called nightingale [*Philomela*], as if in second place. But it would have been more appropriate if they had given second place to

Orpheus [*Illi*]. For just as a parrot deserves first place, and the noisy magpie second, so Homer conquers Orpheus [*iste vincit illum*]. This symbol can refer to those people who cannot reach the rung of highest praise but through their virtue reach the one that follows it [*sed inde | Virtute mox sequentem*].][32]

At its most elementary level, Renaissance emblem writing requires that all three elements of a composition ratify each other. Here, the poem extends the meaning of the emblem's title by suggesting that Orpheus is held in higher esteem *only* because he is the "elder" poet: Orpheus "takes first place" because he "comes first" in time. Broaching the problem of value in this way, the poem seems to argue the modern is superior to its ancient counterpart. Homer normally belongs with the latter, but here, in his relation to the antiquity of Orpheus, he becomes a figure for the modern. While Orpheus is prior to Homer, the picture shows that he is also younger than his successor; Homer follows Orpheus but is older than his ancestor. If Homer's old age is not a claim that value degenerates as it passes from ancient song to modern writing—and in this emblem, the title and the poem exclude that possibility—then perhaps it suggests that value increases and matures as it descends through time. To this possibility a later text by Francis Bacon provides a gloss: "[True] antiquity should mean the oldness and great age of the world, which should be attributed to our time, not to a younger period of the world such as the ancients. True, that age is ancient and older in relation to us, but with respect to the world itself, it was new and younger. We expect from an old man greater knowledge of things human and a more mature judgment than from a young man, both because of his experience and because of the store and variety of things which he has seen and heard and thought about."[33]

On the other hand, the greater part of this emblem's subtlety and interest lies in its effort to synthesize the different terms of the dichotomy that it proposes. Even when we read Sambucus in light of Bacon's claims, we may not infer that the modern entirely relinquishes the ancient in the process of superseding it. For in the *New Organon* the modern is partly indebted to Antiquity for contributing to its treasury of accumulated "things." Here, in the same way, Homer is beholden to Orpheus for the song that he inscribes in his book. Seen from this vantage, every element of the emblem may be said to work toward another goal: namely, to prevent the reader from concluding that the ancient and the modern differ. Indeed, for his contemporaries, the distinction of Sambucus's writing likely inhered in its conspicuous tendency to assimilate the ancient and the modern, placing them in a sympathetic relationship that figures, for Foucault, the fundamental resemblance of all things within Renaissance thought: "Sympathy is an instance of the *Same* so strong and so insistent that it will not rest content to be merely one of the forms of likeness; it has the dangerous power of *assimilating*, of rendering things identical to one another, of mingling them, of causing their individuality to disappear."[34]

How does Sambucus unify the apparent oppositions of the emblem? Take the word *gradus* ("rung" or "step") which tries to represent in space the hierarchy of value that the emblem's picture and poem unfold in time: Orpheus comes first and Homer second. Nothing could be easier to understand, but as the poem moves toward its conclusion, it becomes more difficult to know where the ancient and the modern stand in the graduated field that the text imagines. We could interpret the statement "Homer follows Orpheus" to mean that he lies in Orpheus's future ("he comes next");[35] or as a metaphor for Homer's inferiority as a poet ("he lags behind"); or we could read the passage ironically, since the poem also claims that "Homer conquers Orpheus." Sambucus invests the final word, *sequentem* ("following"), with such an abundance of contradictory meanings that it, and *gradus,* cannot make specific distinctions between Orpheus and Homer in respect of place, time, or value. The word *gradus* is used only once in the accusative (*gradum*), but significantly, it refers to two different things: Neither the "first rung" nor "the rung that follows," it pertains to both of them, simultaneously. By the end of the poem, it is impossible to discern what comes *first* or *second,* in any sense, because the "following rung" ("gradum . . . sequentem"), to which the virtuous climb, may either be below or above, before or after, the "first rung" of "praise" ("gradum . . . laudemque . . . primam"). And grammatically, they are the same.

The poem's avian metaphors obey this distinctive logic too. Once again, the very language that differentiates the ancient and the modern paradoxically suggests their identity. Here, the terms of difference that overcome themselves are not "young" and "old," or "first" and "second," but "original" and "imitation." For in the tenth book of *Historia naturalis,* Pliny the Elder attributes the capacity for composition to swans and nightingales,[36] which are singing birds, while to parrots and magpies, which "merely" speak, he ascribes a capacity for mimicry.[37] Framed by this suggestive ornithology, the relationship between the ancient and the modern seems like a dichotomy. But Orpheus is not just a swan: The poem insists that he is a magpie too. Homer is both a nightingale and a parrot. These baffling contradictions block our efforts to read the emblem dichotomously, and they oblige us to think about the relationship between the ancient and the modern in another way. Indeed, they confront us with the possibility that *both* Orpheus and Homer occupy the first *and* the second place: the ancient place and its modern counterpart, the place of inventors as well as mimics, and of song as well as writing. According to this reading, Orpheus and Homer represent different temporalities of value—as indeed they must, if the emblem is to function as a genealogy of modern composition from ancient sources. At the same time, however, the picture's symmetry suggests that the poets and the temporalities that they represent are inherently identical. Orpheus is the image of a young antiquity, Homer of an old modernity: In this regard, they are reflections of each other. Or, taking the emblem for a mirror, we could say that Orpheus and Homer are different versions of the same desire to create the present in the image of the past, and so to make the ancient new again.

The second picture of Orpheus in this book—the one that Whitney later chose for his anthology—follows in an appendix of numismatic images. There, Orpheus appears on the reverse side of a Roman medal (see figure 17).

This picture is drawn from a real object that was struck in bronze between 142 and 145 C.E., in order to commemorate the reign of Antoninus Pius; one of the emperor's many names, Marcus Aurelius Augustus, appears in Greek lettering on the obverse side, along with his profile portrait. The triangle near Orpheus's left knee is the Greek letter delta, for "Dyrrhacium," the Illyrian city in which the object was produced. This identifying mark is visible on a surviving example of the medal.[38] By including this detail in the woodcut, Sambucus presumably tells the reader that he has seen the object and that his copy, therefore, is authentic.[39]

When we scruple about authenticity, however, we make a distinction between the ancient and the modern, or in this

17. Page of ancient medals showing Orpheus, from Johannes Sambucus's *Emblemata, cum aliquot nummis* (Antwerp, 1564).
By permission of the Folger Shakespeare Library.

case the "original" and the "copy," that this image of Orpheus, like the one before it, is determined to subvert. The printed medal obviously differs from the ancient object that it imitates. It is made of different materials, for example, and belongs to another time. The appearance of both sides of the medal in a single visual field clarifies that the artifact and its picture exist in different dimensions. On the other hand, these distinctions should not be overstated, since the appendix also cleaves to the idea that ancient medals and modern books are fundamentally the same. Examples of this commonplace abound in the antiquarian literature of the sixteenth century. Though printed books are made of ink and paper, moveable type, like coinage, is cut from metal; and so through Gutenberg, who was a goldsmith, the modern technology of printing traces its origins to the precious substances that ancient minters used for making coins and medals. In other versions of the analogy, Aldus Manutius takes his printer's mark from a Roman medal that Pietro Bembo gave him;[40] Guillaume Budé's *De asse* (1514), the first printed numismatic text, displays the image of a working press on its title page, as another printer's mark; Sambucus decorates the title of the *Emblemata* with images of the muses drawn from ancient coins (see figure 18).

Playing on this technological affinity, the appendix in the *Emblemata* suggests that no numismatic image is more original than any other—though one may *come before* and be made of *more enduring* stuff. For a coin or medal, like a printed page, is the likeness of something else, impressed in matter in reverse. Whether minted or printed, ancient or modern, all coins and medals are therefore implicitly counterfeit, in the sense that they are made in contrast to other objects (*contra facere*).[41] The force of this analogy partly overcomes the real features that differentiate coins and medals from their printed copies. When

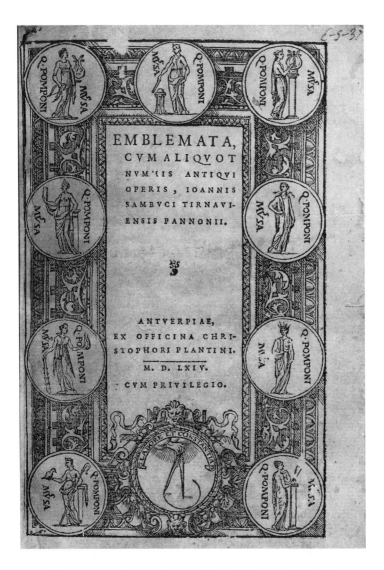

18. Title page showing ancient medals with figures of the Muses, from Johannes Sambucus's *Emblemata, cum aliquot nummis* (Antwerp, 1564). By permission of the Folger Shakespeare Library.

books and coins become the same kind of thing, printed texts like the *Emblemata* not only represent numismatic objects but also extend them into the present time and place. (This is the counterfeit's other meaning as true likeness or exact replica.) While coins and medals, as the durable remains of the classical world, remain continuous with Antiquity and make it present, humanist books adopt a numismatic rhetoric of precious durability in order to overcome the temporal gap that separates them from the things that they copy. As the book marks "the persistence of the thing . . . in *being there*,"[42] it becomes one with its objects of study and thus with the past that is present in their matter. For Guillaume Rouille, the author and printer of *Promptuaire des medalles* (1577)—a popular compendium of ancient medals—the modern book was less a supplement for absent artifacts than it was an antiquarian collection, through which the past disclosed itself to the senses in a marvelous plenitude of presence: "[You, reader,] will consider [the ancients] to be present in effigy; [you] will hear them speaking through writing; [you] will contemplate their eminent deeds through history; and they will bring back the past times of all human memory to [your] century. . . . [I]n recollecting the things that [you] have read here, it will seem that [you] have been, before the time of [your] birth, living with those who are no more."[43]

Displayed in the appendix of the *Emblemata* like the printed pages of an open book, the Roman medals announce the ancient genealogy of the modern text in which they appear. Like other antique objects, they are also proof that Antiquity itself is immanent in the Renaissance book. Sambucus's coins, statues, ruins, and obelisks are elaborately framed and mediated; they enjoy a figurative materiality only. But within those limits, they change this anthology of emblem poems into a "humanist reliquary."[44] These objects reify the ancient past; their presence overcomes its otherness; they take possession of it for the modern writer. Moreover, as objective correlatives for the language that frames them, they also constitute a morphology of the text's accomplishment, authority, and kind. Benedetto Varchi observed in the 1550s that "words cannot be separated from things . . . and things cannot be expressed without words."[45] Illuminated by this logic, and by the logic of the emblem genre (title = picture = poem), the exhibition of ancient artifacts and modern verses in this book insists on their equivalence. In the emblem "Musarum, ex antiquis numis Q. Pomponii, verae effigies" (The true effigies of the Muses, from an ancient coin of Q. Pomponius), the reverse side of a Roman coin is a picture of ancient composition, which it represents as the music-making of Apollo and the Muses (see figure 19).

At the same time, the coin is a picture of the neo-Latin poem that renders it ecphrastically. This is the same coin from which Sambucus draws the numismatic portraits of the muses on the title page, a further suggestion that his ancient collections and his modern anthology consist of the very same things. Thus the ability of the modern book to transport its readers across a certain distance—between past and present, thing and word, *pictura* and *poesis*—is calibrated to another representational process, whereby ancient objects become symbols not only for the past but also for the text that appropriates them as hieroglyphs of its own origin, value, and distinction.

The analogy between ancient things and modern words that Sambucus emphasizes in his text enjoyed a long life, despite the arrival of empiricism with Bacon's argument that an "affectionate study of eloquence and copie [*copia*] of speech" had misled men to "hunt more after words than matter."[46] In calling for a redefinition of language in its relation to the nat-

Mufarum, ex antiquis numis Q. Pomponij, veræ effigies, & etymologica vis ex Virgilio,

Ad Hannibalem Cruceium.

CLIO *gefta canens transfactis tempora reddit,*
Melpomene tragico proclamat mœsta boatu.
Comica lasciuo gaudet sermone Thalia.
Dulciloquos calamos Euterpe flatibus vrget.
Terpsichore affectus citharis mouet, imperat, auget,
Plectra gerens Erato saltat pede, carmine, vultu.

Carmina

19. Apollo and the Muses taken from an ancient medal, from Johannes Sambucus's *Emblemata, cum aliquot nummis* (Antwerp, 1564). By permission of the Folger Shakespeare Library.

ural world, Bacon held that words and things are intrinsically different.[47] By the mid-seventeenth century, the Book of Nature was—for Gallileo, Robert Hooke, and others—"an essentially non-verbal text."[48] When Henry Peacham attempts to reconcile antiquarian studies to the doctrines of the New Science, he therefore begins by denying that "Antique Coynes" and "bookes" are related in the way that earlier humanists, like Sambucus, had proposed. "[B]ookes and histories and the like," argues Peacham, "are but copyes of Antiquity, bee they never so truely descended unto us," while coins and medals "are the very Antiquities themselves" and "the very same individuall things which were in use so many ages agoe." This is to juxtapose things and words in a way that forces them to relinquish the inextricable connection that Sambucus takes for granted, and so to reinvent antiquarian historiography in the image of a reformed natural science.

Eager to establish that antique coins are empirical facts, Peacham deprives them of their fungibility as symbols and figures. Reduced to "individuall" material things, whose meaning is exhausted by their former "use," coins surrender their capacity to represent anything but themselves. Texts, meanwhile, take on the vaporous condition of hearsay and perception, since they are only verbal "copyes" of the physical "things which were in use so many ages agoe"—what Peacham might have called (had he been Bacon) "the stuff and material of true induction."[49] Whereas the privilege of coins as historical evidence depends on the chaste confinement of their meaning to Antiquity's "bare 'was,'"[50] and on the relative immutability of their inscriptions over time, "bookes and histories and the like" are excluded from this objective truth by the different circumstances of their transmission through handwriting and the printing press—to which, since they are open to adulter-

ation, Peacham imputes the taint of a promiscuous subjectivity: "[B]ee they never so truely descended unto us." Here, however, at the moment of its most forceful articulation, the new
antithesis of words and things breaks down. For imitation is
the only language that Peacham has for describing the value of
ancient coins and medals as material objects.

> [W]ould you see a patterne of the *Rogus* or funerall
> pile burnt at the canonization of the Romane Em-
> perors? would you see how the *Augurs* Hat . . . was
> made? Would you see the true and undoubted
> modells of their Temples, Alters, Deities, Columnes,
> Gates, Arches, Aquaeducts, Bridges, Sacrifices, Ves-
> sels, *Sellae Curules,* Ensignes and Standards, Navall
> and mirall Crownes, Amphytheatres, Circi, Bathes,
> Chariots, Trophies, Ancilla, and a thousand things
> more? Repayre to the old coynes, and you shall find
> them, and all things else that they ever did, made, or
> used, there shall you see them excellently and lively
> represented.[51]

Marx's observation that the "symbolic existence" of the
coin "so to speak absorbs its material existence"[52] may help to
explain what is happening in this passage, where Peacham's
enthusiasm for the "severall figures stamped on . . . Antique
Coynes" suddenly undercuts the value that he has been assigning exclusively to numismata as though they were matter but
not material objects made by human hands. Peacham previ-
ously discriminated between "use" and "copy" with the same
emphasis that Bacon distinguishes things from words, but at
the end of his essay he cancels that difference and shows that
during Antiquity the use of coins and medals was, in large

part, representational. This reversal restores to "copy," "mod-ell," and "patterne" the ambiguity that they enjoyed in Renais-sance English, where they belonged to a group of words that could refer to any point along a continuum from "original" to "imitation."[53] In the process of reaffirming the very same anal-ogy between words and things that he sets out to expunge, Peacham rediscovers the poetics of the ancient artifact that is emerging in the pages of Sambucus's *Emblemata*.

The influence of Peacham's essay is difficult to measure. As an attempt to imagine an empirical method for an anti-quarian science, its impact was negligible. On the other hand, Peacham was also a maker of emblems,[54] and as a text that manages to transmit precisely the humanistic archaeology that it rejects, "Of Antiquities" may have enjoyed more success than its author would have liked; Leonard Barkan reminds us that "the founders of a humanistic approach to classical remains" treated "archaeology as a subset of the study of texts."[55] Fol-lowing Peacham, English antiquaries like John Evelyn hearken to a dispensation of words and things whose inflection is pat-ently more Renaissance than modern. "And verily," writes Eve-lyn in *Numismata* (1697), "if we consider *Medals* in respect of the Matter; they are, for ought appears, the most lasting and (give me leave to call them) Vocal Monuments of Antiquity." He specially observes, with regard to the reverse side of medals, that the ancient artifact is a kind of writing and therefore a lin-guistic matter—the thing being an image of the word, and vice versa: "[H]aving relation to *Symbol* only, [*Reverses*] require particular explication, as do other *Emblems, Devises,* and *Hi-eroglyphicks*."[56] From Evelyn's influential text, John Pointer in-ferred in *Britannia Romana* (1724) that there is a "great Affinity between Coins and Poems," while Joseph Addison regarded the "medallic eloquence" of ancient numismata as a passport

to historical truth and a benchmark for excellence in the contemporary verbal arts.[57]

The texts from which I have drawn these passages are the
distant progeny of early humanism's efforts to correlate the
textual and nontextual remains of the ancient world and so
produce a certain vision of the past.[58] Accordingly, they tack
toward the sensibilities of the *Emblemata* and, like it, deploy
ancient artifacts as symbols for Antiquity's value in its most
general sense: a value that humanism projected onto the past
in order to reclaim it later for itself, in the form of countless
precious fragments. But in a turn that the influence of neither
Sambucus nor Peacham adequately explains, these passages
also make the analogy between ancient coins and medals and
verbal compositions much more explicit than we have had occasion to observe. Evelyn's reference to antique medals as
"Vocal Monuments" not only grants a voice to matter. Since
"monument" can mean a written document or record as well
as a memorial object that is uninscribed, it also implicates that
voice in the materiality of writing.[59] In this way, Evelyn pre-
pares the reader for the equally remarkable analogy that he
makes between ancient medals and the emblem, device, and
hieroglyph: genres of inscription that the Renaissance esteemed
for the emphasis they placed on the exchangeability of word
and thing. For Costalius, the eloquence that Orpheus embodies refers exclusively to the excellence of ancient speech; in "Vis
eloquentiae," eloquence is a distinction that is does not yet
apply to modern printed texts, though this may be the direction in which Costalius is headed. The very fact that Addison
can extol the eloquence of ancient things, as though they were
poetic texts, suggests that modern textuality has appropriated
to itself the terms of value that once belonged to antique speech;
or even that speech has partly taken on the density of the things

that objectify it in Renaissance emblems, and of the print technology that was turning all human thought, ever more literally, into matter. How this shift occurred—how ancient coins and medals might have come to resemble verbal compositions and to serve as metaphors for the eloquence of writing—is another matter, and in order to explore it, we must return to Whitney's *Choice of Emblemes*.

The Antike Pieces of English Eloquence

> The search for descent is not the erecting of foundations: on the contrary, it disturbs what was previously considered immobile; it fragments what was thought unified; it shows the heterogeneity of what was imagined consistent with itself.[60]

"Orphei Musica" is the second of two emblems that Whitney dedicates to Stephen Bull, a "doctissimus vir" about whom nothing more is known. The title of the first, which immediately precedes it, is "Scripta non temerè edenda" (Writing should not be published hastily).[61] As a prologue to the Orphic music that follows, this emblem reveals a scene of writing (see figure 20).

At the left, an old man prevents a younger one from handing a paper to a third person, who gazes at the symbols written on it. Equipped with wings and a horn, this classical figure personifies the "fame" that the "younglinge" writer impatiently "desire[s]" for his text.

The poem beneath the picture identifies the old man as Quinctilius, "a graue and reuerende sire." Prompted by the Latin gloss in the right margin, we recognize him as Quintilius Varus, the ancient Roman whom Horace praises for being a ju-

Ad doctiſſ. virum D. Sᴛ. Bᴠʟʟᴠᴍ.

Quinſtilij Var. cen-
ſura de ſcriptis edē-
dis Horat. Art.poët.

Lᴏ, here Qᴠɪɴᴄᴛɪʟɪᴠs ſittes, a graue and reuerende ſire:
And pulles a younglinge by the arme, that did for fame deſire.
For, hee with pace of ſnayle, proceeded to his pen;
Leſt haſte ſhoulde make him wiſhe (too late) it weare to write againe.
And therfore ſtill with care, woulde euerie thinge amende:
Yea, ofte eche worde, and line ſuruaye, before hee made an ende.
And, yf he any ſawe, whoſe care to wryte was ſmall:
To him, like wordes to theſe hee vſd, which hee did meane to all.
My ſonne, what worke thou writes, correcte, reforme, amende,
But if thou like thy firſt aſſaye, then not Qᴠɪɴᴄᴛɪʟɪᴠs frende?
The fruicte at firſte is ſower, till time giue pleaſante taſte:
And verie rare is that attempte, that is not harm'd with haſte.
Perfection comes in time, and forme and faſhion giues:
And euer raſhenes, yeeldes repente, and moſt diſpiſed liues.
Then, alter ofte, and chaunge, peruſe, and reade, and marke:
The man that ſoftlie ſettes his ſteppes, goes ſafeſt in the darke.
But if that thirſt of fame, doe pricke thee forthe too faſte:
Thou ſhalt (when it is all to late) repente therefore at laſte.

Ouid. 3. Faſt.
Differ, habent paruæ
commoda magna moræ.

Senec. Agam.
Proinde quicquid eſt, da
ſpacium & tempus tibi:
Quod ratio nequit, ſæ-
pe ſanauit mora.

a   *Orphei*   ꝛ

20. A scene of writing, from Geffrey Whitney's
A choice of emblemes (Leiden, 1586).
By permission of the Folger Shakespeare Library.

dicious critic.[62] Quinctilius is a quotation of the Horatian text that preserves his memory, and in its voice he admonishes the younger man—possibly, he stands for Whitney—to have a care for the value of his own writings: "*My sonne,* what worke thou writes, correcte, reforme, amende." Quinctilius may be an image of Quintilius Varus, of Horace, or of Antiquity in general, but he also bears a striking resemblance to Homer, at least as we have seen him in the emblem "In secundis consistere laudible quoque," where he has beard, cap, and pen (see figure 16). Thus Quinctilius comes into focus as the intersection of Whitney's ancient and modern sources—*Ars Poetica* and *Emblemata*—and as a picture of the different kinds of authority that Whitney tries to exercise: on the one hand, the authority of antique Latin literature; on the other, of a continental humanism and a neo-Latin poetry that have come between the English emblem and the ancient objects of its desire. "Scripta non temerè edenda" expresses Whitney's claim on these older texts and traditions as an affiliation. It also conveys a certain ambivalence about the logic of genealogy that it deploys. For Quinctilius impedes the very text that he offers to improve: "Perfection comes in time, and forme and fashion giues: | And euer rashenes, yeeldes repente, and most dispised liues. | Then, alter ofte, and change, peruse, and reade, and marke. . . ." As a representation of Whitney's classical and humanist precursors, the elderly Quinctilius is the only figure in the emblem who is able to discern the value of a text, and the only one who holds a pen. Through him, Latinity extends the promise of perfectibility and value to each new piece of writing. Does the emblem also suggest that in order to achieve "Perfection" the young man must make his writing in the image of Quinctilius himself? And would this be to make the ancient *anew* or merely *again*?

Whitney obliges the reader to interpret this emblem in light of the one that follows it. Apart from their dedications to Stephen Bull, both texts are written in alternating lines of twelve and fourteen syllables, a meter called Poulter's Measure; both refer to Horace's *Ars Poetica* in the margin and to Sambucus's *Emblemata* in the picture; both are centrally concerned with the relationship of ancient to modern, and of Latin to vernacular, poetics. Their physical locations in the book also suggest that they are inextricable in their meaning: "Scripta non temerè edenda" and "Orphei Musica" are printed on opposite sides of a single page. Seen as one thing, semi-independent of the *Choice*'s other emblems, they form an object like a coin or medal, of which the picture of Orpheus on page 186 is in more than one sense the reverse side.

Moving forward from "Scripta non temerè edenda" to "Orphei Musica," Whitney's text tells a story about its own origins and composition. Like the young man's paper, the *Choice* is here recalled to the ancient authors and emblem writers that precede it: to Costalius and Sambucus as to Horace, and to the iconography in which Orpheus represents the mythical origins of human civilization in eloquent speech, and antique objects symbolize the historical past of Rome. This return results in transformation. For as it crosses the threshold of page 185, the imperfect composition that Quinctilius snatches from the hand of Fame arrives, in a perfected form, as "Orphei Musica"—a text that claims to be both sound and writing, music and a piece of matter. We turn the page and pass from *scripta* into voice and song, the privileged modalities of antique composition. As it hearkens to the voice of Orpheus, Whitney's written text assimilates itself to the ancient category of *eloquentia*, which Renaissance humanism associated primarily with the tongue rather than the hand or the pen.[63] Orpheus, mean-

while, undergoes inscription, not once but three times: first
upon the Roman medal, then in the appendix of Sambucus's
book, and finally by Whitney here. His song is transmuted into
a monument, and in this way eloquence, a category of ancient
speech, accommodates itself to the materiality of modern,
vernacular writing. It is an achievement that in 1555 Costalius's
Pegma, a neo-Latin text, has not yet imagined.

This is the first time that an antique medal illustrates an
English poem. To my knowledge, it is also the first time that
"the material knowledge of old Rome"[64] introduces a new distinction to the field of English Renaissance writing—which,
conceived in the broadest sense of "poesy," has sometimes been
thought to be indifferent to such distinctions.[65] We have already seen how Orpheus, in his first appearance in an emblem,
is associated with the artist-deities of *Metamorphoses* and
Genesis and so with the power to differentiate. In this emblem,
Whitney recurs to those associations and uses Orpheus as a
way of asserting the eloquence and fame of his English text.
The obscurity into which his poems have subsequently fallen
makes this assertion rather more remarkable than less. For in
this emblem Whitney permits the *Choice* to find the reflection
its own modernity, Englishness, and matter, purged of every
taint, in the image of an ancient object—in an artifact that
represents the continuity of Whitney's writing with Orphic
song and Roman culture, and thus the categorical difference of
its eloquence from other kinds of contemporary vernacular
composition.

Like other emblem books by Renaissance humanists,
Whitney's *Choice* aspires to close the distance between the ancient and the modern, arrogating to itself the value that it creates through its fascination with the past and its remains. But
unlike Costalius and Sambucus, Whitney writes in English.

This, too, is a distinctive choice, making him the first English-man to compose and publish an emblem book in his native language.[66] For the remainder of this chapter, I would like to explore a few of the consequences of this choice as they are il-luminated by "Orphei Musica." I want to argue that in juxta-position to the English text beneath it, the medal that at-tributes ancient eloquence to modern writing also exposes a counterclassical—and, properly speaking, a *vulgar*—impulse in Whitney's poetry, as powerful as the affinity for classical texts and antiquities that we have been examining. The ancient object is therefore a promise not only that Whitney's emblems differ from other kinds of English writing but also that they differ from the ancient texts that they imitate.

In a double return to *Ars Poetica* and to the emblem on the previous page, the poem in "Orphei Musica" begins by par-aphrasing Horace. (If Whitney is the writer of this text, is he also its author?) The first twelve lines explain that Orpheus's "musicke sweete" is not a musical performance in the literal sense but a figure for "sweetenes of [the] tonge"—which is to say, for eloquence: a condition of language in which verbal composition exceeds the limits of ordinary speech and be-comes more than the individual words from which its fabric is woven. These lines also take the Horatian view that the ani-mals, plants, and rocks that Orpheus gathers to himself are metaphors for "most rude," "fierce," and "brutishe" men, the primitive humanity from which eloquence fashions civiliza-tion. Here, however, at the poem's midpoint, Whitney abruptly turns from his Horatian model, turning at the same time from Orpheus as a sign of superlative verbal achievement. Address-ing Stephen Bull, or possibly the reader, Whitney celebrates one "E. P. Esquier," whose initials appear in the margin. This "Apollos darlinge" dwells not in Thrace—Orpheus's birthplace—but "so neare your home." In the same way that Whitney contrasts E. P. with Orpheus in regard to their geographical origins, he differentiates between the verbal powers that they exemplify. E. P. is described as an "impe," or offshoot, of Orpheus, but he "farre excelles" him. His excellence is not only in degree but also, apparently, in kind. For "if his musicke [eloquence] faile: his curstesie is suche, | That none so rude, and base of minde, but hee reclaimes them muche."

It is difficult to know what "curtesie" means. Logically, it functions as a term of differentiation in the same way that "home" is opposed to "THRACIA." The sense of the passage is that "curtesie" is a translation of *eloquentia,* that it is synonymous with "musicke" and achieves the same results, only to a greater degree. Whitney also implies, however, that "curtesie" refers to a different category of value and thus to a different kind of composition: to the native and the modern *as opposed to* the foreign and the ancient. For just as "curtesie" marks the difference between E. P. and the "rude, and base" men whom he "reclaimes" with words, so it marks the otherness of English writing to its antique precursors. To the modernity and Englishness of "curtesie" Whitney juxtaposes the antiquity of a "musicke" (eloquence) that originates in Thrace, a remote region that ancient writers associate with barbarity. This is to reshuffle the terms of the dichotomies that normally place England in an inferior position to Rome—ancient and modern; classical and gothic; civil and savage—and so create the possibility of new relationship. Orpheus's Thracian roots, like E. P.'s "curtesie," imply that the ancient is not in every case synonymous with the civilized, nor the modern with the savage. At the same time, the link between Orpheus and Thrace also points to the potential of an English literature that has not yet emerged: Civilization, the myth reminds us, has always sprung from vulgar sources.

So while the Roman medal is the symbol of an ancient pedigree, it also discloses Whitney's ambivalence about the terms and categories of value that he appropriates from Antiquity, a turn that sets Whitney apart from neo-Latin emblem writers like Costalius (Coustau) and Sambucus (Zsámboky) as clearly as his English name. Whitney's reference to E. P. Esquier as an "impe of ORPHEUS" imagines the encounter between the ancient and the modern in a similarly ambivalent way. Both natural and artificial, their meeting point is a figure of hybridity: a grafting (imp) of two plants of different stock. This hybridity finds its formal equivalent in the juxtaposition of classical and vulgar languages throughout the emblem, as it does in Poulter's Measure: the alternation of twelve-syllable lines, imitating Latin hexameters, with fourteeners, a rhythm drawn from vernacular ballads. "Ambivalence," "appropriation," "hybridity," and "otherness" are all terms of consequence in contemporary postcolonial theory.[67] I use them deliberately in order to suggest something about the appearance of the category of eloquent English writing at the end of the sixteenth century. I would argue that in the process of retrieving from Antiquity the terms and concepts that introduced new distinctions to the field of English writing, vernacular writers were obliged to confront the radical alterity of England to the ancient world, and of English to the languages and aesthetic canons that they wanted to assimilate. Is it possible, then, that during the Renaissance the distinction of English literature first emerged from the perception that vernacular writing occupied a subaltern position to its antique models? Is the imitation of classical sources that we have come to recognize as the dominant procedure of literary making in this period the symptom of a postcolonial relation?

As I suggest in the introduction to this book, the wider context for these questions is the unprecedented strain that England's relationship to Rome was suffering in the 1580s and 1590s. At the same time that humanist philology granted classical Latin and Latin literature a preeminent importance in the school curriculum and in matters of style generally, the legend that Britain was descended from Brutus, the offspring of Aeneas, entered its final decline, as Reformation antiquaries worked to sever the genealogy that apparently tied England to Rome, the seat of Anti-Christ. In 1586, the year that Whitney published the *Choice* in English, William Camden published *Britannia* in Latin. Generally diffident about the credibility of Geoffrey of Monmouth, this book was nevertheless a monument to the hybridity of Roman and British culture. It was also the first antiquarian text by an Englishman to include numismatic illustrations, pictures of the "treasure" that the Romans "buried . . . within the ground" before departing from the island in the reign of Valentinian III. The section on coinage follows a long essay, "Romans in Britaine," which Camden draws to a close with some speculations about the racial and ethnic character of modern Britons ("How the Britaines are decended from the Trojans"):

> In writing of these matters, . . . whiles I consider and thinke otherwhiles with my selfe, how many Colonies of Romans were in so long a time brought hither, how many souldiers continually transported over hither from Rome to lie in garrison, how many sent hither to negotiate either their own business, or the affaires of the Empire, who joyning in marriage with Britans, both planted themselves, and also

> begat children here (For, *Wheresoever the Romans
> winneth,* saith Seneca, *there he woneth, and inhab-
> iteth:*) I enter oft times into this cogitation, That
> Britans may more truely ingraffe themselves into
> the Trojans stocke, by these Romans, who are de-
> scended from Trojans. . . . And meete it is that we
> should beleeve, that the Britans and Romans in
> so many ages, by a blessed and joyfull mutuall
> ingraffing, as it were, have growen into one stocke
> and nation. . . .

To this argument—which draws on the same botanical
metaphor as Whitney's emblem—Camden appends eight pages
of numismatic images, since "there ariseth very muche light to
the illustration of ancient Histories, out of ancient Coines"
(see figures 21 and 22).[68]

The first three pages of this section are devoted to British
coins, the rest to Roman coins. Taken together, they make a
picture of the hybridity that Camden describes in the earlier
passage. The blank coin at the very end represents all the coins
that are yet to be discovered—the missing pieces, if you will,
of a genuinely Roman Britain that time has ruined.[69] On the
other hand, that absence and the explanations that follow suggest that these coins represent two different cultures that failed
to integrate themselves, despite their long acquaintance. Making a distinction between "Coniectures" about British coins and
"Notes" on Roman ones, Camden also points to a difference between the histories that these objects can illuminate: on the one
hand, an ignominious native past in which Britons "first came
under subjection of the Romanes"; and on the other, a foreign
past of Roman imperium and "of Roman Emperours" themselves.[70] The section on coinage is an afterword to Camden's

21. A page of ancient British coins, from William Camden,
Britain (London, 1610).
By permission of the Folger Shakespeare Library.

Nummi antiqui Romanorum qui ad historiam Britannicam præcipue spectant

69

22. A page of ancient Roman coins with blanks, from William
Camden, *Britain* (London, 1610).
By permission of the Folger Shakespeare Library.

vision of Britano-Roman hybridity, but it is also a prologue to the essay that follows, "The Downfall or Destruction of Britain." For Camden, the exhibition of these "antike peeces"[71]—though he offers it them as testimony to the synthesis of cultures— leads, ineluctably, to a different thesis: namely, that Romans and Britons were never joined organically. For once the Roman Empire had withdrawn from the most remote of all its colonies, Britain could no longer defend itself against the barbarians, by whom it was absorbed.

Whitney's Orphic medal resembles Camden's "antike peeces" in the sense that it too cogitates a Roman origin for modern English culture, during a time when the relationship between England and Rome was increasingly precarious, implausible, and vitiated. On the other hand, Whitney's choice to use this particular object as an illustration for a vernacular poem that celebrates a native poet's "curtesie," also mitigates against its classical resonance. That is to say: The humanist philology, antiquarian research, and revisionist Protestant history that transformed England's relationship to the ancient past did not prevent writers like Whitney from using Orpheus as a symbol for the classical origins and aspirations of their texts. They did, however, also make it possible for Orpheus to symbolize the origin of vernacular writing in another way. In contradistinction to classical Latin, northern vernacular languages were commonly described, even by English writers, as rude, barbarous, uncouth, brutish, gothic, and vulgar. When Reformation antiquaries demolished the legend of Brutus, they inadvertently opened a space in which writers were free to rethink the terms of England's relationship to Rome, and how English related to Latin, and thus to give those terms new value, if not to reject them entirely. In this context, Whitney's medal, quite apart from its function as a symbol of the classical past, represents a vernacular eloquence whose inherent vulgarity differentiates it from *eloquentia,* on which it is conceptually dependent. This is the difficult idea that Whitney articulates when he contrasts E. P.'s "curtesie" with the Orphic "musicke" of which it is, and is not, an echo.

William Webbe's *Discourse of English Poetrie* (1586) also takes an important step toward rehabilitating the vernacular in this way when it invokes the figure of Orpheus. Like other humanist writers, Webbe traces modern vernacular poetry to a period of the utmost antiquity. But when his narrative arrives there, he discovers Orpheus in a situation rather more primitive than classical:

> [T]he first that was first worthelye memorable in the excellent gyft of Poetrye, the best wryters agree that it was *Orpheus,* who by the swete gyft of his heauenly Poetry, withdrew men from raungying uncertainly, and wandering brutishly about, and made them gather together, and keepe company, made houses, and kept fellowshippe together, who therefore is reported (as Horace sayth) to asswage the fiercenesse of Tygers, and mooue the harde Flynts. After him was *Amphion,* who was the first that caused Citties to bee builded, and men therein to liue decently and orderly according to lawe and right. Next was *Tyrtaeus,* who began to practise warlike defences, to keepe backe enemies, and saue themselues from invasion of foes.[72]

This passage partly recurs to a familiar, Horatian logic. Each poet represents a moment at which human beings divided themselves from the natural world or from each other;

once again, the concept of eloquence (in Webbe's text, "poetry") implies the concept of difference, and vice versa. Where Horace stresses the resemblance of Orpheus and Amphion, however, Webbe seems to weigh the difference between them. Orpheus is the most ancient figure here, and for Webbe that means that he must also be the least civilized. Poet and poetry alike belong to a time before the foundation of cities and states and of the imposition of the law, and the community that Orphic eloquence creates is scarcely more defined than the featureless terrain out of which he summons it. Little more than a group of human bodies, clustered together in "company" and "fellowshippe," this first version of civilization cleaves to the natural world from which it is divided only by the wall of a house. Here, the eloquent figure of Orpheus awaits the kind of civilization that the Renaissance could regard as classical.

English writers at the end of the sixteenth century could look to at least one other contemporary source for the idea that Orpheus's eloquence was indivisible from his barbarity. Referring to Costalius's *Pegma,* I earlier linked the Orpheus of "Vis eloquentiae" to the creator of the world by a chain of associations that leads from Amphion (mover of rocks) to Orpheus (mover of beasts) to the Prime Mover. Looking again at Costalius's emblems, it could be said that Orpheus does not resemble the god of *Metamorphoses* and Genesis as clearly as Amphion does (see figures 4 and 7). Orpheus does not wear a crown, for example. His hair is unkempt, he goes barefoot, and his clothes seem tattered. His appearance ties him more closely to the forest on the left than to the city on the right. It would be difficult, in fact, for him not to be related to the wilderness behind him. For in "Vis eloquentiae" the forest takes up half of the space in the picture. Orpheus is both the alternative to this place and its extension, a blossom on the solitary branch that crosses the center of the field. In "Pax," by contrast—which comes before this emblem but represents a later moment—the wood has retreated from Amphion's song and the expanding city walls. Dwindled to a single tree, it recalls in the negative the one and only spire at the right-hand side of "Vis eloquentiae."

If we return one final time to "Orphei Musica," allowing Costalius and Webbe to shed some light on it, we may therefore want to ask again where Orpheus is sitting in this portrait. The emblem's Horatian subtext implies that we find him, in his usual spot, on the threshold of human history, and several elements suggest that this is an image not of a vulgar primitivism but of the classical, in all of its sophistication. This Orpheus is clean shaven in contrast to his counterpart in *Pegma*, who has a tangled beard. Although he is barefoot, he wears a Roman toga instead of rags. The Δ to the right of Orpheus's leg is the mint mark of Dyrrhacium, a flourishing city in the Illyrian provinces of Antonine Rome. Polydore Vergil explains that this letter is also the pattern for the first lyre.[73] Here, as writing literally becomes its instrument, eloquence passes into matter and so becomes coextensive with the Roman civilization that this object represents, as with the modern English poem that Whitney makes in its image.

The Δ, on the other hand, also recalls the pyramid on the right-hand side of "Vis eloquentiae." As a symbol of urban sophistication and literacy, it marks a boundary between the written and the oral, the civil and the savage, that Orpheus has not yet crossed in an image that is more static than its counterpart in Costalius's *Pegma*. If Orpheus is not inside the city walls, perhaps he has retreated to the forest. One emblem book, published between Costalius's *Pegma* and Whitney's *Choice*, puts him there: Nicolas Reusner's *Emblematum* (1581), in the emblem "Musicae, & Poëticae vis" (see figure 23).

Quíq, tot egregios heroas vicit, & armis
Perdomuit toties : vna nunc vincitur ira:
Inuictumq, virum vincit dolor, atq, cupido.
Sic nemo Aiacem potuit superare, nisi Aiax:
Dum nimis impatiens, grauioris morte, repulsæ:
Lethiferum condit sua per præcordia ferrum.
O quantum decus est, se vincere posse per iram:
Maxima, si nescis, victoria vincere seipsum est.

Muſicæ, & Poëticæ vis.

EMBLEMA XXI.

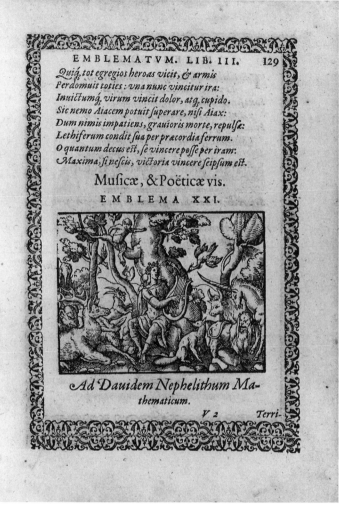

Ad Dauidem Nephelithum Ma-
thematicum.

V 2 Terri-

23. Orpheus, from Nicolaus Reusner's *Emblemata* (1581).
By permission of the Folger Shakespeare Library.

So do contemporary editions of Ovid's *Metamorphoses* (see figure 15). In this context, it is no longer possible to confine Orpheus to *Ars Poetica* or to the kind of civilization whose origins he is made to figure there. Deep within the woods, surrounded by beasts, this might be the Orpheus of Virgil's *Georgics* and Ovid's *Metamorphoses*—in which case we find him at the end of his story rather than the beginning of ours. Granted, it seems unlikely that we are meant to interpret this portrait as an image of failure and imminent catastrophe: Every other element of "Orphei Musica" points in the opposite direction. But perhaps we are meant to interpret it as the portrait of an enabling difference. For in turning to the Latin classics for their origins, English Renaissance writers not only discovered the heterogeneity of their own writing to ancient literature. They also discovered how heterogeneous classical writing was with respect to itself. The debt that vernacular writing owes to Antiquity is therefore more than the sum of the conventions that it appropriates. It is, rather, the debt of an internalized difference itself. The sylvan Orpheus of Whitney's emblem represents, in this sense, both a classical and a counterclassical genealogy—without which it would have been impossible for the hybrid kind of English writing, what I have been calling vulgar eloquence, to separate itself from the Latin literature that it imitated or from the vernacular compositions that cast its distinction in relief.

II
Shakespeare's "Wild Musick"

Marvelous Bondage

[I]t is the ravished object who is the real subject of rape; the *object* of capture becomes the *subject* of love; and the *subject* of the *conquest* moves into the class of loved object.[1]

Long before the 1590s, when it first alighted on Shakespearean branches, the nightingale was a trope that differentiated eloquence from other linguistic events, a symbol for the genealogy and excellence of the texts in which it appeared.[2] For the Greek poet Myrsilos, who lived in the fourth century B.C.E., the nightingale was linked to Orpheus, whose eloquence passed from human beings to animals and plants when his head came to rest on Lesbos, in a grove where the nightingale builds its nest.[3] In the context of English poetry at the end of the sixteenth century, the nightingale is the sign of a particular affluence, associated with the literature of ancient Greece and Rome. On the other hand, its value as a symbolic currency and mark of distinction depends just as much on its widespread availability and usage as a bromide as it does on its restrictive identification with a minority of prestigious foreign texts.

Like the other forms of conventional wisdom that the Renaissance rarely tired of repeating (the proverb, *sententia*, and emblem), the nightingale owes its fungibility as a metaphor for textual value to the fact that during the sixteenth century the primary definition of "commonplace" had not yet become "clichéd," "platitudinous," or "trite."[4] Indeed, referring to the "goods" ("bona") left behind in writing by the noblest intellects, Seneca held, in an influential passage, that the value of this textual property is augmented rather than diminished by its ubiquity, "for the more persons you share it with, the greater it will become" ("maiora fient, quo illa pluribus diversis").[5] Highly prescriptive in the way that it assigns value to texts ("this is the best"), yet available to everyone (any writer can use it), the nightingale serves, throughout the period of its migration that concerns me, not only as the vessel of an elite literary culture, established in its value from time out of mind. For Shakespeare's generation, it was also the harbinger of a new kind of English composition, paradoxically older than the ancients, that arrogated to itself the eloquent status that its temporal, geographic, and linguistic difference from classical Antiquity appeared to deny it.

If the nightingale is a sign of wealth in this sense, "intended to be evaluated and appreciated," it is also a sign of authority, "intended to be believed and obeyed."[6] In Petrarch's metrical epistles, the nightingale is "regina canentum | Phebeium" (the queen of Phobean singing); Spenser appeals to it, in *The Shepheardes Calender,* as "the souereigne of song."[7] Though Shakespeare invokes the nightingale as a way of as-

serting the independence of his vernacular writing from ancient literature, this gesture is never entirely free from the influence of the classical authors who first adopted this bird as a
figure for the kind of verbal art that was their own. How could
it be, when these allusions to the nightingale are partly moti-
vated by the desire to affiliate vernacular writing with classical
literature, which during the sixteenth century came to seem
more alien the more familiar it became? In this regard, the
Renaissance practice of imitation would appear to suspend
Shakespeare between the privilege that the nightingale be-
stows on vulgar composition and the sense of abjection that
arises from that very endowment. In Ovid's *Metamorphoses,*
the nightingale is a figure for precisely this tension—a way of
acknowledging that whenever writers submit themselves to a
tradition that is larger than themselves, they are both augmented and diminished by the experience. For Ovid's nightingale not only "bears" the literature that it represents, in the
sense of "conveying" it like a precious cargo from one period,
language, and writer to another. Because its song originates in
rape and mutilation, it also "suffers" the tradition that it embodies, thereby "giving birth" to new texts in which an older
writing reproduces and diversifies itself.

This is to point, in a preliminary way only, to the link between the pervasive sexual content of Ovid's version of the
nightingale myth and the poet's evident concern, in that critical episode, with the process by which Roman literature is be-
gotten from heterogeneous sources. Mindful of the debt that
his "modern" Latin poem bears to "ancient" Greek literature,
Ovid suggests that the literature to which the nightingale assimilates the different kinds of writing through which it passes
is itself a crossing of Greek and Latin, civil and savage, and foreign and familiar elements. This crossing the poet influentially

renders, time and again, as sexual congress (marriage) and sexual coercion (rape). While I would not want to argue that marriage and rape are identical, even for Ovid, they certainly resemble one another as metaphors for a poetic process that yokes its parts together and, from their difference, makes a hybrid composition.[8] Philomela's tapestry, the banquet in which Procne concocts her revenge, the complaint of the nightingale: all of these exquisite mixtures are figures for Ovidian composition. Notably, they are also the offspring of an eroticized encounter between Athens and Thrace, in which conquest obliges Pandion to surrender his daughters, as the spoils of war, to a barbarian called Tereus. Thus the rape of Philomela and Procne's passage into wedlock and childbirth are the figures of an Ovidian literary history: two explanations for what happened to Greek literature and Latin writing when Rome conquered Greece and was infused with its victim's civilizing stock.

In Ovid's parable about the foreign origins of Latin literature, both Tereus and Philomela are figures for the Roman writer *and* for the Hellenistic literature to which Roman writing succumbed when conquest imported it from Greece. Later, this aspect of Ovid's tale greatly influenced the way that Shakespeare came to understand and represent the relationship between classical literature and his own kind of writing in *Titus Andronicus*. For when Ovid establishes that poets are like rapists and like the victims of rape, he teaches Shakespeare to think of violence not only as the effect of writing but also as its precondition. On the one hand, the tale of Tereus and Philomela likely appealed to Shakespeare as a framework for imagining how a barbarous, English writing could take possession of a much more sophisticated Latin literature and engender something new on it. In this context, Aaron and the Goths are figures for the playwright, Lavinia for the classical corpus that he violently deflowers in the process of making a new vernacular text. But in contrast to this interpretation of the play, which Jonathan Bate has made familiar, I would argue that Ovid's tale also provides Shakespeare with a way of reversing those relationships, and of casting England and English writing as the fortunate victims of a Roman conquest.[9] For in the same way that Philomela represents Ovid in *Metamorphoses,* Lavinia represents Shakespeare; and when Lavinia is a figure for the vernacular poet, Aaron and the Goths serve as analogues for the classical literature that English writers came increasingly to experience as alien, ingenious, seductive, forceful, and cruel.[10]

From the fact that Shakespeare chose a raped and mutilated girl to symbolize his identity as a poet, we may infer an unusual idea. He appears to have believed that in order to be eloquent, he not only had to conquer Latin literature but also to be conquered by it. Possibly that idea helps to explain why Mulcaster describes England's relationship to Rome as a "meruellous bondage," and why Posthumus, a pivotal Britano-Roman character in Shakespeare's *Cymbeline* (c. 1611), embraces confinement near the end of the play, saying, "Most welcome, bondage, for thou art a way, | I think, to liberty" (5.4.3–4).[11]

We are accustomed to speaking of aesthetic excellence in terms of ravishment, and in that sense to acknowledging that the condition of ravishment is productive as well as destructive.[12] Even so, the idea that brutal domination produces artistic virtuosity—or more generally, that victims stand to benefit from violence and coercion—is shocking to us. It was, however, much less shocking to classical Rome and Renaissance England. Of the relationship between Rome and Athens, for example, Horace taught the Renaissance that "[c]aptive Greece made her savage victor captive, and brought the arts into rustic Latium" (Graecia capta ferum victorem cepit et artis | in-

tulit agresti Latio).[13] The argument here is not simply that the
Roman Empire improved itself by annexing Greece and plun-
dering its riches. To the contrary: Horace would also have us
understand that Rome enjoys the benefits of Hellenistic culture only to the extent that Rome itself surrenders to its cultivated victim. During the English Renaissance, this logic supported, and was supported by, the belief that learning and
authority had migrated westward since the fall of Troy (*trans-
latio studii et imperii*), following the path of conquest from
Asia to Greece, from Greece to Rome, and thence to England.
In this context, radical defeat is just the opposite of what we
think it ought to be: Conquest breaks ground for a new foundation, marking the beginning and enrichment of civilization,
rather than its demise. Through surrender, the dispossessed
obtain something from their masters that is, by definition,
more valuable than anything of theirs.

Of course, it required some ingenuity to fit these ideas to
the context of England's own antiquity. For those writers who
adapted Horace's text to the history that they were inventing
for English eloquence and English civilization (and by now it
is should be clear that eloquence and civilization are meto-
nyms for each other right across this period), it must have been
painfully clear that ancient Britain was no Athens, and that
Rome had nothing to gain from it. Thus William Camden observes, of the Roman Conquest of Britain, that benefit flows in
one direction, from victor to victim. Light comes from darkness,
prestige from humiliation, and authority from subjugation:

> This yoke of the Romanes although it were griev-
> ous, yet comfortable it proved and a saving health
> unto them; for the healthsome light of Iesus Christ
> shone withal upon the Britans, . . . and the bright-

nesse of that most glorious Empire, chased away all
savage barbarism from the Britans minds, like as
from other nations whom it had subdued. For Rome,
as saith Rutilius,

>———*Legeferis mundum complexa triumphis*
> *Foedere communi vivere cuncta facit:*
> Compassed the world with triumphs bringing lawes;
> And all to live in common league doth cause.
> And in another place speaking unto the same Rome . . . ;
> *Fecisti patriam diversis gentibus unam.*
> *Profuit iniustis te dominante capi.*
> *Dumque offers victis proprii consortia juris,*
> *Vrbem fecisti quod prius orbis erat.*
> Thou hast of divers nations one entire country
> framed,
> Happy it was for lawlesse folke, that they were by thee
> tamed.
> For offering use, to them subdu'd, of thine own
> proper lore,
> One civill state thou mad'st of that, which was wild
> world before.[14]

Camden is writing history, of course, but during this
period—when the nightingale came to prominence as a figure
for the incipient category of vernacular eloquence—this text
may have seemed like literary theory too; for it treats the Roman
Conquest not only as a historical event but also as a metaphor
that explains the origins and nature of eloquence in England.
A moment later, Camden argues that the "Romanes, having
brought over Colonies hither, and reduced the naturall inhabitants of the Iland unto the society of civill life, . . . trained them

up in the liberall Arts, and [sent] them into Gaule for learne perfectly the law"—and at this point he cites Juvenal as a witness:
"Gaule eloquent of Britans hath good pleading lawyers made."[15]
In *Remaines* (1614), Camden modifies this claim, citing Tacitus
instead of Juvenal. He would have us understand that of all the
races that Rome reduced to tributaries, the Britons were the
most inclined by nature to benefit from defeat, and through
surrender to acquire the kinds of distinction—learning, law,
civil life, and eloquence—that classical Antiquity alone had the
authority to bestow. "Tacitus . . . reporteth that *Julius Agricola*
Governour here for the Roman, preferred the Britans, as able
to do more by witte, then the Gaules by studie: *Ut qui* (saieth
he) *modo linguam Romanam abnuebant, eloquentiam concupis-
cerent*" (As a result . . . they who used to reject the Latin language
began to aspire to eloquence).[16]

    For Camden, the eloquence to which the ancient Britons
may attain, by virtue of their inborn wit, is Latinate rather
than vernacular. But his preference for Latin does not prevent
us from remarking on the similarities between Camden's arguments and the efforts that other writers made, during the
sixteenth century, in order to enhance the status of English
and invent a genuinely vulgar kind of eloquence. Camden is
indebted, for example, to Richard Mulcaster—who argues for
the intrinsic value of English writing, and for its autonomy
from Greek and Latin literature, but also identifies the rise of
eloquence in England with England's historic vulnerability as
a state. Thus while—or *because*—"our state is no *Empire* to
hope to enlarge it by commanding ouer cuntries," English
writers know "the mean . . . to turn to our vse all the great trea-
sur, of either foren soil, or foren language."[17]

    There is, however, another subtext in Camden's *Britain*,
much more significant for our purposes. Camden's argument

that eloquence arrived in England with the Roman Empire would appear to imitate a familiar myth in which the achievement of eloquence is unthinkable apart from the experience of ravishment and surrender. Seen through this lens, the Roman Conquest reenacts the legendary feats of Orpheus, the archaic poet whose eloquence subdued and civilized primitive human beings; distinguished public and private rights, and the sacred from the ordinary; established rules for marriage; built town walls in the wilderness; wrote down laws; and revealed the mysteries of the arts and sciences. In making this allusion, Camden is likely making a claim about the value and distinction of his own text: His history repeats the arrival of Orpheus in the wilderness, and of Rome on British shores, and in that way it positions itself as the receptacle of the precious gifts that Orpheus and Rome forcibly bestow.

More remarkably, however, Camden would appear to suggest that the history of Britain is structured like a literary tradition, in which every text must recapitulate its predecessors in order to succeed them. Camden may have gleaned that idea from Philemon Holland, his translator, who earlier called upon the vulgar writers of his generation "by all means to triumph now over the Romans in subduing their literature under the dent of the English pen, in requital of the conquest sometime over this Island, achieved by the edge of the sword."[18] Here, it is the nature of requital to repeat the injuries that it would redress, and of revenge to copy the events by which it is provoked. Renaissance England's most accomplished translator of Latin texts may have repudiated the Roman Conquest and its influence, but it was evidently a Roman sword that taught his English pen how and what it ought to write.

I think, then, that it is permissible to speak of the antiquarian poetics of Camden's *Britain,* and to observe that this text inserts itself in a conversation about the concept of vernacular eloquence that hearkens to Ovid's *Metamorphoses* and its meditation on the conquest of Roman writing by Hellenistic literature. In defense of that suggestion, I point to the word "yoke" at the forefront of the passage that we have been discussing. "Yoke" is English for "iugum," the word that Camden uses in the Latin original of *Britain:* "Hoc Romanorum iugum quamvis graue, tamen salutare fuit."[19] In Latin, "iugum" not only refers to the harness that teams of oxen wear when ploughing fields, or to signs of servitude in general. It also means the bonds of matrimony ("conjugal") and the beam of a weaver's loom (Ovid uses it thus in reference to Arachne).[20] In the context of these associations, "yoke" and "iugum" mark the place where Camden's *Britain* intersects *Metamorphoses,* finds the object of its antiquarian research reflected in the nightingale myth, and acknowledges a preoccupation that they share: to wit, the threshold at which one thing becomes another; two different things become the same; or several different kinds blend together in order to give rise to new kinds and new distinctions. Like Philomela's loom and Procne's marriage, the "yoke of the Romanes" appears to be a metaphor for a coercive process that changes barbarism into civility, servitude into authority, rape into marriage, and conquest into cultivation; while the vernacular eloquence that arises from this process is like a fabric made from different threads or the offspring of an interracial union. Though Camden differentiated his antiquarian "kinde of argument" from poetry and rhetoric on the grounds that in was "*incapable of all Eloquent speech,*" he apparently discovered that if he wanted to explain how modern English culture arose from British and Roman stocks, yoked together by a violence that acknowledged their distinction, he would need to treat the passage of time as though it were the practice of imitation, and to tell the story of English eloquence in the manner of the nightingale.[21]

The Nightingale's Line of Flight

What if one became animal or plant *through* literature . . . ? Is it not through the voice that one becomes animal?[22]

Possibly it would be more plausible to argue that the tale of Philomela casts a shadow on Camden's *Britain*, instead of intersecting it. Yet there is persuasive evidence, to the contrary, that the nightingale is waiting to be flushed from the thickets of Camden's antiquarian prose. Several English poets that come before Camden, and use the nightingale as a figure for their vulgar eloquence, make a point of linking native invention to foreign conquest with the word *iugum*. In 1533, for example, Robert Saltwood describes the sound of the nightingale's music as "iug," writing that "In manifold notes lyke wonderus," this bird sings "iug/ iug right meruelus." Then he compares the nightingale's virtuosity in disposing of its notes ("Freshe subtly and redy of outerraunce, | Facunde/ elegaunt and of remembraunce") to the strategy of Alexander the Great, "who berith the name | Cesar" and "Whos polycy triumph had ouer all"; and to Sertorius, a crafty Roman general. This is Saltwood's way of claiming that his modern invention is as shrewd as ancient policy, his eloquence as irresistible as conquest. But note: He also professes to be amazed that "So lytel a byrde" could "muse that lesson | So audible/ so tewnable in good facyon." To the extent that his amazement implies the condition of ravishment or abjection, it would appear that Saltwood anticipates Camden by suggesting that English eloquence is characterized by a tension between potency and impotence. Here it is Saltwood himself who falls victim to the "greatest conquest left in wrytting" that "[t]o a lytel body came"; and according to a logic upon which Camden later seized, the nightingale must first enthrall the poet in order to exalt his vulgar writing.[23]

The connection that Saltwood makes between eloquence and conquest is strengthened if we assume that "iug" is a contraction or an echo of *iugum*. George Gascoigne links these words explicitly in *The Complaynt of Phylomene* (1576). Here, the nightingale appears to the poet in a dream, and having summarized Ovid's version of her story, she sings four notes: "Tereu," "Fy," "Iug," and "Nemesis."[24] Each note refers to an aspect of the violence and degradation in which the nightingale's eloquence originates. "Tereu" is Tereus, Phylomene's Thracian rapist. "Fy" is the protest that Phylomene utters. "Iug" is onomatopoetic for her birdsong. "Nemesis" is the name of Just Revenge, who arrives near the end of the text in order to gloss these notes and exhort the poet to "make . . . a metaphor" from all that he has heard.[25] When Just Revenge comes to "Iug," she calls upon "latynists, | By learning to expresse" whether it "should onely *Iugum* meane | Or *Iugulator* [murderer] too." For "Some think that *Iugum* is | The *Iug*, she iugleth so" but "*Iugulator* is the word | That doubleth al hir woe." In this way, "Iug" becomes an acoustical link between the notes of Phylomene's song, the virtuosity with which she sings them ("iugleth"), and an experience of coercion that is indissociable from ancient Rome and the "learning" of "latynists" ("iugum," "iugulator"). And from here it is a short step to the theory of literary production that Gascoigne articulates through the words of Just Revenge in these lines: "At last (by griefe constrained) | [Her conscience] boldely breaketh out, | And makes the hollow wood to ring | With *Eccho* round about."[26]

Whether Just Revenge refers to the yoke of oppression or of marriage when she uses the phrase "should only *Iugum* meane," it is difficult to know. A moment later, she points to both of these possibilities, observing of the nightingale that "when she thinkes thereon [*Iugulator*], | She beares them both in minde, | Him [Tereus], breaker of his bonde in bed, | Hir [Procne], killer of hir kinde." I would suggest, however, that rather than try to clarify this point, we ought to ask why Gascoigne goes to elaborate lengths to make the nightingale's song seem opaque. For anyone who is familiar with Ovid's tale of Philomela—or, for that matter, with Gascoigne's *Complaynt*—will have no trouble deciphering the notes that Phylomene sings. It is therefore noteworthy that the poet himself pretends to find her song ambiguous, and that Just Revenge tends to obscure rather than elucidate its meaning. Gascoigne's insight would appear to be that only by estranging this most familiar convention of Latin literature, and by framing Latin eloquence as animal sounds, can English poets turn the categories of eloquence and literature to new uses and claim the nightingale as the symbol of their vulgar kind of writing. When Just Revenge associates the "Iug" in Phylomene's song with adulteration, bondbreaking, and crimes against kinship, Gascoigne acknowledges that in order to become eloquent, he must return to the scene of an ancient humiliation and augment it through repetition (when "Iug" means "Iugulator," it "doubleth all her woe"). Notably, however, he also represents vulgar eloquence itself as a mixture of kinds and a transgression of boundaries—as a wild music that "boldely breaketh out" from the forest of its classical precursors in order to become *their* model, obliging them to echo it.

To a significant degree, *The Complaynt of Phylomene* established the terms in which later English poets would use the

nightingale in order to distinguish a certain kind of vernacular writing from the classical literature that it imitated. Gascoigne's influence is particularly felt in the "August" eclogue of
The Shepheardes Calender, where the nightingale joins her
voice to the "nightly cryes" of Colin Clout, "the more taug-
ment | The memory of hys misdeede, that bred her woe." Colin
imitates Philomela's "songs and plaintiue pleas" in turn, and
through animal sounds he finds the way to enhance the status
of Spenser's modern English poem and present it as a classical
achievement.[27] Subtler than Gascoigne, though no less drawn
to the imaginative possibilities of philology, Spenser takes his
word "augment" from the Latin verb *augere,* the word from
which *auctor* (author) and *auctoritas* (authority) are also de-
rived, meaning "to increase" in value, status, size, amount, volume, and intensity.[28] Here, "augment" calls our attention to a
basic paradox of Renaissance imitation theory: In order to be
more than your precursors, you must also be the same. Spenser
realizes that paradox in the form of his eclogue, for the song
that Cuddie sings at the conclusion of "August" is a complaint
by Colin Clout that other shepherds have urged him to repeat.
It is, moreover, a sestina: a poem of six stanzas of six lines, in
which the same six rhyme words are repeated in six different
sequences before returning to their original order in a final ter-
cet; here the rhyme words are "woe," "sound," "cryes," "part,"
"sleepe," and the pivotal term "augment." Spenser frames all of
this artifice as a repetition of birdsong, not merely juxtaposing
but synthesizing the sounds that animals make, sounds heard
against the backdrop of "wild woddes," with verse forms of the
utmost sophistication and polish. In this way, he implies that
the "gallimaufray or hodgepodge" of aesthetic kinds (ancient
and modern, classical and vulgar, Roman and Gothic, human
and animal), over which the nightingale presides as "souereign"

and "blessed byrd," is a portrait of the heterogeneity of his own composition—like the "disorderly order" of the *Calender*'s title page, where roman, italic, and black letter type-faces are all employed to make the point that Spenser's text is both familiar and strange, old and new; that it is, as Margreta de Grazia has put it, a "Gothic Classic."[29]

Paradoxical conflations of different "parts" are the hallmarks of Spenserian writing in *The Shepheardes Calender*. Taken together, they are arguably its most consequential feature for the English writers who were Spenser's contemporaries, including Shakespeare. For they provide a framework in which the innate indecorum of Renaissance English—a language that descends from radically different word stocks that "il . . . accorde"— may be seen as giving rise to a new modality of decorum: a vulgar decorum, conceptually dependent on classical aesthetics but as consistently heterogeneous as the "mother tongue" to which even native speakers come as "straungers" and "alienes." In this context, E. K. acknowledges that Spenser's poem is a patchwork fabric of hard, obsolete, and foreign words, but he would also have us understand that it is "knitt[ed]" in such a way that it is as round and flows as smoothly as any classical "Periode." Thus he summons the very corpus of ancient aesthetics in order to defend the changes that Spenser makes to its elementary distinction between decorum and indecorum: "[So] great delight tooke the worthy Poete Alceus to behold a blemish in the ioynt of a wel-shaped body." Thus "oftentimes a dischorde in Musick maketh a comely concordaunce." And thus the "shrieking sound" and "yrksome yells" of "banefull byrds" may be said to "tune" the poet's compositions until they are as sweet as the nightingale's "songs and plaintiue pleas."[30]

I would argue that the sestina in the "August" eclogue is one of Spenser's most important attempts to invent the foundation of a vernacular literature, a new textual distinction which, in its English context, arises from a commingling of "kind" and "unkind." For it is here that Spenser metaphorizes the internal contradiction and self-estrangement of the English language—what the first English lexicographer described as the "difference of English"—as an animal cacophony, erupting from a place beyond the boundaries of the human order.[31] At the same time, Spenser insists that were it not for that noise, there would be no harmony; indeed, for him noise is one of harmony's own parts, or counterparts. Shifting the question of Spenserian decorum from the ear to the eye, E. K. remarks that "[e]uen so do those rough and harsh termes enlumine and make more clearly to appeare the brightnesse of braue and glorious words."[32] From this perspective, and in this light, it is easier to see that for Spenser and the writers who imitated him, among them Shakespeare, the nightingale's beastliness is as critical to her function as a symbol for decorous vulgarity as her historical association with the excellence of ancient literature or with the sweetness of Petrarchan lyric. For as the harbinger of spring, the nightingale is always the *first* musician, and by appealing to her song's primality, English poets asserted that their vernacular eloquence was even older than Antiquity, and of a piece with Nature. Or to reverse the terms of the epigraph with which I began this section: Writers like Spenser and Shakespeare sought the distinction of literature where we might least expect them to find it—in the domain of animals, plants, and stones. And there, through the nightingale, they spoke with remarkably eloquent voices.

Rather than dispense with decorum, or "decencie," as the central criterion for assigning value to verbal compositions, George Puttenham prefers to argue that "decencies are of sundrie sorts" and so to follow Spenser's lead: retaining decorum, for vernacular composition, as "the line and leuell for al good makers to do their business by."[33] In describing decorum as a "line and leuell," Puttenham draws explicitly upon the artisanal discourses of carpentry, surveying, and measurement; elsewhere, he argues that the poet is a maker "like the Carpenter and Ioyner," for "he vseth his metricall proportions by appointed and harmonicall measures and distaunces."[34] But suppose we thought more expansively about the concept of the line, for Puttenham's arguments, like Spenser's verses, subject it, and any taxonomy of value that it might be used to draw, to a certain pressure. In particular, they reveal that in the context of English, decorum's "line" is arbitrary rather than self-evident. Who shall say what divides good from bad compositions, or what makes *this* text precious and *that one* worthless? Acknowledging that "it may be a question who shal haue the determination of such controuersie as may arise whether this or that action or speech be decent or indecent," Puttenham appeals to the resources of "a learned and experienced discretion," which "resteth in the discerning part of the minde, so as he who can make best and most differences of things by reasonable and wittie distinction is to be the fittest iudge or sentencer of [*decencie*]."[35]

We can infer from other sections of the *Arte* that this ideal judge, "the discreetest man," is likely a courtier, since it is the "vsuall speech of the Court, and that of London and the shires lying about London within lx. myles, and not much aboue," that Puttenham would establish as the normative idiom, or "mother speach," of the entire country.[36] But what concerns me here, in his chapter on decorum, are the other possibilities that arise from Puttenham's commitment to the line as a principle of "discretion"—a commitment that he makes at the very moment that he shifts from theory to practice and from precept to example, describing so many instances of "decencie" and "vndecencie" that it becomes impossible to ascertain on what basis "the best . . . differences of things" are finally to be made.[37] These passages suggest that though he chafes against the authority of Greek and Latin aesthetics throughout the *Arte*, Puttenham derives decorum (the standard for measuring the value of every English line) from classical criteria like symmetry, proportion, and definitude. On the other hand, something like the opposite is also true. For in this text the line of decorum implies continuity (lineage) as well as differentiation (borderlines). Indeed, where "[*decencie*] comes to be very much alterable and subiect to varietie," decorum's "line and leuell" will often be nonlinear and perforce indefinite: a boundless limit and an open closure; a rule and its exemplary exception; no less an oxymoron than the vulgar decorum, vernacular eloquence, or English literature whose conceptual foundations Puttenham uses it to sketch.[38]

I would argue that during the 1590s Shakespeare embraced decorum as the "line and leuell" of his verbal art, but also that he practices decorum, like Spenser, in a remarkably equivocal way. Represented by the nightingale and echoed in her song, the vulgar decorum of Shakespearean writing may be described as a paradox—if you will, as a norm and deviation all at once. In this context the line remains a useful figure for understanding the relationship between ancient and modern writing, as Shakespeare frames it in the *Sonnets* and *Titus Andronicus*. For Shakespeare would appear to grasp the concept of decorum not only in terms of what Deleuze and Guattari call "lines of articulation and segmentarity, strata and territories" but also in terms of what they call "lines of flight, movements of deterritorialization and destratification."[39] For Deleuze and Guattari, every book amounts to a combination of these different kinds of lines: "Comparative rates of flow on these lines produce phenomena of relative slowness and viscosity, or, on the contrary, of acceleration and rupture. All this, lines and measurable speeds, constitutes *an assemblage*."[40] In my argument, the nightingale is a figure for both of these senses of the "line," and for a way of thinking that English writing is simultaneously continuous with the classical literary tradition and radically differentiated from it. The nightingale places Shakespeare in a poetic lineage that descends from classical Antiquity; and as a fixed point of reference in the shifting landscape of Renaissance textuality, it guarantees the value of his work by differentiating it from other kinds of English writing, to which it is presumably unrelated even by the mother tongue. On the other hand, as a figure for the process of poetry and its ongoing transmission, the nightingale is also perpetually in motion: a fluctuation rather than a monument, like the "living record" of Shakespeare's lines of verse.[41] I mean that the nightingale not only symbolizes a prestigious literary past, fixed and foreclosed in the succession of historical periods. It also stands for the passage of time within literary tradition, and in this context its line of flight is a metaphor for an indeterminate relationship and change. If the nightingale imposes certain limits on the Renaissance discourse of textual value, it also soars above the terrain of those distinctions, puts them in perspective, and traverses them. I contend that it is from crossings like these that a new breed of English poets takes flight in the 1580s and 1590s—conceived and fledged, like their eloquent vulgarity, beneath the shadow of Philomela's wings.

Warbling

Tu, filomela, potes vocum discrimina mille,
  Mille vales varios rite referre modos.
Nam quaevis aliae volucres modulamina temptent,
  Nulla potest modulos aequiperare tuos.

[Philomela, you are able to repeat the distinctions
of thousands of voices, skilled rightly to render
thousands of varying tunes—other birds may essay
what modulations they like, your melodies none
can rival.][42]

If we want to understand why Shakespeare represented
his English poetry as birdsong during the 1590s, and why he
took the nightingale as a symbol for his kind of writing, we
might begin by observing that the nightingale has always been
associated with crises of classification. In book 19 of Homer's
Odyssey, for example, as her patience reaches its breaking point,
Penelope wonders whether she ought to violate the bonds of
wedlock and marry one of the suitors, or remain faithful to her
absent husband and their son. She asks, in effect, "Who am I?,"
and the implications of the question extend well beyond herself. The answer will not only determine Penelope's identity:
where she belongs, and to whom, and what kind of woman she
is. In the run up to the climactic battle between Odysseus and
the suitors in book 22, her answer will also define, for every
character, what it means to be *philos* or *xenos*, "one of us" or
"one of them." For were Penelope to choose another husband,
there would be no home to which Odysseus could return; and
but for her fidelity, he would be Agamemnon or Menelaus.
Until Penelope decides who she is (Penelope, Clytemnestra,

Helen), Odysseus can be neither one person nor another. In this critical scene, he stands with Penelope at the boundary between reunion and repudiation, in the guise of a familiar-looking stranger.

Penelope compares herself to Aedon as she wavers, the daughter of Pandareos, who killed her own son, Itylos, in error; and whom the gods, aroused to pity by her lamentation, later changed into a nightingale, the bird to whom she gives her name ("Aedon" means "nightingale" in Greek). The allusion is presumably intended to restore stability to Penelope's identity and locate it in a commonplace. But in George Chapman's translation of the *Odyssey*, it has just the opposite effect and prolongs the period of her indecision as metaphor:

> . . . And as all night
> Pandareus' daughter, poor Edone, sings,
> Clad in the verdure of the yearly Springs,
> When she for Itylus, her loved Sonne
> (By Zethus' issue, in his madnesse done
> To cruell death) poures out her hourely mone,
> And drawes the eares to her of every one:
> So flowes my mone, that cuts in two my minde,
> And here and there gives my discourse the winde,
> Uncertain whether I shal with my Son
> Abide still heere . . .
> Or follow any best Greeke I can chuse. . . . [43]

The analogy between Penelope and the nightingale turns here on the word "mone," which Chapman uses for Aedon's cry (ὀλόφυρσις) and for Penelope's heart or mind (θῡμός). Evidently, "mone" is a variant spelling of "moan," meaning "lamentation" or "complaint." It also derives from the Old English verb *gemunan*, which means "to remember" or "to bear in mind"; and thus, in its substantive form, "mone" means "memory" or "thought," from which moaning can arise.[44] Chapman's knowledge of Old English is, of course, an open question, but if we fail to take this more archaic sense of "mone" into consideration, we may be likely to infer that Penelope and Aedon resemble one another because they have suffered similar losses, and bemoan them; and that idea is Petrarchan rather than Homeric. Unlike Aedon, Penelope has not slain her child or even lost him; unlike Shakespeare's Lucrece, who later compares her "deep groans" to Philomela's "sad strain," neither Aedon nor Penelope has been raped.[45] When Penelope identifies her reflection in the nightingale, she may be contemplating the fact that like Aedon she is at risk of slaying her son, by disinheriting him, but she is also identifying change itself. Chapman's ingenious play on "mone" clarifies that for her, the avian voice that emanates from the trees, changeable and various ("τρωπῶσα χέει πολυηχέα φωνήν"), is an acoustical portrait of the ambivalence to which her own mind stirs ("ἐμοὶ δίχα θυμὸς ὀρώρεται ἔνθα καὶ ἔνθα"). Penelope means that the structure of her feeling is the same as the form of Aedon's music—that her mind is simultaneously as fluid ("so flowes my mone") and fragmented ("that cuts in two my minde") as the nightingale's lament, which in Homer's poem is a paradox: a seamless pouring forth of many sounds, each distinguished from the others. In a turn that puts the status of the poet himself at issue, Penelope's question, "Who should I be?" becomes synonymous with Homer's, "How should I sing?"

In framing this relationship between Penelope's state of mind and the formal characteristics of the nightingale's music, Homer makes an important claim about the nature of poetic representation, and about continuity and difference as they bear on the question of a composition's virtuosity. Aedon's song, Penelope's flight into metaphor, and the *Odyssey* itself arise from paradoxes in which the difference between self and other, like and unlike, no longer seems self-evident or viable. As compositions, they are called into being by crisis: by transgressions of boundaries (Aedon kills her own son); by blurred distinction (Penelope may be Odysseus's wife, or his widow); and by the confusion of kind with unkind (even at home Odysseus would appear to be an exile). But thereupon they take up the impossible task of clarifying the very ambiguities that elicit them, and of stabilizing categories that are, perforce, in flux. For to make a metaphor, any metaphor, is to blur the line between one kind of thing and another, or traduce it; in the case of Penelope's allusion to the nightingale, it is the line that separates human beings from wild animals. This is what Homer's extraordinary passage teaches Roman poets and rhetoricians and what they, in turn, teach their Renaissance readers. In precisely this context, Puttenham calls metaphor "the figure of *transport*" and "a kinde of wresting of a single word from his owne rightfull signification, to another not so naturall, but yet of some affinitie or coueniencie with it."[46] Homer's insight in the *Odyssey* is that crisis is the precondition and the product of poetry, and when we see it through the prism of his nightingale, poetry itself would appear to be crisis. For the nightingale's song and Penelope's metaphor are like the shroud that Penelope makes and unmakes every day. They postpone the resolution toward which they point; and in doing that they expose a fundamental tension between poetry's heterogeneous materials and the poetic movement that blends them all together.

Homer's description of the nightingale passed through many different genres on its way to the English Renaissance, depositing its influence in each and in that way accruing more. When the ancient zoologist Aelian discusses the range and variety of the nightingale's voice, for example, he quotes *Odyssey* 19.518–21.[47] Behind Aelian there also stands Pliny, who held that the nightingale, alone among the birds, enjoyed "a perfect knowledge of music" ("perfecta musicae scientia") as its natural endowment.[48] I would argue that Pliny refers to Homer's *Odyssey* as well, amplifying the relevant verses in this way, in Philemon Holland's translation:

> [S]hee alone in her song keepeth time and measure truely; shee riseth and falleth in her note just with the rules of musicke and perfect harmonie: for one while, in one entire breath she draweth out her tune at length treatable; another while she quavereth, and goeth away as fast in her running points: sometime she maketh stops and short cuts in her notes, another time shee gathereth in her wind and singeth descant between the plaine song: she fetcheth her breath againe, and then you shall have her in her catches and division: anon all on a sodaine, before a man would think it, she drowneth her voice, that one can scarce heare her: now and then she seemeth to record to her selfe; and then shee breaketh out to sing voluntarie. In summe, she varieth and altereth her voice to all keyes: one while, full of her largs, longs, briefes, semibriefes, and minims; another while in her crotchets, quavers, semiquavers, and double semiquavers: for at one time you shall heare her voice full and lowd, another time as low; and anon shrill and on high: thicke and short when she list; drawne out at leisure againe when she is dis-

posed: and then (if shee be so pleased) she riseth &
mounteth up aloft, as it were with a wind-organ.
Thus she altereth from one to another, and singeth
all parts, the Treble, the Meane, and the Base.[49]

Holland follows Pliny here and fashions a single period
from a remarkable range of subordinate clauses. The passage
is a mimesis of the formal characteristics of the nightingale's
song and exemplifies the acoustical phenomenon that it would
explain.[50] Pliny's superbly crafted sentence became the standard text for scientific queries about the nightingale's voice
during the Renaissance; Pierre Belon's *L'histoire de la Nature
des Oyseaux* (1555) quotes it verbatim.[51] Unsurprisingly, perhaps, considering its subject matter and delicacy of composition, and its debt to Homer, it also came to have authority in
the discourse of rhetoric and poetics—authority that we can
trace in the pages of another Renaissance ornithology, the *Ornithologiae* of Ulisses Aldrovandi (1599–1605).

For Aldrovandi, the nightingale is more than a bird with
musical abilities, more than the most eloquent of birds. It is
the emblem of eloquence itself: "A hieroglyphic," he writes,
"not only for the best poet but for the perfect orator too" ("Non
solum autem optimi poetae, sed perfecti oratoris hieroglyph-
icum dici potest Luscinia").[52] In defense of this claim, Aldrovandi
quotes *Exercitatio linguae latinae*, a grammar-school text by
Juan Luis Vives, a contemporary philologist. Published in 1539,
and printed in more than one hundred editions by the turn of
the following century, this collection of Latin dialogues about
life in the humanist curriculum is meant to teach a method for
speaking and writing well. In one of the dialogues, a figure
called Ioannius argues that for every human sense, God fur-
nishes some outstanding pleasure in which it may be steeped

("egregia aliqua voluptate perfundatur"). With respect to hearing, he says that this pleasure is birdsong, and the harmony of the nightingale's music above all others ("concentus avium et potissimum lusciniae"). Vives supplies a paraphrase of Pliny's sentence at this point, in order to describe that music[53] (later, Henry Hawkins translated it into English in an emblem called "The Nightingal").[54] And thus, renovated by Vives, Pliny passes into the curriculum of the language arts, where his text about the nightingale's virtuosity becomes a theory and *exemplum* of eloquence for the generation of schoolboys that included Shakespeare. In particular, it becomes an authority for the concept that eloquent compositions, though they are made from many parts, are also indivisible; that eloquence is not reducible to *this* or *that* part of writing but arises as a certain dynamic relationship between them. This is the difficult idea that the Richard Niccols strains to capture in 1607, when he contrasts the monotony of the cuckoo's song, which has "no varietie, no change, no choice," with the "warble" of the nightingale, which "all at once with many parts in one, | Diuid[es] sweetly in diuision."[55] It is small wonder, in this context, that Antony refers to Cleopatra as "my nightingale," since every "defect" contributes to "perfection" in the "infinite variety" of her speech.[56]

As my quotation from Niccols will testify, it was the common practice of English writers in this period to refer to the peculiar eloquence of the nightingale's song as "warbling," and possibly there is no vulgar word more copious in its metaphorical reference to the act of poetic composition. For as it entered English from the Old French *werbler*, the word "warble" came to refer to a variety of related movements: the plucking of strings on musical instruments; the quiver of a bird's tongue as it sings; the rustle of feathers when a bird alights on a perch or mounts aloft; the trill of streams over obstacles in their paths; and the blowing of wind through trees.[57] Through an English corruption of the word "whorl," "warble" also meant "spindle" and so referred to a weaver's movement at the loom.[58] In each of these cases, it is a tiny step from eye to ear, from the way that a vibration looks to the sound that it makes.

Over and above the synesthesia that it names, "warbling" also points to the relationship of apparently antithetical activities: to the link between composure and discomposure, organization and disruption, making and unmaking—or, recalling the arguments that I made earlier, between destruction and creation. It implies the idea, unusual for us, that artists must disturb their materials in order to put them together—in the same way that birds shake their wings in order to arrange them, or that water breaks over rocks that it submerges in its flow. As an image of what a composition should be, a warble is therefore a coming apart and a coming together. In *A Midsummer Night's Dream*, Helena uses warbling in order to describe her "schoolday's friendship" with Hermia: "an union in partition," when they were "two artificial gods" who made "one flower | Both on one sampler," "Both warbling of one song, both in one key," as if their different "hands, . . . voices and minds | Had been incorporate" and only "seeming parted."[59] This is to find in warbling the master trope of imitation, and in the nightingale an image of the process by which poets construct their writing from pieces of many different texts. For in Shakespeare's play the "ancient love" of Hermia and Helena represents one way that different artists may relate to each another when they share the same material. Framed as warbling, that relationship reveals itself as an oscillation: neither an identity nor an absolute difference, but a resemblance.

In this context, it behooves us to remember that Milton once referred to Shakespeare as a warbler: "sweetest Shake-

speare," he calls him in *L'Allegro*, "fancy's child," who "Warble[s] his native wood-notes wild."[60] Shakespeare's association
with the nightingale in this poem is not coincidental. Comparing *L'Allegro* to *Il Penseroso*, we find that Shakespeare stands
in apposition to Philomela, whom Milton also calls the "sweetest" musician, resorting to another alliterative verse in order to
describe her "Most musical, most melancholy" song.[61] The
lines about Shakespeare in *L'Allegro* are resonant in their own
right, and their explication must await a reading of *Sonnet* 102,
the Shakespearean text that Milton ruminates. But as a prologue to that reading, I want to point out that "Warble," "wood-
notes," and "wild" are all pivotal and overdetermined words in
relation to the question with which we began, the same question that Milton asks in this poem as he weighs the merits of
one poetic model against another: "What kind of writer is
Shakespeare?"

From Milton's perspective, Shakespeare's poems are
"wood-notes" because an English nightingale has sung them,
and because they sit against the backdrop of a forest of earlier
writing that Milton is felling for its poetic timber. The forest in
L'Allegro is also an image of the time of Shakespeare's writing,
a way of suggesting that Shakespeare is ancient in relation to
the modernity of Milton's text, though Milton was born during Shakespeare's lifetime. For Milton, as for many English
writers of his period, the forest represents a primitive moment, before the dawn of classical civilization, when a vulgar
and "native" kind of poetry first arose from nature—or is it, in
this case, from Shakespeare, whose works (in Milton's estimation) become synonymous with nature, achievements never to
be repeated? Of the "prioritie of time" in relation to the origins
of English eloquence, Puttenham significantly remarks that
"our maner of vulgar Poesie is more ancient then the artificiall

of the Greeks and Latines, ours coming by instinct of nature, which was before Art . . . , and vsed with the sauage and vn-ciuill, who were before all science or ciulitie."[62] In this context, it is easier to see that the "wood" in "wood-notes"—by virtue of its association with "madness," "ferocity," and "violence"— also points emphatically to "wild," the word that modifies it at the end of the line, and indeed that all of the definitions of "wood" that Milton puts in play consequentially derive from the Old English *wod*, meaning "song," "poetry," or "excited" in the sense of being "inspired."[63] It is also easier to see that Milton is making a comment about the specifically vulgar character of the Shakespearean writing that he emblazons with a classical topos: Milton's eulogy for Shakespeare's sweetness is a critique of the origins of English eloquence, as Shakespeare has come to represent them in Milton's own poem. For in the process of displaying Shakespeare as an ancient poet, Milton's allusion to the nightingale obliges us to regard Shakespearean antiquity with a certain ambivalence. These lines reason that while it may be superlatively sweet, Shakespeare's music is perforce as wild as the primeval past from which it springs, and as bestial as the animal in which the poet finds his predecessor's voice. Milton invites us to imagine that Shakespeare's wild music is as different from the classical measures of his own poetry as Shakespeare's native fancy is from "Jonson's learned sock."[64] In this context, Shakespeare is "antic" whereas Milton aspires to be "antique"; the Renaissance spelled and pronounced these different words in the same way.

Contemporary readings of the *Sonnets* tend to emphasize the balance, delicacy, and control that these poems exhibit, and rightly so. But from Milton's perspective, it might have seemed that Shakespeare's affinity for paradox and bold reversal was indicative of a very different kind of eloquence: of a vulgar eloquence, or a warbling, that was wildly inclined to violate distinction and generate what Shakespeare himself calls "compounds strange" (76.4). The dynamic quality of Shakespearean verse in this respect, by turns sophisticated and ferocious, is everywhere in evidence in the *Sonnets*. Arguably, however, no single poem is more given to "variation and quick change" (76.2) than 102, where the nightingale—which is both male (102.7) and female (102.10)—captures in its body the extreme hybridity of Shakespeare's warbling and his "wood-notes wild."

The nightingale's arrival in *Sonnet* 102 coincides with a familiar crisis of value and problem of distinction that the poem's opening lines bring to the forefront of our attention:

> My loue is strengthened though more weak in
>   seeming,
> I loue not lesse, though lesse the show appeare,
> That loue is marchandiz'd, whose ritch esteeming,
> The owners tongue doth publish euery where.
>   (102.1–4)

In this context, the nightingale appears (but only appears!) to symbolize Shakespeare's affiliation with a tradition of vernacular complaint poetry that the English Renaissance credited to Petrarch.[65] Dressed in the nightingale's familiar plumage, and complaining about love, the poet implies that he and all sonnet writers, after Petrarch, are birds of a feather. On the other hand, he also disclaims the affiliation that he displays by conspicuously assigning his birdlike song to a moment *in the past*, when his poetry and his love were fledglings and Petrarchan fruit did not yet cloy the palate. The poet argues that when "[o]ur loue was new, and then but in the spring," he "was

wont to greet it with [his] laies, I As *Philomell* in summers front
doth singe, I And stops his pipe in growth of riper daies . . ."
(102.5–8). Although the summer is not "less pleasant now I
Then when her mournefull himns did hush the night," he says
that times have changed: A "wild musick burthens euery bow, I
And sweets growne common loose their deare delight" (102.9–
12). Therefore, lest his "songe" and subject grow "dull," losing
the distinction that sharply sets them off from other lovers and
other works of art, Shakespeare chooses, "like her [*Philomell*],"
to "some-time hold [his] tongue" (102.13–14). While his reference to blunted and to blunting tongues recalls the most grue-
some and familiar passages of Philomela's story, it also differentiates Shakespeare's poem from his sources. In the same way
that Spenser distances himself from Petrarch and his poetic
brood by allowing Colin Clout to break the "oaten pype" on
which he made his "complaints of loue so louely," Shakespeare
stops his own pipe and ties his own tongue in *Sonnet* 102. Thus
he points to the line that separates his writing from the vernacular and classical traditions that it invokes, all the same, as
its own kind.[66]

It is only at the end of the poem, then, that we come to
appreciate its most remarkable feature: The nightingale stands
not for Shakespearean singing but for silence—a silence that
silences all other sounds by virtue of its eloquence. According
to a contemporary proverb, "It is a speciall vertue to speake
little & well," and "Silence is a sweet eloquence."[67] Where apparent weakness is real strength and prodigality cheapens the
objects of its expense, we may infer that poverty is wealth,
dearth abundance, reticence loquacity, and silence *copia*. Cicero
would have it that eloquence is "wisdom speaking copiously"
("copiose loquens sapientia"), wisdom "accommodated to the
emotions and sensibilities of the common herd" ("ad motus

animorum vulgique sensus accommodatior").[68] But in *Sonnet* 102 Shakespeare reverses this dictum by arguing that his refusal to sing is more copious, and thus more eloquent, than any poem of "ritch esteeming," precisely because his "speechless song" (102.3, 8.13) is utterly uncommon—though it may be vulgar. Earlier, in *Sonnet* 85, Shakespeare argued that his "dumb thoughts" about his lover were just as "good" as any "polished form" produced by "golden quill" and "well-refinéd pen" (85 passim). In *Sonnet* 102 he claims that his silence is more valuable still, because it reaches back beyond Petrarch's vernacular lyrics to Ovid, and from classical literature recovers the silence that Philomela suffered as form of poetic agency: as a self-silencing that defines a difference not only between the poet and his vernacular rivals but also between his text and the Latin poem that it revises and supplants.

This is to treat silence in a way very different from Shakespearean drama, where the phrase "stop [the] mouth" is commonly associated with acts of passion that deprive another person of voice; or, indeed, from *Sonnets* 100 and 101, where the poet's Muse is "truant" and his silence indicates a failure to represent the lover adequately. There, the Muse admonishes the poet that "Truth needs no colour with his colour fixed. | Beauty hath no pencil beauty's truth to lay." She reasons, to the contrary, that "best is best if never intermixed" (101.1, 6–8). These lines keep faith with another Renaissance commonplace that is significant for our purposes: "Eloquence ought to be lyke gold which is then of greatest price and value, vhen [*sic*] it hath the least drosse in it."[69] In this context, the silence into which Shakespeare says that he has lapsed in *Sonnet* 102 would appear to be an unadulterated failure.

Except that nothing is unadulterated in the *Sonnets*, particularly in this poem. As we have had many occasions to observe, the nightingale never appears, but it represents a crisis of classification in which kind and unkind are distinguished only by their paradoxical resemblance. It is only the lover who "present'st a pure unstained prime" (70.8) somewhere beyond the contingencies of language. By contrast the nightingale, that more worldly harbinger of spring, tells another kind of time. It compounds rather than distinguishes different temporalities ("then" with "now," the antique past with the antic present), and in this way it points to a hybridity that distinguishes Shakespeare from every kind of writing on which he draws.

That is to say: *Sonnet* 102 appears to argue, straining credibility in the effort to represent an ideal love, that the poet's copious silence differs categorically from the "wild musick" of his rivals—differs in the same way that the nightingale's softly aspirated "*h*imns [that] *h*ush the night" differ acoustically from the low growl and dental clatter of the line with which that music is associated: "sweets *g*rown *c*ommon lose their *d*ear *d*elight" (italics mine). It is, of course, Milton, rather than Shakespeare, who calls Shakespeare's music "wild." Yet we must not forget that these are *both* Shakespearean verses, both elements of the selfsame poem. In the compounded text of *Sonnet* 102, the nightingale's presence reminds us that the poet's silence, like the hymn that the nightingale used to sing, is a version of the bestial music from which it has been differentiated, and vice versa. Conflations of this kind are the result of the exacting poetic discipline to which Shakespeare confines himself in the *Sonnets*, but they also require an extreme freedom—the very freedom that Geffrey Whitney identifies with the singing of the nightingale in an emblem called "Animi scrinium seruitus" (Bondage is the prison of the mind) (see figure 24).

Whitney observes that the nightingale "that chaunteth all the springe, | Whose warblinge notes, throughout the

His wordes, and deedes, that beares the face of frende,
Before you choose, suche one for your delite.

And if at lengthe, yow trye him by his tuche,
And finde him hault, whereby you stand in dout,
No harte, nor hand, see that you ioyne with suche
But at the first, bee bould to rase him out.
  Yet if by proofe, my wordes, and deedes agree,
  Then let mee still within your tables bee.

*Fabula, nox terris ab-
sentia longa diremit,
Nec perimet; toto licet
abstrahar orbe, vel æuo:
Nunquam animo di-
uisus agam; prius ipsa
recedet
Corpore vita mea, quã
vester pectore vultus.
Horat.1. Serm.1.
At pater vt gnati, sic
nos debemus amici,
Si quod sit vitium non
fastidire, &c.

Animi scrinium seruitus.

Ad ornatum virum, D. ELLISEVM GRYPHITH.

THE Prouerbe saithe, the bounde muste still obey,
 And bondage bringes, the freest man in awe:
Whoe serues must please, and heare what other saye,
And learne to keepe *HARPOCRATES his lawe:
 Then bondage is the Prison of the minde:
 And makes them mute, where wisedome is by kinde.

The Nightingall, that chaunteth all the springe,
Whose warblinge notes, throughout the wooddes are harde,
Beinge kepte in cage, she ceaseth for to singe,
And mournes, bicause her libertie is barde:
 Oh bondage vile, the worthie mans deface,
 Bee farre from those, that learning doe imbrace.

    N 3   *Multis*

*Silentij deus
apud Aegyptos.

24. A nightingale in a cage, from Geffrey Whitney's
A choice of emblemes (Leiden, 1586).
By permission of the Folger Shakespeare Library.

wooddes are harde, | Beinge kepte in cage, she ceaseth for to singe, | And mournes, because her libertie is barde." This proverbial wisdom suggests that for Shakespeare wilderness and wildness may have been the only contexts in which the nightingale, and the English poetry that she comes to represent, could be said to be eloquent. For warbling is indissociable from the liberties that it takes with language. It is, if you will, a form of a poetic license that violates the very limits that it posits. And in this sense it serves to think contradictions like silent singing and bestial eloquence; and therefore to pronounce the "wild musick" of the *Sonnets* and the "stretchèd metre of [Shakespeare's] antique song" (17.11).

Writing Destruction

. . . grande doloris
ingenium est, miserisque venit sollertia rebus.[70]

The wit that misery begets is great:
Great sorrow addes a quicknesse to conceit.[71]

From the eighteenth century to the present day, Shakespeare criticism has tended to assume that the poet's life was the basis of his work; and that his poems, like his plays, are much less indebted to his education or his art than they are to his apprehension of nature, a category to which Shakespeare himself is often assimilated. Following Ben Jonson, who distinguishes the uncanny verisimilitude of Shakespeare's writing from the poet's "small Latine and less Greek,"[72] Samuel Johnson attributes Shakespeare's "excellence" to "his own native force" rather than "the common helps of scholastick education, the precepts of critical science, and the examples of ancient authors." "There has always prevailed a tradition, that Shakespeare wanted learning," writes Johnson, "that he had no regular education, nor much skill in the dead languages. . . . Some have imagined, that they have discovered deep learning in many imitations of old writers; but the examples which I have known urged, were drawn from books translated in his time; or were such easy co-incidencies of thought, as will happen to all who consider the same subjects; or such remarks on life or axioms of morality as float in conversation, and are transmitted through the world in proverbial sentences." He continues in this vein until there is nothing to be done but to turn Shakespeare into nature; and at that point, the wildness of the natural world serves Johnson as a metaphor for the "barbarity" of Shakespeare's period, the unruliness of the English language at that time, and the "extravagance" of the poetic license that Shakespeare took. While "the work of a correct and regular writer is a garden accurately formed and diligently planted, varied with shades, and scented with flowers," Johnson argues that "the composition of Shakespeare is a forest, in which oaks extend their branches, and pines tower in the air, interspersed sometimes with weeds and brambles, and sometimes giving shelter to myrtles and to roses; filling the eye with awful pomp, and gratifying the mind with endless diversity."[73] Arguably, the passage hearkens to *L'Allegro*, and Milton would appear to have taught Johnson that while the sweet strains of Shakespeare's music stand out from the backdrop of the forest, the forest also frames them, gives them meaning, tells us what kind of sounds they are. As a warbler of woodnotes, Milton's Shakespeare more closely resembles a wild animal or a plant than he does a human being.

In contrast to this influential way of representing Shakespeare, I have argued that the poet's compositions, at least the early ones, arise from his studious engagement with the classical literature that he read in the Elizabethan grammar school.[74]

Stephen Booth dismisses Shakespeare's reference to the nightingale in *Sonnet* 102 as a trivial matter, writing that "*Philomel*" is "used simply as a poetic name for the species, with no active reference to the myth of Philomela."[75] My argument obliges us to give it much more weight. Though Jonson and Milton are apt to distinguish themselves from Shakespeare by pointing to the difference between his talent and their learning, Shakespeare's allusion to the nightingale suggests that classical literature was as instrumental in shaping his sense of vernacular poetic identity as it was in shaping theirs. The impact of the classics in this respect may be felt in Shakespeare's plays as well as his poems, but I would suggest that it is felt with particular acuity in *Titus Andronicus*, where Ovid's version of the nightingale myth receives its fullest elaboration as a topos for Shakespeare's imitative writing.

As we turn to that play, however, let us pause over *Sonnet* 23, a text that extends and complicates the meditation on eloquence that Shakespeare conducts in *Sonnet* 102. We are now in a position to see that *Sonnet* 23 also calls upon the nightingale as a symbol for the poet's vulgar eloquence. In its situation "between" *Sonnet* 102 and *Titus Andronicus*, it illuminates a transition that the category of eloquence is making through Shakespeare's early work: a transition not only from the ancient to the modern or from Latin to English but also from utterance to writing and from lyric to drama. In this context, the nightingale is more than a claim that Shakespeare's texts are eloquent. It is also a way of imagining the changes that *eloquentia* had to undergo in order to retain its pride of place within the hierarchy of value that English writers translated from classical Antiquity and adapted to the modernity of their vulgar compositions.

At the beginning of *Sonnet* 23 the poet solicits our attention by comparing himself, first, to "an vnperfect actor on the

stage," who cannot speak his lines from fright; then, to "some
fierce thing repleat with too much rage," whose "strengths
abondance weakens his owne heart" (23.1–4). I am like this
speechless actor and this wild beast, he argues, because "for
fear of trust, [I] forget to say, | The perfect ceremony of loues
right," and "in mine owne loues strength seeme to decay," when
I am, in fact, "[o]re-charged with burthen of mine owne loues
might" (23.5–8). By juxtaposing strength with weakness and
speech with silence, this poem echoes (or anticipates) *Sonnet*
102, though the first quatrain puts these leitmotifs in a different relation. While things are no more what they seem to be in
Sonnet 23 than in *Sonnet* 102, here the poet says that strength is
not belied by weakness; rather, it betokens it. Whereas in *Sonnet* 102 silence expresses his deliberate decision not to speak or
sing, in 23 it would appear to be a spasm, involuntary and in-
eloquent.

In the context of these reversals, Shakespeare uses the
word "eloquence" for the first and only time in the *Sonnets*,
linking it to writing as well as speech. "O let my books be then
the eloquence," he pleads, "And domb presagers of my speak-
ing brest, | Who pleade for loue, and look for recompence, |
More then that tonge that more hath more exprest" (23.9–12).
These lines change the direction in which the poem seemed to
be going when it described the poet as "vnperfect actor," whose
silence exposes his failure to play a part. Tacking instead toward the sentiments of *Sonnet* 102, they endow the poet's mute-
ness with "eloquence," a term of value that the poem promptly
assimilates to the inscription of a written text. The reassign-
ment of eloquence from the domain of audible speech to silent
writing occurs in conjunction with a noteworthy allusion to
the nightingale—a figure that is conjured here by the "tongue"
that Shakespeare uses the trope of synecdoche to sever from

the mouths of his poetic rivals, and even more so by the poet's
"speaking brest." According to a convention of Medieval poetry,
the nightingale makes its music by pressing its breast against a
thorn; it thereby gives voice to feelings that arise from within
its body, feelings that are, simultaneously, imposed from without. This is the convention that Philip Sidney uses as an image
of his own craft as a sonneteer, comparing himself to the nightingale, who "Sings out her woes, a thorne her song-booke mak-
ing," and "Her throate in tunes expresseth, | What griefe her
breast oppresseth."[76] In this figure of speech, Shakespeare follows him. For when Lucrece addresses the nightingale in the
aftermath of her rape and promises "to imitate thee well" (eloquence arises, once again, from ravishment), she means that
"against [her] heart" she will "fix a sharp knife," while "against
a thorn thou bear'st thy part" (*Lucrece* 1135–41). That promise
she fulfills at the moment of her death—and when suicide is
framed as an imitation of the nightingale's "part," we may describe it as an eloquent composition, even though it brings a
period to the broken speech, full of "many accents and delays, |
Untimely breathings, sick and short assays," that would appear
to be the opposite of warbling (*Lucrece* 1719–20).

Sonnet 23 suggests that when thorns are pens and blood
is ink, the nightingale's loquacious breast will solicit interpretation not only as membrane that exhalation crosses on its way
to becoming voice. It is also a surface on which a text is being
written. In this context, the phrase "speaking brest" may change
Shakespeare into a musical instrument, like a nightingale or a
pipe, through which inspired breath can blow; and in *Lucrece*
our heroine makes a version of this point when she describes
Philomela's thorn and her knife as "frets upon an instrument."
But "speaking brest" also conspicuously conveys the eloquence
that Antiquity reserved to the acoustical properties of music or

speech *upon writing*, which may be seen but not heard—
unless of course we use our eyes to hear it, as the poet urges us
to do in the sonnet's final couplet: "O learne to read what silent
loue hath writ, | To heare wit eies belongs to loues fine wit"
(23.13–14).

Referring to the paradoxical relationship between utterance and writing in the *Sonnets*, Joel Fineman argues that Shakespeare constructs a "disjunctive conjunction of, on the one
hand, a general thematics of vision and, on the other, a general
thematics of voice." Or to put it another way: The *Sonnets* trace
the decline of an "ontology of literary vision," which Fineman
associates with the idealizing praise of an epideictic tradition
"that reaches back to the invention of the 'literary' as an intel-
ligible theoretical category," into an "ontology of literary voice,"
in which "the very speaking of language" prevents the "literary
subjects of verbal representation" from revealing "their ideal
and visionary presence." In Fineman's view, the distinction of
Shakespearean poetry derives from this "historically significant entropic evacuation of the poetics of idealization," and
from the novel "literary subject" and "determinate poetic per-
sona" that "opens his mouth to speak in the aftermath of
praise." For him, Shakespeare's break with the classical tradition of epideixis is what it means for the *Sonnets* "to be literary" within the broader context of late sixteenth-century writing: to "recharacterize language as something duplicitously
and equivocally verbal rather than as something truthfully and
univocally visual," or "explicitly [to] put the difference *of* language into words."[77]

I think that these arguments are unsurpassed in their el-
egance and explanatory power so far as they concern Shakespeare's transformation of epideictic poetry and its premises.
But I also think that the difference of the *Sonnets* could be ad-

dressed in other terms—particularly if by "difference" we mean Shakespeare's tendency to flaunt the very features of his poems that pay the tribute of imitation to the classical texts from which he distinguishes his own. I want to suggest that in the process of using the nightingale in order to cross-couple hearing and vision, speech and writing, eloquence and silence, *Sonnets* 23 and 102 trace the opposite of the movement that Fineman describes as literary: a movement from the tongue and the ear to the hand and the eye. I would argue that this is precisely the path that Latin *eloquentia* follows as it changes into England's vulgar eloquence, the preeminent category of value for a new, vernacular writing. Possibly the movement of eloquence from speech to writing, and from poetry to drama, in early Shakespearean writing may be easier to gauge if we consider the degree to which Shakespeare's *Sonnets* depart from familiar paradigms of eloquence that the Renaissance inherited from Roman rhetoric. In the *Orator*, for example, Cicero stipulates that were it not for utterance, it would be impossible to conceive of eloquence, for the former is inherent to the latter. The word *eloquentia* comes from the verb *eloquor*, he reasons, meaning "I speak," and therefore the only term that may comprehend the full perfection of "the perfect orator and the highest species of eloquence" ("perfecti oratoris et summae eloquentiae species") is one that grants privilege to orality—like "eloquence" itself. For Cicero, "the all-inclusive word" that differentiates the ideal orator from other proficient users of language is "orator," and it can "not [be] *inventor* or *compositor* or *actor*," since "in Greek, [it is] *rhetor*, from 'speaking' [*eloquendo*], and in Latin he is called 'eloquent' [*eloquens*]."[78] Shakespeare's decision in *Sonnet* 23 to associate the eloquence of a "speaking brest" with silence and writing stands in sharp contrast to the Ciceronian arguments on which it would appear to be dependent.

Whether *Sonnet* 23 foreshadows *Titus Andronicus* or echoes it is not possible to know, but I would suggest that the resemblance between these texts is striking in one respect: *Titus Andronicus*, like *Sonnet* 23, represents the arrival of classical eloquence in Shakespearean writing as a relationship between an imperfect actor, or a wild animal, and an eloquent book. In a pivotal scene at the beginning of act 4, Shakespeare presents a raped and mutilated Lavinia as this actor and this animal, and Ovid as the ancient book from which the vulgar eloquence of his play silently arises as a written text. Using her lips to "[quote] the leaves" of "Ovid's *Metamorphosis*," which her nephew brings on stage, Lavinia reveals that "the tragic tale of Philomel" is her story, and that she is Shakespeare's nightingale: like Aaron and Titus, a portrait of the artist at his work. A moment later, shifting from quotation to inscription, Lavinia begins to write. Placing a staff in her mouth, she inscribes the word "Stuprum" and the names "Chiron" and "Demetrius" on a "sandy plot." Thus Shakespeare makes a conspicuous gesture to the sensibilities of writers like Saltwood, Gascoigne, and Camden, and he figures the origins of his English writing with the Latin word for rape.[79]

As this meditation on the process by which Renaissance poets turned their ancient reading into modern texts unfolds, Shakespeare contrives to touch Lavinia's mouth to the raw materials and instruments of writing, and in this way he presents her as a relay between the Latin eloquence of Ovid's poem and the new kind of eloquence that arises from the plot of *Titus Andronicus*. *Strictu sensu*, Lavinia's mangled body presents the playwright's relationship to Ovid in terms of emulation rather than imitation. For his text augments its model rather than copies it, a distinction that Titus would appear to make when he declares to Chiron and Demetrius, in the comparative degree, that "worse than Philomel you used my daughter | And worse than Procne I will be revenged" (5.3.194–95). Note, however, that Shakespeare tries to establish that his play is *more than* its model by showing that *even less* remains of Lavinia than remained of Ovid's Philomela. Lavinia is raped not by one man but by two; Chiron and Demetrius not only pluck out her tongue, they also cut off her hands. Here, the gratuitous reduction of Lavinia's body paradoxically betokens an increase in the value of the Shakespearean composition that this body represents. When Aaron pauses to exult over the success of his ingenious plots, he uses the word "trim" in relation to this paradox. In Shakespeare's English, "trim" has a meaning like "polished" and "filed," words that not only refer to artistic virtuosity (in the sense of eloquence, elegance, and perfection) but also define that virtuosity as a tension between "taking away" (cutting, smoothing, burnishing) and "putting on" (adorning, decking, garnishing):

AARON   They cut thy sister's tongue, and rav-
        ished her,
        And cut her hands, and trimmed her as
        thou sawest.
LUCIUS O detestable villain! call'st thou that
        trimming?
AARON   Why, she was washed and cut and
        trimmed, and 'twas
        Trim sport for them which had the
        doing of it. (5.1.92–96)

We recognize the idea that surfaces in this grisly exchange from Saltwood's poem about the nightingale, Gascoigne's *Complaynt of Phylomene,* and Camden's *Britain.* It is that every gain depends upon a prior loss—or if you will, that subtraction is addition. At the same time, Aaron's play on "trim" in relation to Lavinia's mangled body also seems to modify that concept. With respect to the excellence of Shakespeare's plot, to which Aaron's boast is pointing in this scene, it would appear that greater losses result in even greater gains, that the condition of eloquence is only as lofty as the humiliation from which it stems is low. This is the calculus that explains why Marcus dilates upon Lavinia's missing limbs and tongue when he discovers her in the woods, a body more deforested than deflowered. Revealed in the immediate aftermath of rape, Lavinia's body is an image of the Andronici, a family tree that a "stern ungentle hand I Hath lopped and hewed and made . . . bare I Of her two branches"—an allusion, perhaps, to Martius and Quintus, whom the emperor condemns to die in the previous scene (2.4.16–18). Lavinia also bears a striking resemblance to "Musicke," as Stephen Gosson figures it in *The Schoole of Abuse* (1579), a victim of "unthrifty scholars that despise [the] good rules of their ancient masters & run to the shop of their own deuises": "Musicke with her clothes tottered, her fleshe torne, her face deformed, her whole bodie mangled and dismembered," "stricken to death, in danger to perishe, and present in place the least part of her selfe."[80] And yet, with respect to the *copia* of Marcus's speech and the pointed allusions that it makes to Ovid's tale of Philomela and to Orpheus, Shakespeare apparently intends for us to understand of Lavinia's wounds that devastation is the source of the most fecund eloquence—or at least of what he considers eloquence to be in this play, where conquest mingles different bloodlines and confuses one kind with another (Roman and Goth), even to the point of obscuring an ethical distinction between the conquerors and the victims of conquest. As Lavinia flees from her uncle, seeks refuge in the woods, and turns into a tree, she becomes the Daphne to the new and vulgar Apollo that Shakespeare, through Marcus, is becoming. When Marcus urges her to speak, she warbles blood, and in this form her injuries become the source of all the plots that follow. From Marcus's ecphrasis to Titus's banquet, they trace their origins to these woods, "By nature made for murders and for rapes," and to this tongueless mouth, where "a crimson river of warm blood, I Like to a bubbling fountain stirred with wind, I Doth rise and fall between thy rosèd lips, I Coming and going with thy honey breath" (2.4.22–25). Once we see that Shakespeare cannot think of his vulgar eloquence apart from Roman violence, it will come as no surprise that his nightingale should bear the name of the woman for whom Aeneas fought a devastating war and upon whom he fathered Rome. For from Shakespeare's subaltern perspective, the story that Virgil tells about the origins of an imperial civilization and the story that Ovid tells about origins of eloquence likely seemed to be the same.[81]

III

The Ancient Neighborhood of Milton's *Maske*

When through the old oak forest I am gone,
Let me not wander in a barren dream.... [1]

Sylvan Eloquence

Of all the metaphors that Milton borrows from Antiquity as a framework for his relationship to classical literature, perhaps none illuminates his attitude toward imitation more clearly than the woods. Literally speaking, the Latin words *nemus* and *lucus* refer to woodlands that have open glades for cattle and to thickets of trees that are sacred to the gods, while *saltus* refers to a forest in hilly or mountainous country, or to a narrow passage through such a place. The word *silva*, however, which refers in a general way to forest or uncultivated land, has a wider range of meaning than any of these terms, whose significance is mainly confined to the physical places that they describe. As a translation of the Greek ὕλη, *silva* also refers to the raw material, unshaped stuff, or unworked mass of matter from which other things are fashioned—like *materies,* the word that Vitruvius uses for "timber."[2] It is through this word that the Romans came to associate other arboreal expressions with verbal composition, and to include them in the lexicon of their poetics. So fertile was this way of thinking about the woods that seventeen centuries later, in one of the first scientific texts about the forest, John Evelyn would describe the tree's biological functions as though they were the processes of an imitation. "Consider how it *assimilates, separates,* and *distributes* [its] several supplies," he writes, "how it *concocts, transmutes, augments, produces,* and *nourishes . . .* and *generates* its like."[3]

Roman authors use the word *silva* in order to describe a specific form of textual organization. In Antiqutiy, *silvae* were those gatherings of writing, whether in prose or verse, that address a variety of topics or are written in different styles. In the erudite miscellany that we know as *Noctes Atticae,* Aulus Gellius reflects that ancient writers use the name *Silvarum* for the "varied, manifold, and as it were indiscriminate learning" ("variam et miscellam et quasi confusanem doctrinam") that they collected.[4] Gellius may be referring here to the lost work of Lucius Ateius Philologus, who left a collection of textual commentaries called *Hyle;* or of Marcus Valerius Probus, another ancient grammarian, who produced a *Silvam Observationum Sermonis Antiqui* (A Grove of Observations on our Early Language).[5] Statius's *Silvae,* an anthology of thirty-two occasional poems, written in different meters, is the only example of the genre to survive Antiquity.

It is likely, therefore, that Ben Jonson had Statius in mind, in 1616, when he published *The Forrest* and again, somewhat later, when he composed the head notes to *The Underwoods* and *Timber: or Discoveries* (1641): "[The] ancients called that kind of body Sylva, or Ϋ"λη, in which there were workes of divers nature, and matter congested; as the multitude call timber-trees, promiscuously growing, a Wood, or Forrest."[6] Here, in the process of defining *silva* as a congestion of matter, Jonson associates the arboreal metaphor for his own text with the creation of the world, in Ovid's *Metamorphoses,* from Chaos, a "rudis indigestaque moles | nec quicquam nisi pondus iners congestaque eodem | non bene iunctarum discordia semina rerum"; in Arthur Golding's memorable translation, "a huge rude heape, and nothing else but even | A heavie lump and clotted clod of seedes togither driven, | Of things at strife among themselves, for want of order due."[7] This resonant connection between *silva* and the primordial matter of the universe was made by Isidore of Seville in the seventh century.[8] In Jonson's lifetime, it survived in a variety of places, including Henry Peacham's *Minerva Britanna* (1612). Peacham's emblem "Nulli penetrabilis" (Impossible to penetrate) urges a courtier called "*SILVIUS*" to be as inscrutable as the "SHADIE Wood, pourtraicted to the sight, | With vncouth pathes, and hidden waies vnknowne: | Resembling *CHAOS*. . ."(see figure 25).[9]

As it proliferates through Latin literature, the metaphor that associates the woods with the raw material of written composition, and of creation generally, ramifies new versions of itself. For some writers, it helps to clarify differences between closely related modalities of discourse. Tacitus, for example, identifies the woods with poetry in distinction to rhetoric; in his *Dialogus de oratoribus,* a rhetorician called Aper argues that poets, "[i]f they want to work hard and produce something worthy, . . . should give up the conversation of friends and city pleasures; they should forsake every other duty and retire into the solitude, as they themselves say, of woods and groves."[10] For this speaker, the poet's otiose retreat

A SHADIE Wood, pourtraicted to the fight,
With vncouth pathes, and hidden waies vnknowne:
Refembling *C H A O S*, or the hideous night,
Or thofe fad Groues, by banke of *A C H E R O N*
With banefull *Ewe*, and *Ebon* overgrowne:
   Whofe thickeft boughes, and inmoft entries are
   Not peirceable, to power of any ftarre.

Thy Imprefe *S I L V I V S*, late I did devife,
To warne the what (if not) thou oughtft to be,
Thus inward clofe, vnfearch'd with outward eies,
With thoufand angles, light fhould never fee:
For fooles that moft are open-hearted free,
   Vnto the world, their weakenes doe bewray,
   And to the net, the firft themfelues betray.

Cc1· *Vnum*

25. The woods, from Henry Peacham's
Minerva Britanna (London, 1612).
By permission of the Folger Shakespeare Library.

into the forest is a sign that poetry is inherently inferior to rhetoric, which thrives in the *negotium* of the law courts, and also that the poet is unfit to perform the orator's public offices. According to Maternus, however, who is a poet, poetry's affinity for the woods is an index of its superiority to every other kind of discourse, and to rhetoric especially. For him, the woods represent the time out of mind that authorizes, and gives meaning to, forensic oratory as a practice of argumentation based on precedents. Poetry is, in this context, the most ancient form of human communication, and because it is prior to cities, it may be said to constitute the civic institutions on which rhetoric depends. The poet's "spirit retires into pure and harmless places and in these sacred dwellings, takes delight. These places are the origins of eloquence and its innermost shrines. In this first condition, adapted to mortals, [eloquence] flowed into unblemished hearts, free from any vice. Thus did the oracles speak." [11] Here, the poet's superiority to the orator partly stems from poetry's philosophical character as a mode of contemplation; partly from its privileged relation to the founding moment of human civilization, which the poet's *animus* ("spirit" or "mind") accesses through the religious act of memory (in the sense of *religare,* meaning "to be tied back to").[12] Lorenzo Valla later uses these arguments in order to turn Ovid's tale of Philomela into a fable about the different disciplines that humanism identified as sister arts within the *studia humanitatis.* Reading Ovid through the lens of Tacitus, Valla finds that Procne is an emblem of rhetoric, or "urbane eloquentie," because as a swallow she haunts the rooftops of the city that she once ruled as queen; Philomela, he reasons, by virtue of her retreat into the forest as a nightingale, symbolizes the "eloquentie nemorali" (sylvan eloquence) that Tacitus taught him to recognize as poetry.[13]

In another influential reference to *silva,* drawn like the last from the domain of rhetoric, Quintilian declines to use the woods as a way of asserting that one kind of discourse is prior or superior to another. [14] Instead, he prefers to make a point about the concept of priority in its relation to authorship. "[W]e should not lend a ready ear to those who think that woods and groves [*nemora silvasque*] are the most suitable places [for composition]," Quintilian argues against Tacitus. For "the pleasant woodland scene [*silvarum amoenitas*], the stream gliding past, the breeze whispering in the branches, the song of the birds, and the very freedom of looking all around—these are all attractions, the pleasures of which (as it seems to me) relax rather than concentrate the thought [*cogitationem*]" (*The Orator's Education* 10.3.17–25).

We could infer from these sentences that Quintilian takes Aper's side against Maternus, and claims that poetry is a form of licentiousness for which the woods, unregulated by any urban plan, are a conducive setting and an outward sign. Or, taking a different approach, we can ask how Quintilian's meditation on the woods contributes to the theory of imitation that he elaborates in the tenth book of *Institutio oratoria.* In this encounter with Tacitus, the woods refer specifically to the passages in *Dialogus de oratoribus* to which I drew our attention; but they also refer, in a general way, to prior writing as the context from which all new compositions, regardless of their kind, must either emerge or fail to emerge. The woods in this sense are a picture of the curriculum of authoritative texts that Quintilian prescribes for his pupils. Earlier, when he observes that *auctores* like Tacitus are the only source of copious expression, Quintilian frames the excellence of their writing as an incentive to emulate rather than imitate them, for it is "a disgrace . . . to be content merely to attain the effect that you are imitating" (*The Orator's Education* 10.1.8, 10.2.7). Now, however, he appears to claim that the literature that the forest symbolizes, precisely by virtue of its excellence, is as likely to curtail new writing as to engender it. That is because in the context of the imitation theory that Quintilian uses the woods in order to elucidate, "the activities of reading and writing become virtually identified."[15] Every writer is a reader who runs the risk of being immobilized by the experience of studying other texts—immobilized or possibly converted, through admiration and pleasure, into a copy of the past, utterly devoid of the critical subjectivity (*cogitatio*) that for Quintilian distinguishes writers from their sources, as he here distinguishes himself from the Tacitean wood into which his arguments have led him.

The idea that writing is obliged to find its *silva* in texts written by other people, and that imitation thus incurs a crisis of self-delimitation, is not, appropriately enough, original to Quintilian. Ovid formulated these concepts earlier in *Metamorphoses*. Consider, for example, the scene in book 10, in which Orpheus gathers a shady wood to an empty clearing. [16]

> There was a hyll, and on the hyll a verie levell
>   plot,
> Fayre greene with grasse. But as for shade or
>   covert there was not.
> As soone as that this Poet borne of Goddes, in that
>   same place
> Sate downe and toucht his turned strings, a
>   shadow came apace.
> There wanted neither Chaons tree, not yit the
>   trees to which

> Fresh Phateons susters turned were, nor Beeche,
>   nor Holme, nor Wich,
> Nor gentle Asp, nor wyveless Bay, nor lofty
>   Chestnuttree. . . .
> . . . Moreover thither came . . .
> The tree to Cybele, mother of the Goddes, most
>   deere. For why?
> Her minion Atys putting off the shape of man, did
>   dye,
> And hardened into this same tree. Among this
>   companee
> Was present with a pyked top the Cypresse, now a
>   tree,
> Sumtime a boay beloved of the God that with a
>   string
> Doothe arme his bow, and with a string in tune
>   his
> Violl bring. (Golding 10.93–116)

The narrative that unfolds from this passage is partly an imitation of the familiar myth about the origins of civilization that Horace paraphrases in *Ars Poetica*. There, Orpheus symbolizes eloquence in its purest and most archaic form: as the music that moves human beings to abandon their primitive ways, come together in communities, and construct dwellings from the trees under which they once huddled as though they were wild beasts.[17] Here, however, in a move that foreshadows Orpheus's fate, Ovid takes apart that story and tells it in a different way. In the new version of the myth, Orpheus flees from urban space in order to assemble a forest outside city walls that once were built from timber. Thus is set in motion a chain of events in which maenads eventually dismantle the *silva* that

Orpheus composes, and use its pieces to dismember him, before they are themselves reintegrated into the woods as oak trees—in which condition they represent Ovid's imitation of Horace as a completed text and make it available as raw material for future compositions.

We could argue, then, that Ovid's version of the Orphic myth is a story about writing rather than civilization—a story that anticipates Quintilian, who later places the origins of all composition "elsewhere," in texts that are prior and extrinsic to the writer's own text: in the *silva,* if you will, into which Orpheus retires in order to tell the stories whose variety the woods represent as nature. On the other hand, the very nature of imitation makes this distinction largely hypothetical. What counts as being intrinsic or extrinsic to a piece of writing, or what can the difference between a model and a copy amount to, when writing itself is imagined as incorporation? Referring to the writer's reading as a foodstuff (*cibum*) rather than a forest (*silva*), Quintilian says that we must "go over the text again and work on it. We chew our food and almost liquefy it before we swallow, so as to digest it more easily; similarly, let our reading be made available for memory and imitation, not in an undigested form, but, as it were, softened and reduced to pap . . ." (*The Orator's Education* 10.1.19).

Given the remarks that Quintilian later makes about *silva,* I think that we must interpret the breaking down of distinction between *auctor* and imitator, in this passage, as a form of analysis that is intended, ultimately, to clarify that distinction rather than obscure it. For Ovid, however, the opposite seems to be true: New compositions are generated from the confusion of precisely the categories whose difference, for Quintilian, is paramount. It is impossible to discern a position of priority in Ovid's meditation on the woods, in the sense that

Orpheus is the model for Ovid's poetry from time out of mind, but he also imitates Ovid by telling stories of metamorphosis; Ovid follows Orpheus and is the author of the fiction that creates him. By the same token, the woods that Orpheus composes with his music, the woods that are meant to represent the raw materials of Ovid's writing, are an image of *Metamorphoses:* Every tree that rises in this forest is a placeholder for a tale that Ovid has already told. So when the story of Orpheus reaches its conclusion, we could infer that the poet's disintegration beneath the canopy of trees that he has created is a parable about his failure to differentiate himself from the texts that he imitates, or from the texts that he writes, as a subject differentiates itself from objects. On the other hand, and in contrast to Quintilian, Ovid implies that it is only through such "failures" that writers become the subjects of their writing, and authorities in the tradition that endows them with value. For *auctor* and imitator are produced by the self-same act: The story of Orpheus shows that the taking apart of the one is the putting together of the other. Or to put it another way: In this meditation on *silva,* there is no time or place before the text that can guarantee its value, and so the only way out of the woods lies through them.

"Veil of Wildness"

Even this cursory survey of references to *silvae* in Roman discussions about the nature of composition and tradition will serve to underscore the importance of the woods as a recurring trope in Milton's early writing. For that writing is preoccupied with the question of the poet's autonomy from his sources—and also with the implications of the fact that during the Renaissance, classical literature and English writing had converged through the practice of imitation and in this way produced England's first vernacular literature as a vulgar eloquence.

One of Milton's first meditations on the woods occurs in the *Seventh Prolusion* (pub. 1674), a Latin declamation in favor of the argument that "Learning makes men happier than ignorance" ("Beatiores reddit homines ars quam ignorantia"). Milton begins by introducing the woods as a representation of an actual place: the neighborhood around his father's country house in Hammersmith. At the same time, the "glades and streams" ("lucos et flumina"), "beloved elms" ("dilectas . . . ulmos"), and "remote woodlands" ("semotos saltus") that Milton associates with "happy memories" ("juncunda memoria") and the "highest favor of the Muses" ("summam cum Musis gratiam") also stand for the writing that he studied there (*Seventh Prolusion* 248–49).[18] The woods are the symbolic aggregate of all the books whose leaves he voraciously consumed, a kind of metaphorical vegetation to which he later returned, in the opening lines of "Lycidas," to "pluck [its] berries" and "shatter [its] leaves" ("Lycidas" 3–5).[19] In this sense, they represent the matter, or *copia,* of Milton's own writing, and they make visible, as space, the time of the education in which he culled it: a "secluded interval" ("occulto aevo"), beyond the business of academic life, where "it seemed that I could grow" ("crescere mihi potuisse visus sum") (*Seventh Prolusion* 250–51). "The literature of antiquity," one critic writes, "was to Milton's genius what soil and light are to a plant." [20]

In a very subtle turn, even by the standards of this precocious academic exercise, Milton establishes the value of his own text by returning to the Latin phrases of one of its classical sources. Referring to the secluded interval away from Cambridge, he alludes to a passage in the twelfth poem of Horace's first book of odes, where the poet predicts that the fame of Marcellus, Augustus's son-in-law, will "grow imperceptibly, as a tree grows" ("crescit occulto velut arbor aevo").[21] Milton also acknowledges the prior reception of this Horatian verse by one of his vernacular predecessors. For simultaneously he alludes to *Henry V,* where that verse is translated in a passage that describes Hal's growth from adolescence into manhood. Early in the play, the Archbishop of Canterbury expresses his amazement that the young king should be capable of such "sweet and honeyed sentences," since (unlike Milton) there was "never noted in him any study, | Any retirement, any sequestration | From open haunts and popularity." The Bishop of Ely responds that "the Prince obscured his contemplation | Under a veil of wildness; which no doubt | Grew like the summer grass, fastest by night, | Unseen, yet crescive in his faculty."[22] Here, the nonce word "crescive"—which seems to be arrested in its passage between Latin and English—recalls Horace's "crescit" and later, in the *Seventh Prolusion,* it is remembered by Milton's "crescere."

The meaning of Milton's double allusion is partly obvious and obviously grandiose. Milton does not scruple to imply that he, like Marcellus and Henry V, is a boy who has recently become a man, on whom the future of his country depends. Woven together, these different threads of Roman and English history and poetry become the fabric of a bold self-endowment. On the other hand, the memory of these Latin and English verses in Milton's text suggests, perhaps, the opposite: his continuing minority and dependence on other writers for value. Referring to his sources in the *Seventh Prolusion,* Milton writes, "I am oppressed by this excessive abundance of evidence; the supplies themselves make me helpless; the means of [defending eloquence] render me defenceless" ("hac ego argumenti foecunditate nimia laboro, ipsae me vires imbecillum, arma inermem reddunt") (*Seventh Prolusion* 252–53). Thus, at the moment when Milton's splendid double allusion notifies his Cambridge audience that he has left his father's house and emerged from the forest of his reading, in order to claim the authority and fame to which learning and eloquence have entitled him, the allusion also draws him back within a patriarchal field whose outward sign is plant life. From the woods in the *Seventh Prolusion,* we are able to follow Milton's Latin not only to Horace's "arbor" but also to Shakespeare's "summer grass," and so it would appear that as Milton passes through the woods, en route to his destiny as an author, he encounters ancient literature in two notably different aspects. The double allusion places Shakespeare in the middle ground between Horace and Milton, and in this situation obliges Milton to see his Roman predecessor through a "veil of wildness"—as it were, through the lens of an earlier vernacular poetics and its vulgar response to the classics; Gilbert Murray, referring to the survival of "the classical tradition" in Shakespeare's work, describes it as "a disguised form," "overgrown" and "hidden by new matter." [23] The consequences of Shakespeare's intervention here are not specifically articulated. It appears to concern Milton, more directly, that the mediation of ancient by modern writing does little to diminish the transforming influence of either. For if he is like Marcellus or Henry V, then by analogy he is also like a tree or a clump of grass. At the end of this passage, the virtuosity of which is intended to announce Milton's distinction from earlier writers, we find that Milton has lost his human shape and become the kind of vegetation that he prunes and ruminates in his speech.

Is this a figure for early maturity or prolonged adolescence? Does Milton's double allusion mark a distinctive re-

sponse to the tradition that precedes him, or is it just a dupli-
cate, twice over, of what has come before? Milton may be arguing here that he is a writer who, despite his youth, deserves
to be regarded as a textual authority, a tree whose timber should
be harvested in the same way that he has culled some lines
from Horace's ode and Shakespeare's play. Or he may be wor-
rying that his audience will not be able to see the tree of his accomplishment for the prodigious forest of earlier writing in
which it has taken root. Likely, the *Seventh Prolusion* is doing
both of these things at once, and the ambivalence of Milton's
self-assertion is instructive. For it tells us as much about the relationship between his classical and vernacular models as it
does about his perception of his relationship to them. The very
fact that Milton is able to trace a line of descent from Horace
to Shakespeare to himself means that the categories of value
that the Renaissance mainly regarded as incommensurable
(ancient and modern, foreign and native, classical and vernacular, Roman and English) have somehow overcome their difference and mixed together in a single genealogy. If you will, a
vulgar eloquence reverberates in Milton's writing ("crescere"),
even as it prefers Horace's Latin ("crescit") to Shakespeare's
English ("crescive").

The woods in the *Seventh Prolusion* are the setting in
which this declension of readers unfolds, and a backdrop
against which *fama* (a Roman category of value) passes into
the sweetness of Shakespeare's sentences, whereupon it is dis-
assembled and recomposed as the formidable learning of Milton's arguments in Latin. In this context, they are a measurement of the hybridity of Milton's writing, or a way of saying that
it arises from two different points of origin that have since converged: on the one hand, the antiquity of Greek and Roman civilization; on the other, the wild and primeval places to which

Renaissance linguists traced the beginnings of vernacular languages.

The woods in the *Seventh Prolusion* also allow us to see this hybridity as the symptom of an internalized conflict in Milton's early writing. For while they represent the literary tradition as an utterly familiar place—familiar in the sense of a family home and of the *loci communes* of well-known texts—they also reveal it to be strange and forbidding. The woods symbolize classical learning as lush and fecund, and therefore as a place of refreshment, rest, and edifying pleasure. But they also identify Antiquity with the time of prehistory and the domain of the subhuman, revealing its pleasant groves of erudition to be a wilderness of ignorance. "If we go back to antiquity," writes Milton, "some of the most ancient indigenous people are said to have wandered in the woods and mountains, seeking the advantage of food after the manner of wild beasts."[24] Where "savagery and frightful barbarism rage about," there "no arts flourish," and "all knowledge is banished" (*Seventh Prolusion* 258–59). Thus he takes us from the *locus amoenus* that he began by praising and transplants us to another place entirely. These are the savage woods from which the Horatian Orpheus, whom we glimpse in Milton's text as the full complement of "Arts and Sciences" ("*Artes & Scientiae*"), inspires the first human beings to build city walls, establish laws, and separate themselves from the beasts. To these "deepest forests" ("sylvis penitissimis") Milton banishes the nightingale, the avatar of a poetry whose "sweet strains" ("suavas modulos") he makes indivisible from a worse-than-bestial idleness. In this place, ancient writing is the liquor in Circe's cup, and in that form threatens to dissolve rather than edify the self (*Seventh Prolusion* 272–73, 280–81). So woods in the *Seventh Prolusion* not only point to the raw material of Milton's defense of learning. They also make a surprising ethical claim about it. If literature can make you better, Milton would appear to say, it can also make you worse.

"My Daily Walks and Ancient Neighbourhood"

> I acknowledge how easie it is to be *lost* in this *Wood*, and that I have hardly power to take off my *Pen* whilst I am on this delightful *Subject*. . . . [25]

The forest in Milton's *Maske Presented at Ludlow Castle* (1634) is an expansion of the woods in the *Seventh Prolusion,* and that earlier text helps us to understand its meaning.[26] As a metaphor for the writing that precedes him, these woods also serve Milton as a way of engaging the classical and vernacular authors that inform his venture. They spatialize those relationships and frame them as territorial disputes within an "ancient neighbourhood" that is, by turns, familiar and strange (*Maske* 313). The landscape of the masque is a tissue of allusions to the "Greek and Latin classics," to the "perusal" of which, Milton wrote, he was "entirely devoted" during his retirement in Hammersmith and Horton.[27] At the same time, they are far from being the "kind hospitable woods" to which the Lady and her brothers, lately "nursed in princely lore," look for nourishment and the way home (*Maske* 186, 34). This is an "ominous wood" thickly sheltered with "black shades," a "leafy labyrinth" recalling Dante's *selva oscura,* and the "ruthless, vast, and gloomy woods" in *Titus Andronicus,* where Lavinia is "[r]avished and wronged as Philomela was" (*Maske* 60–61, 276).[28] So when the Lady says that the "blind mazes of this tangled wood" are apt to lead her feet astray, she speaks not only to the problem of not knowing where to turn in the woods but also to the danger that simply being there, in the presence of those trees, will turn her into something else, utterly unlike herself (*Maske* 180). The Attendant Spirit warns that travelers in the woods may not only get lost but also lose themselves, give up their human shape, and "all their friends and native home forget, | To roll with pleasure in a sensual sty" (*Maske* 76–77).

In this context the woods represent at least two different ways of losing oneself during the encounter with literature: by having either too many choices or too few. In one sense, Milton's wide reading creates the conditions for all of the promiscuous and errant footwork in the *Maske;* but in another the woods, which represent that reading, may be said to dictate the conventions of knowledge and experience, and so to determine, rather more narrowly, the direction that every course must take. The Lady's dilemma is a version of the crisis that Milton acknowledges in the *Seventh Prolusion,* where his references to Horace and Shakespeare both open and foreclose the possibility of referring to the self. In the *Maske,* the way home lies through the forest of past writing, and neither the Lady's footsteps nor Milton's poetry, to which her pedestrian rhetoric refers, may depart for that destination from any other spot: "O where else," asks the Lady, "[s]hall I inform my unacquainted feet?" (*Maske* 179). Here, the pun on "queint" in "unacquainted" points to a connection between the Lady's ignorance and her virginity, raising an important question about the nature of reading and writing, which Milton partly represents as copulation—copulation in the sense of an intercourse with other writers that reproduces texts, traditions, and genealogies of authorship. By way of complicating the sharp dichotomy between learning and ignorance in the *Seventh Prolusion,* Milton asks whether it is worse to be ignorant (to be lost) from having too much knowledge or too little, and in this way he begins to theorize virginity and chastity, the Lady's celebrated virtues, as new ways of relating to the literature that the woods embody, and as new kinds of imitation in which it is possible to learn how to write without losing oneself in the bargain.

More emphatically, then, than that of the *Seventh Prolusion*, the sylvan topography of the *Maske* suggests that some prior text, tradition, or authority—in a phrase, "the sure guess of well-practised feet"—is the precondition of Milton's poetic motion (*Maske* 309). What makes the wood particularly menacing in this respect is the difficulty of defining exactly what that authority is, where it comes from, how it works, and what its limits are, since it seems to foliate in all directions. From one perspective, the "bosky bourn" of Milton's *silva* gives the widest orbit to the errancy and "stray attendance" of the characters (*Maske* 312, 314). From another, it is susceptible of description as confinement and enclosure: a "pinfold," "maze," "labyrinth," "dungeon," "snare," and "wild surrounding waste" that closely regulates all movement through it (*Maske* 7, 180, 277, 348, 566, 403). Apart from its physical dimensions, the wood is notably indefinite in other ways. No one, not even Comus, is native to the wild wood, and no one can account for its origins. It is part neither of England nor of Wales in the masque, lying instead between them as a necessary passage, apparently not subject to a particular authority. Like so many other places in this text—"the starry threshold of Jove's court," the Severn's "rushy fringed bank," and the "green earth's end," to which the Attendant Spirit flies at the conclusion of the masque—"the perplexed paths of this drear wood" are a liminal space, somewhere in between *here* and *there* (*Maske* 1, 889, 1013, 37). The *silva* represents the past of literature, but it also marks a transition in the present. In its aspect as a limit, the wood is therefore impossible to define precisely, and the constant dilation and contraction of wooded space in the *Maske* allows us to glimpse something basic about Milton's encounter with textual traditions that constantly outflank his writing and, in this way, threaten to inhibit it.

For Milton, the question of writing is primarily a question of jurisdiction, and ironically his breadth of study likely made his sense of the predicament of imitation more, rather than less, acute. John Manwood's influential treatment of arboreal law may have made it sharper still. Published in 1589, and continuously available throughout the eighteenth century, Manwood's *Treatise and Discourse on the Lawes of the Forrest* mainly conceptualizes arboreal space as an assortment of jurisdictional problems.[29] For Manwood, a forest is a "certen Territorie of wooddy grounds & fruitfull pastures, priuiledged for wild beasts and foules . . . to rest and abide in, in the safe protection of the King, for his princely delight and pleasure" (1ʳ). It is "the most highest fraunchise of noble, and princely pleasure, that can be incident unto the Crowne and Royall dignitie of a prince" (7ʳ). While only a monarch can "make" or "have" a forest (Manwood explains that when a forest is granted to a subject, it becomes another kind of property altogether), forests typically encompass other kinds of woodland, held by the King's subjects: parks, chases, and warrens, among other "Lordships, liberties, & precincts that are full of woods" (16ʳ–20ᵛ, 2ᵛ). This is the crux of the jurisdictional issue that Manwood explores in his *Treatise,* and possibly the most resonant aspect of the work for Milton. For forests retain their integrity and privilege only if they are not cultivated by the subjects who hold property freely within them: "[To] destroy the couerts of the Forrest, is to destroy the Forrest it selfe," writes

Manwood. "Also, to conuert the pasture grounds, meadows, and feedings [within the forest] into arable land, is likewise to destroy the Forrest" (2ᵛ). Since a covert is the habitation and "safe abyding place for [the] wilde beasts" that give the prince his pleasure, and since a forest cannot be a forest if it lacks wild animals for hunting, Manwood argues that "if any man haue woods within any Forrest, although that the soile, wherin those woods do grow, be his own freehold, yet he may not cut downe nor fell his woods nor couerts there" (14ᵛ, 41ʳ). Here, he hastily attempts to rearticulate the distinctions of the arboreal lexicon that his text has muddled—a rhetorical symptom of the confusion that is endemic to the territories and spheres of authority that he means to differentiate: "[Note] that woods and couerts, are al one in some sence & signification, but in some sence and signification they do differ" (41ʳ).

In Manwood's text, the forest thus implies a crisis in signification itself. For by its nature it creates a situation in which the limit between *this* and *that* place cannot be perceived, though this difference must be enforced in order to affirm the whole system of territorial distinctions that makes the king's authority and subject's freehold meaningful. "A Forrest doth lie open, and not inclosed with hedge, ditch, pale, or stone-wall . . . yet, in the eie and consideration of the Lawe, the same hath as strong enclosure . . . as if there were a brick-wall to inu-iron the same" (3ᵛ). Quite apart from its relevance to English law, the question of jurisdiction and difference to which Manwood constantly returns, illuminates the problems of tradition, authorial identity, literary authority, and textual value that Milton encounters in the woods. How will he ever discover and preserve the peculiar distinction of his writing if all his footwork must fall within the bosky orbit of the literary past? Looking forward to the *Maske* from Manwood's *Treatise*, we can see that the difference between the literature that Milton has read and the literature he hopes to write is, like the boundary of the forest, both emphatic and elusive—like "the sun-clad power" of the Lady's chastity, an invisible membrane between Milton and the traditions that Comus and the woods seductively embody (*Maske* 426, 781).

"My Mother Circe"

I would not want to overstate the analogy between legal jurisdiction and literary authority that I have drawn here,[30] but I do think that Manwood's treatment of wooded space, to the extent that it seeks to differentiate between two spheres of sovereignty that overlap and resemble one another, provides an intriguing framework for thinking about Milton's sense of imitation and the implications of the past for his autonomy as a writer. In that spirit, let us continue to examine the spaces of the *Maske* as a way of bringing his attitude more sharply into focus. Though its action mainly occurs out of doors, in the forest, on 29 September 1634 the *Maske*'s first production took place inside Ludlow Castle, situating Comus's "wild wood" within the narrower confines of a building that served as the provincial seat of the Lord Lieutenant of Wales. This noteworthy conflation of indoor and outdoor space points to Milton's affinity for several ancient texts in which the overlaying of woods and buildings underscores a tension between the old and the new within composition itself.

The confounding of the woods and Ludlow Castle may be an allusion, for example, to the house of Pelops in Seneca's *Thyestes*, a building whose "golden beames so bright" prevent one from seeing the "privie Palaice [that] underlieth" it, "in secret place aloe": a "ditch ful deepe that doth enclose the wood of privitee," where Atreus butchers his nephews and feeds them to their father.[31] It may also refer to Ovid's tale of Philomela, in which the rooms of Tereus's palace ("a place within the house far off and far above the ground") become a forest where Procne, taking revenge for Philomela's rape, murders her son and makes her husband eat him: "She dragged Itys after hir, as when it happens in Inde | A Tyger gets a little Calfe that suckes upon a Hynde | And drags him through the shadie woods."[32] These references are significant for our purposes. In leading us to them Milton also takes us back to a still more ancient text that brings "the identity-difference crux" of imitation theory to the forefront of his writing.[33] For the quality of space in Ovid's text and Seneca's alludes to the house of Circe, which arises in the woods of Homer's *Odyssey* and Virgil's *Aeneid* as a frame for incommensurable kinds of place and states of being, and in this sense partly serves as an image of poetic composition. In Ovid's poem and Seneca's play, the collapse of distinction between building and forest, the partial transformation of people into beasts, and the ingestion of sons by fathers would appear to recur to the house of Circe in order to depict the process of imitation as a confusion of things that should be kept apart. I intend to show that for Milton the myth of Circe may have illuminated not only the practice of imitation but also the hybridity of England's vulgar eloquence in a similar way.

On the island of Aeaea, midway between Troy and Ithaca in the *Odyssey*, Circe's house is a congestion of raw materials, finished compositions, and works-in-progress.[34] A palace "of bright stone built in a conspicuous way," it stands, where it cannot be seen, "in a grove | Set thicke with trees" (*Odyssey* 10.190–91, 281). The building is occupied by wild animals, and it flourishes with potent herbs: It is, in this sense, an outgrowth of the "uncut consecrated woods" in which it is embedded (*Odyssey* 10.464). Nevertheless, the house exemplifies the polished artifice and exquisite cultivation that Homer associates with the Circe's singing and weaving, which we never experience as products, only actions (*Odyssey* 10.190 passim). Renaissance mythography partly glossed these contradictions by associating Circe's name with the Latin word *miscendo,* a periphrastic construction "meaning 'what must be mixed.'"[35] George Sandys explained that "commixtion in generation is properly *Circe,*" since, as the "issue" of the sun and the ocean, she is related to the combination of heat and moisture from which all life forms are created.[36] These readings suggest that Circe is much less a person in the story that Odysseus tells than she is an embodiment of his dynamic telling. Like her "sylvan Iland," Circe stands at the threshold between the strange and the familiar, and in this pivotal situation she symbolizes a way of making transitions between different places (Troy and Ithaca), states of being (human and animal), and kinds of matter (sound and song, thread and fabric) that closely resembles the activity of Homer's narration (*Odyssey* 10.413). Circe, her spell craft, and her dwelling place are emblems of the *Odyssey*'s process of composition, in which different points of reference become unfixed and change their bearing in order to extend the horizon of meaning beyond the forest that represents the materials and the pretexts of the poet's work.

Later, having reached its turning point in book 7, the *Aeneid* appears to turn away from the *Odyssey,* the model for its first six books, for Aeneas makes no landfall on Aeaea.[37] Virgil, however, lingers over this scene of transition, as though he were straining to capture in his Latin lines the measures of Circe's "constant song," which "reverberates" from the island's "impassable groves" ("inaccessos . . . lucos | adsiduo resonat

cantu"): as sweet as the bark she burns for incense ("odor-
atam . . . cedrum") and as subtle as the fabric on her loom
("tenuis . . . telas") (*Aeneid* 7.11–14). In the first complete English
translation of Virgil's epic, Thomas Phaer and Thomas Twyne
describe the sound that emanates from the forest in terms of
the "clattring" of the "tooles [that Circe] works & turns" at her
loom, deep within the "sounding saluage woods" (Phaer and
Twyne 7.12–13).[38] In this way, they guide the reader back
through the Homeric vibrations of the *Aeneid* to the wood of
Homer's own poem, where Circe's song and tapestry reflect
one another in a captivating story about art that art inspires itself to tell, while Circe "breathes a voice divine I as she some
web wrought, or her spindle's twine I She cherisht with her
song" (*Odyssey* 10.305–07). This is precisely the path that Virgil would forbid himself, Aeneas, and us to take, for he regards
the sensory plenitude of Circe's island as an obstacle no less
formidable to his own invention than to Aeneas's homecoming. On the other hand, in order to avoid that path, it would
also seem that we are obliged to take it. After an interval of
some twenty lines, during which we pause with Virgil and Aeneas to savor the beauty of Homeric imagery, Neptune must
dispatch us with a "prosperous wind" toward Italy, and toward
a paradox that can scarcely be imagined without the benefit of
Circe's magic: the paradox of Aeneas "coming home" to a place
where he has never been (Phaer and Twyne 7.22).

Odysseus cannot learn the way home without becoming
Circe's lover, and though Aeneas has no such intercourse with
her, I would suggest that in the grammar of Virgil's poem she
is an indispensable conjugation. For having bid a last farewell
to his dead friends and kinsmen in the underworld, Aeneas is
obliged to form alliances with Latinus, king of Latium, and
Evander, the leader of a Greek community at Pallanteum—al-

liances that mix different bodies, languages, and cultures, and from the old create the possibility of the new. The discovery that Dardanus, Troy's legendary founder, is the ancestor not only of Priam but also of Latinus and Evander initially appears to make these efforts moot and to confirm that Circe has been excluded from the ethnic and literary genealogies that the poem constructs as its fulfillment (*Aeneid* 7.240–41, 8.135–42). According to the paradigm of family that Dardanus embodies as "first father" ("primus pater"), Trojans, Latins, and Greeks are inherently the same kind of people (*Aeneid* 8.134). But we could also say that because he symbolizes a perfect endogamy, Dardanus is unable to account for the heterogeneity of Virgil's historical vision, or of his formal achievement in the *Aeneid*. To the contrary, because he represents the poem's movement as revolution rather than evolution—"hinc Dardanus ortus, I huc repetit" ("Here Dardanus was born, I here he returns again")—Dardanus comes to represent something like the opposite of Virgil's Rome (*Aeneid* 7.240–41). A figure for return rather than progress, or for stasis rather than change, Dardanus resembles those collateral societies in the *Aeneid* that identify so intensely with the past that they become a self-regarding parody of their ancestors—a repetition of the old, rather than a procreation of the new: like the "little Troy" and "copy of great Pergamus" that Priam's last living son establishes at Epirus ("parvam Troiam simulataque magnis I Pergama") (*Aeneid* 3.349–50).

In contrast to Dardanus, Circe provides a solution in which new kinds of culture and poetry arise from the mixture of different genealogies, so thoroughly commingled that with respect to their progeny "no difference more them both shalbe betwixt" (Phaer and Twyne 12.896). Here, in a passage that refers to the offspring of Aeneas and Lavinia, Phaer and Twyne freely translate the phrase "commixti corpore" (mixed in body), which conceptualizes the process of composition in terms very different from Ovid or Seneca (*Aeneid* 12.835). The Dardanus myth implies that from generation to generation all kith remain essentially one and the same kin, but when Virgil emphasizes that the marriage between Aeneas and Lavinia is exogamous, he depends on the logic of the myth of Circe to tell a different story about Roman origins and the creation of a Latin litera- ture. This marriage is a promise, ratified by Jove, that the great- ness of the Roman Empire, and of Latin poetry, shall inhere in the difference that it internalizes (Troy and Greece), as against the difference that it excludes (Carthage), the Latin *genus* being "blended from the blood" ("mixtum . . . sanguine") of all the different parties to the war (*Aeneid* 12.834 – 40). As it tacks toward idea that there can be no endogamy without ex- ogamy, no homecoming but for foreign places, and no Latin literature without the imitation of Greek music, the *Aeneid* cannot help but find its progenitrix in Circe. This is literally true, for if we trace the line backward from Aeneas's bride, to her father Latinus, to his father Faunus, whom Circe bore to Picus, we shall find that Circe is Lavinia's great-grandmother.

Virgil underscores Circe's continuing relation to the form and teleology of his epic by setting the betrothal of Aeneas and Lavinia in a laurel grove that grows inside Latinus's ancestral home (*Aeneid* 7.59 passim). Later, the alliance between Aeneas and Evander gives rise to a vision in which the woods of Pal- lanteum reveal the outlines of urban Rome, and Evander's hut becomes the future location of the Forum (*Aeneid* 8.184 – 370). These commensurations of different kinds of space, and of dif- ferent moments in time, exemplify a protocol of mimesis that Virgil learns from the Circe episode in Homer. Framed by these scenes, an extraordinary passage draws our attention to the river

Tiber, where we find another version of this protocol. As the oars of Aeneas's sailors "cut" the reflection of the trees that grow along the bank ("viridisque secant placido aequore silvas"), Virgil presents the wood of his poem—in the sense of the raw material that he culls from other texts—as influential imagery (from the Latin *fluere,* to flow), mixed by the motion of his poetic bark (*Aeneid* 8.96). The poet clarifies that the relationship between Homer and himself is like a passage or a fluctuation, and in this way he suggests that Circe is not only the framework on which the *Aeneid*'s seamless composition hangs, more than the sum of all its different threads, but also a figure for the logic of the literary tradition into which he writes his poem.

As many of Milton's readers have remarked, his allusions to Circe—particularly at the beginning of his career—seem to tell a cautionary tale about being seduced by antique writing and forcibly remade in its image.[39] But I would also suggest that they provide less xenophobic ways of parsing the ancient texts that Milton foregrounds in his verses: less xenophobic in the sense that the very presence of such allusions in the *Maske* acknowledges the degree to which Milton's vernacular writing is a mixture that can no more be divided into its constituent parts (ancient and modern, alien and native) than a child can be divided into its parents. As Comus's mother, Circe occupies a place at the periphery of the *Maske.* But as a star that shines on its horizon, she casts her influence into the middle of the woods, where Milton follows Homer and Virgil in putting the most basic distinctions into question; by blending "here" with "there" and "I" with "you"; and by obliging every term of difference to imply its opposite. In this landscape, "home" is a matter of perspective: While all of Milton's characters speak English, none of them is indigenous to the island. The Attendant Spirit comes from heaven; Sabrina from Troy (through her father, Brutus); the Lady and her family from another kingdom; and Comus from the Mediterranean, by way of Spain, whence his journey resembles the westward migration of the ancient "lore" in which the Lady has been "nursed," as though it were her mother (*Maske* 34). These characters impress us and each other as being both familiar and foreign, utterly different yet uncannily alike, and they manifest this paradoxical condition in speeches that mix rhymed and unrhymed verse, confounding the acoustical properties that many Renaissance theorists regarded as the basis for distinguishing absolutely between the English language and Greek or Latin. Like the *Maske* itself, Comus, the Attendant Spirit, Sabrina, the Lady, and her brothers are all the progeny of a union between classical and vernacular writing that is the vulgar eloquence of Milton's time. If the Circe myth helps Milton to articulate the hybridity of his own compositions, it must also compel him to recognize that there is a contradiction between the kind of writing at which he excels and the kind of writing that aspires to be new. For as it reaches its apex in Milton, the vulgar eloquence that synthesizes antithetical categories of origin, kind, and value perforce implies that every text must ring with echoes of older voices—even this one, though it would tell "[w]hat never yet was heard in tale or song | From old, or modern bard, in hall, or bower" (*Maske* 44–45).

"Home-Felt Delight," "Foreign Wonder," and "a Small Unsightly Root"

[T]here are more ways to the *Wood* than one. . . . [40]

It is not passing through these Learnings that hurts us, but the dwelling and sticking about them.[41]

The metaphor of woods allows Milton to emplot his text within ancient literature, and to exhibit the value and distinction of his composition, in the broader context of vernacular writing, as a function of those distant origins. But there is also a sense in which the forest presents Antiquity as a dead end, from which Milton must diverge or emerge if it is to have any meaning as *his*. Though the "ancient neighbourhood" in the masque is ostensibly a passage to one's home, it is also, as we have seen, a field of textuality in which one can go astray—a field that would integrate the poet's work into itself and, in this way, deprive it of the difference that for Milton issues from the vital singularity of every writer. "Books are not absolutely dead things," he observes in this regard, "but doe contain a potencie of life in them to be as active as that soule was whose progeny they are."[42]

Milton's treatment of the Circe myth extends his equivocal thinking about classical literature to the vernacular writers that he imitates in the *Maske*—or rather, to the practice of imitation generally. For the Circe myth is a way of understanding that the classical and vernacular traditions have come to be the same. Framed by Virgil as a parable about imitation, the myth represents, as an overcoming of distance and a yoking together of heterogeneous parts, the process by which ancient literature was itself composed from disparate pieces of Greek and Latin writing; and, as it traveled westward, continued to assimilate other kinds of writing to itself, including (it might be said) the English kind that I have been calling "vulgar eloquence." Seen from this perspective, the heterogeneity of England's vernacular writing in the seventeenth century may have impressed Milton as a distinction without a difference; and his own achievement in demonstrating the continuity of the ancient and the modern, as a failure to distinguish his work from its sources in a clear and radical way.

I turn now to two scenes in which Milton is remarkably ingenious in his efforts to differentiate the *Maske* from its classical and vernacular models, and to think the concepts "imitation" and "tradition" in novel ways. The first turns on something that the Lady says to Comus, the second on her refusal to say anything to him at all. Barbara Lewalski rightly argues that it would be naïve to infer, from the fact that Milton was apparently called "the Lady of Christ's [College]," that the Lady herself speaks unequivocally for him.[43] But it would also be wrong to deny that this character stands at the center of the *Maske* and plays a uniquely important role in its vocational drama. As we have seen, Milton uses the Lady as a way of conceptualizing his situation as a writer, and from her experience in the woods he fashions an allegory about his own encounter with literary history. In this context, the Lady's song makes a special claim on our attention, not in the least because it is intended to make her stand out from the "tufted grove" of older writing to which it is addressed (*Maske* 224):

> Sweet Echo, sweetest nymph that liv'st unseen
> > Within thy airy shell
> > By slow Meander's margent green,
> And in the violet-embroidered vale
> > Where the love-lorn nightingale
> Nightly to thee her sad song mourneth well.
> Canst thou not tell me of a gentle pair
> > That likest thy Narcissus are?
> > > O if thou have
> > Hid them in some flowery cave,
> > > Tell me but where
> > Sweet queen of parley, daughter of the
> > > sphere.

So mayst thou be translated to the skies,
And give resounding grace to all of heaven's
  harmonies (*Maske* 229 – 42).

Comus and the Attendant Spirit sing and speak, by turns, in rhymed and unrhymed verse, but alone among the characters of the *Maske,* the Lady combines these different forms into a single composition that is unique if not, strictly speaking, sui generis. The rhyme scheme of her song is *abaccbdeffgghh,* and in its final six lines, as the rhymes intensify in a series of couplets, they give up their acoustical resemblance for the ocular identity of eye rhyme: have, cave; where, sphere; skies, harmonies. The threshold for this transformation is exactly midway through the poem, at lines 7 and 8, where the end words "pair" and "are" rhyme in neither the ear nor the eye—though they resemble each other closely enough that, for a moment, we think they should. This is to enact, in the acoustical and orthographical features of the Lady's song, the crisis of distinction between originals and imitations that occurs in the tale of Narcissus, to which the song alludes. As a technical solution to that crisis, lines 7 and 8 improvise a boundary, on either side of which the song both looks and sounds different. These formal differences reinforce our awareness of a broader distinction between one kind of composition, represented by the Lady, that restores to vernacular writing the musical plenitude of ancient poetry and makes the old new; and another kind, exemplified by Echo, who merely listens to the nightingale's "sad song," that consists of the reception and repetition of older texts (*Maske* 234). The fact that the Lady receives no response from Echo also underscores a distinction that "slow Meander's margent green" elaborates in space (*Maske* 231). Ordinarily, an echo will locate a speaker *here* and *there* at the same time, but the Lady's extraordinary "noise" identifies her with one, and only one, position—which is, in this case, within the forest but beyond the pale of Echo and Philomela (*Maske* 227). When Milton declines to provide an answer to it, he suggests that the Lady's song, as a figure for his own writing, is unanticipated and inimitable. Earlier, I observed that Virgil points to the difference between the *Odyssey* and *Aeneid* by displaying his Homeric models as reverberating sounds, pungent odors, and as after-images thrown back from the surface of his text. In this scene, Milton reverses that technique by suggesting that the value and distinction of the Lady's music inheres in the fact that it casts no reflection whatsoever.

The Lady's song demonstrates the virtuosity of Milton's hybrid writing, but more importantly, it announces a sea change in his attitude toward earlier practitioners of vulgar eloquence. In a complex return to Shakespeare's *Tempest,* for example, Milton draws an analogy between the Lady's song and a song that Ariel sings about the transformation that the King of Naples undergoes after death: "Nothing of him that doth fade | But doth suffer a sea change | Into something rich and strange" (*Tempest* 1.2.400–02).[44] These compositions bear no resemblance to each other in terms of their occasion, content, or style. Taking a wider view, however, we can see that Milton frames the Lady's song with conspicuous allusions to passages that bracket Ariel's song in Shakespeare's play. In both cases, it is Comus who makes the allusions. First, he reveals a desire to breed children with the Lady: "I shall ere long | Be well stocked with as fair a herd as grazed | About my mother Circe" (*Maske* 151–53). Here, his language recalls the rape that Caliban dreams of committing on Miranda: "O ho, O ho! Would't had been done! | Thou dids't prevent me; I had peopled else | This isle with Calibans" (*Tempest* 1.2.349–51). Later, after the Lady has finished singing, Comus declares that he would rather serve than over-power her: "I'll speak to her I And she shall be my queen" (*Maske* 263–64). This passage recalls Ferdinand's promise that if Miranda is still "a virgin, I And [her] affection not gone forth, I'll make [her] I The Queen of Naples" (*Tempest* 1.2.348–50).

Recurring to *The Tempest* in this way, Milton presents his relationship to Shakespeare as a miscegenation that follows from rape and as a profession of sympathy and love. This am-biguity creates a certain distance, as it were between the *Maske* and the allusions that it makes. From this imaginary perspec-tive, outside the vernacular tradition in which the text impli-cates itself, Milton is able to hypothesize the radical difference of the Lady's song from the kinds of composition that it imi-tates. It falls to Comus to say how the Lady's song is different in this regard, and partly he displays the distinction of her vul-gar eloquence in himself. Whereas Ariel only refers to change, the Lady changes Comus in a literal sense, changing the way that he looks and sounds, along with the way that he feels. Comus also says that he has never experienced "such a sacred, and home-felt delight, I Such a sober certainty of waking bliss," and he hails the Lady as a "foreign wonder I Whom certain these rough shades did never breed" (*Maske* 261–65). The paradoxes of these lines are important and instructive. Though the Lady's song impresses Comus as being more "home-felt" than his mother's music, he tells us that the song is completely new to him, and unlike anything that he has ever heard on Circe's island. "[F]oreign" to every place with which he is ac-quainted, it appears to come from neither here nor there, and thus solicits "wonder" instead of understanding. This is to put the Lady's song in a category almost beyond signification, where every point of reference is disoriented, and all *deixis* baffled. In this passage, language strains to circumscribe the unknown within the known, but finally it is the poverty of the literature that Comus himself embodies that points to the richness and strangeness of the Lady's music. Comus is Milton's most vibrant imitation of Shakespeare, and through him Shakespearean writing is made to frame a composition that it is notably inadequate to comprehend. Having gone to these elaborate lengths to show that the Lady's song and the kind of writing that it represents are unlike any other kind, Milton would now remind us that it is only through imitation that this distinction is achieved, and the limits of the past made visible.

The *Maske*'s dramatic form presents the literature that Milton imitates not only statically, as the image of a forest, but also dynamically, as an intercourse that would turn every participant into a version of itself. It therefore makes sense that the Lady should finally refuse either to speak or to copulate with Comus, since Milton associates speech and copulation with a concept of tradition in which the self is lost in the process of inventing its origins through the imitation of older texts. Possibly, the Lady's silence (which persists even after Comus has been driven off, and the Lady freed from her captivity) is a sign that Milton fails to find an alternative to this concept. Or possibly it is the alternative itself. For the Lady's silence places her, and what she has to say, outside the language of the *Maske*. From this perspective, the limitations of Comus's discourse are revealed, once again, *as though* it were a different discourse from the Lady's, when in fact they both belong to Milton. The Lady argues that Comus "hast nor ear, nor soul to apprehend | The sublime notion, and high mystery" of what she calls "the sage | And serious doctrine of virginity." Thus she consigns him to a category ("thy present lot") that marks a difference between his "dear wit, and gay rhetoric" and her sagacity (*Maske* 783–89).

What virginity means in the context of Milton's meditation on imitative writing is difficult to say. In my opinion, it is a sign of the poet's effort to imagine, in contrast to the English writers who preceded him, and to Shakespeare in particular, the possibility of eloquence without ravishment, and of ravishment without rape. "Shakespeare," observes John Guillory in this context, "invariably associated poetic production with procreation, a conventional trope that Milton resisted."[45] The final confrontation between Comus and the Lady is a performance of this resistance. Confining the Lady to her chair, Comus threatens to make her, "as Daphne was | Root-bound, that fled Apollo" (600–01). Here, Milton conjures and repudiates an image not only of an Ovidian source but also of his roots in Shakespeare; this passage is evidently an allusion to the scene in *Titus Andronicus* when Marcus discovers Lavinia in the woods, a tree whose severed branches provide the timber for his eloquent ecphrasis (2.4.11–57). In this context, and referring more to the withholding of relations than to a relationship itself, virginity partly functions as a metaphor for the autonomy and distinction that Milton's writing is always groping toward through imitation. It also stands in relation to the Lady's silence as a theory of imitation might to an imitative practice. Silence, arising from virginity, becomes its perlocutionary act. It posits a way of conversing that is not open to conversion, and in this sense it is a placeholder for a new kind discourse, immanent but elsewhere, that is inside the woods of Milton's *Maske* and extrinsic to them too:

> Thou art not fit to hear thyself convinced;
> Yet should I try, the uncontrolled worth
> Of this pure cause would kindle my rapt spirits
> To such a flame of sacred vehemence,

> That dumb things would be moved to sympathize,
> And the brute Earth would lend her nerves, and
>   shake,
> Till all thy magic structures reared so high,
> Were shattered into heaps o'er thy false head.
>   (*Maske* 791–98)

This is to fall silent for reasons very different from those of the speaker of Shakespeare's *Sonnets*, who would not "dull" his lover "with his song" (102.14). Comus says that "some superior power" is speaking through the Lady here (*Maske* 800). Her word "sacred" gives us an idea where that power comes from. Like the "sacred" that Comus uses earlier, in reference to the pleasure that her singing gives him, it describes an otherworldly origin and identifies her inspiration with a place outside the boundaries of literary history—and with a text like Psalm 137, in which the Israelites, as they sit in captivity "by the riuers of Babel," hang up their harps and refuse to make the "songs and mirth" that their captors require of them: "How shall we sing, *said we,* a song of the Lord in a strange land?"[46] This gesture notwithstanding, the Lady's speech also invokes a more mundane authority, for she is imitating Ovid's *Metamorphoses,* a stream whose influence she here directs into channels of her own devising. The Lady imagines that if she spoke the "mystery" that she withholds from Comus, she would speak like Orpheus and move "dumb things . . . to sympathize" with her. In making this claim, she draws an analogy, and a distinction, between herself and Philomela, to whom the Attendant Spirit, remembering her song, compares her in an earlier passage: "O poor hapless nightingale thought I, | How sweet thou sing'st, how near the deadly snare!" (*Maske* 565–66). For on the verge of being raped, Ovid's Philomela goads

Tereus into killing her by vowing that if she should "have power to come abrode, [thy doings] blase I will | In open face of all the world. Or if thou keepe me still | As prisoner in these woods, my voyce the verie woods shall fill, | And make the stones to understand" (Golding 6.695–99). Tereus prefers to sever Philomela's tongue, and significantly for Milton, it goes on talking—articulate even after it has been silenced and cast, like debris, upon the forest floor: "The stumpe whereon it hung | Did patter still. The tip fell downe and quivering on the ground | As though it had murmured it made a certaine sound" (Golding 6.710–12).

The difference between the Lady and Philomela, and therefore between Milton's text and the Latin poem that it closely tracks, is the difference between self-restraint and censorship, or between subjectivity and objectification. But let us not forget that Philomela's suffering is the price that she must pay in order to become an artist and a subject. As he does in his treatment of the myth of Orpheus, Ovid suggests that in order to make objects, you must first become one, and thus only by losing her tongue can Philomela find it again, at the end of her story (or is it the beginning?), in the eloquence of the nightingale. It is a strength of Milton's writing in the *Maske*, and a sign of his integrity as a student of classical literature, that he refuses to lose sight of the implications of this story, which the Lady magisterially prevents from being told, yet again, as hers. When the Attendant Spirit and the Lady's brothers arrive to rescue her from Comus, Milton places the tale of Philomela before our eyes one final time, in the form of haemony, "a small unsightly root" (*Maske* 628). Since the eighteenth century, no single feature of the *Maske* has solicited more interpretation, and mainly those interpretations have turned on the observation that haemony is a version of moly, the plant that

Hermes gives to Odysseus in the *Odyssey*, so that he may enjoy Circe's enchantments without being enchanted by them.[47] In order to appreciate haemony's relevance to Milton's meditation on the tale of Philomela, we would need to realize that "root" is the English translation of the Latin word *radix*, which Ovid uses for Philomela's severed tongue: "radix micat ultima lin- guae | ipsa iacet terraeque tremens inmurmurat atrae" (The root quivers, and the tip of the tongue falls to the dark ground where, trembling, it murmurs) (*Metamorphoses* 6.557–58, trans- lation mine). In this context, haemony performs its prophy- lactic function as it were *against* the literature that it symbol- izes. Here, the eloquence of ancient writing is brought to light as a form of mut(e)ilation.

Like the Lady's song and silence, haemony points back- ward to the kinds of literature that Milton reads in order to point forward to the different kind of literature that he would write. Or to put it another way: Haemony is a symbol for the dialectical process of imitation in Milton's writing, a root that emancipates him instead of binding him. As we return from this plant to the tropes with which we began, it may be helpful to consider the use that Gilles Deleuze and Felix Guattari make of botanical metaphors in their attempt to theorize traditions of thought as systems of either repetition or difference. For them, the tree and the root, as images for writing ("the root- book" and "the radicle-system"), are two manifestations of a single logic of transmission: what they call "the law of reflec- tion, the One that becomes two" in an endless ramification of identical copies of itself. Against the arborescent thinking that the tree and root symbolize, they set the rhizome, "a subter- ranean stem [that] is absolutely different from roots and radi- cles." The rhizome represents tradition as heterogeneity and vertiginousness. It "has no beginning or end; it is always in the middle, between things, interbeing," and "any point of a rhizome can be connected to anything other, and must be." This is "very different from the tree or root," they continue, "which plots a point, fixes an order. . . . The tree is affiliation, but the rhizome is alliance. The tree imposes the verb 'to be,' but the fabric of the rhizome is the conjunction, 'and . . . and . . . and . . .' This conjunction carries enough force to shake and uproot the verb 'to be.'"[48]

Only trees and roots spring from the soil of the *Maske*, but I would like to suggest that Milton uses them to work toward a rhizomatic relation to the past. The Attendant Spirit says that he received haemony from "a certain shepherd lad," who "loved [him] well" and "oft would beg [him] sing," hearkening "even to ecstasy" (*Maske* 618–24). Uprooted from its original location "in another country," where it bears "a bright golden flower," haemony appears to be a transplant to "this soil," where now it is distinguished by its "darkish" leaves and "prickles." These morphological differences draw our attention to certain changes in form and value that literature has undergone in the course of its transmission westward. In its new shape, haemony is both "Unknown, and like esteemed," but it also flourishes more abundantly than it used to do, for "the dull swain | Treads on it daily with his clouted shoon"; in the process of becoming less apparently desirable, it has become "more med'cinal" as well (*Maske* 630–35). These lines allude to *The Shepheardes Calender* and, more generally, to the kind of writing that descends from Spenser, the point at which the ancient literary tradition passed into English, took root in its soil, and gave rise to the vulgar eloquence that at the end of the sixteenth century could still refer to itself as "uncouth, unkiste," or, in Samuel Johnson's disparaging phrase, "studied barbarity."[49] Or it might be more correct to say that this passage tells a story about the transmission of literature from the ancient to the modern that emphasizes its difference at every point along the way, as well as the amity with which it is conducted from one time, place, and language to another, growing ever more fungible as it came to be held in common. At the critical moment when Comus prepares to "try [the Lady] yet more strongly," and the *Maske* is poised to become a mere copy of its Ovidian model, haemony points us out of the "wild wood" of Milton's sources to the "fresh woods" that he surveys at the end of "Lycidas," and to the "Sylvarum liber" of Greek and Latin verses in which the first phase of Milton's poetic career reaches its culmination in the *Poems* (1645) ("Lycidas" 805). Thomas Warton praised Milton's *liber* for being full of "legitimate classical compositions," but more to the point, it is fully of legitimately Miltonic compositions.[50] In this new wood, to show that Milton is, at last, upon an equal footing with his fathers, literary and otherwise, *Ad Patrem* imprecates John Milton *père* to approve the younger Milton's choice to become a poet, but of course the poet has already made that choice, on his own authority, and there is no going back. Emerging from the forest, he elects to make a music (like Orpheus's) that "gives ears to oak trees" ("quercubus addidit aures") and compels the past to listen, rather than the kind of eloquence that is appropriate to the "woodland choristers" ("Silvestres decet iste choros"), like Comus (like Shakespeare), that he has left behind.[51]

Notes

Introduction

1. John Florio, *Queen Anna's new world of words, or dictionarie of the Italian and English tongues, collected, and newly much augmented* (London, 1611), s.v. "diserto."

2. There are several studies that address antiquarian activity during the English Reformation and the problematic status of Geoffrey of Monmouth's text: Margaret Aston, "English Ruins and English History: The Dissolution and the Sense of the Past," *Journal of the Warburg and Courtauld Institutes* 36 (1973): 231–55; Herschel Baker, *The Race of Time: Three Lectures on Renaissance Historiography* (Toronto: University of Toronto Press, 1967); Leonard Dean, *Tudor Theories of History Writing* (Ann Arbor: University of Michigan Press, 1947); Arthur Ferguson, *Clio Unbound: Perception of the Social and Cultural Past in Renaissance England* (Durham: Duke University Press, 1979), and *Utter Antiquity: Perceptions of Prehistory in Renaissance England* (Durham: Duke University Press, 1993); F. Smith Fussner, *The Historical Revolution: English Historical Writing and Thought, 1580–1640* (London: Routledge and Kegan Paul, 1962); T. D. Kendrick, *British Antiquaries* (London: Methuen, 1950); Joseph Levine, "Tudor Antiquaries," *History Today* 20 (1970): 278–85; Gerald MacLean, *Time's Witness: Historical Representations in English Poetry, 1603–1660* (Madison: University of Wisconsin Press, 1990); May McKisack, *Medieval History in the Tudor Age* (Oxford: Oxford University Press, 1971); Stan Mendyk, "*Speculum Britanniae*": *Regional Study, Antiquarianism, and Science in Britain to 1700* (Toronto: University of Toronto Press, 1989); Graham Parry, *The Trophies of Time: English Antiquarians of the Seventeenth Century* (Oxford: Oxford University Press, 1995); Stuart Piggot, *Ancient Britons and the Antiquarian Imagination: Ideas from the Renaissance*

to the Regency (London: Thames and Hudson, 1989); J. G. A. Pocock, *The Ancient Constitution and the Feudal Law: English Historical Thought in the Seventeenth Century* (New York: W. W. Norton, 1967); James Simpson, "Ageism: Leland, Bale, and the Laborious Start of English Literary History, 1350–1550," *New Medieval Literatures* 1 (1997): 213–36; and Bart Van Es, *Spenser's Forms of History* (Oxford: Oxford University Press, 2002).

3. According to Geoffrey of Monmouth, Brutus is the illegitimate son of Silvius, Aeneas's grandson, by a cousin of Aeneas's second wife, Lavinia. Technically speaking, England's legendary descent from Rome and Troy is thus collateral or analogic, rather than direct—though that distinction was not of interest either to Geoffrey's supporters or detractors in the Renaissance. See Geoffrey of Monmouth, *The History of the Kings of Britain*, trans. Lewis Thorpe (London: Penguin Books, 1988), pp. 53–74.

4. This despite the efforts of several English writers to defend Geoffrey of Monmouth against a series of skeptical attacks that included William of Newburgh's *Historia Rerum Anglicanarum* (twelfth century), Polydore Vergil's *Anglica Historica* (London, 1534), and Thomas Fenne's *Fennes frutes vvhich vvorke is deuided into three seuerall parts . . . The third* [of which argues], *that it is not requisite to deriue our pedegree from the vnfaithfull Troians, who were chiefe causes of their owne destruction* (London, 1590). See, for example, John Leland, *Assertio inclytissimi Arturii, The Famous Historie of Chinon of Middleton . . . to which is added* The Assertion of King Arthur, ed. Walter Mead, Early English Text Society, o.s. no. 165 (London: Oxford University Press, 1925 for 1923); and Richard Harvey, *Philadelphus, or A Defence of the Brutes, and the Brutans History* (London, 1593). I am grateful to Jeff Dolven for bringing Fenne's treatise to my attention.

5. Here I would disagree with Quentin Skinner that the attitude of Renaissance humanists toward "the major texts of classical eloquence" indicates that they "lack any sense of the past as a foreign country" and that "they approach [those texts] as if they are contemporary documents with an almost wholly unproblematic relevance to their own circumstances." Quentin Skinner, *Reason and Rhetoric in the Philosophy of Hobbes* (Cambridge: Cambridge University Press, 1996), p. 40.

6. On the status of English during this period, see Paula Blank, *Broken English: Dialects and the Politics of Language in Renaissance Writings* (New York: Routledge, 1996); Richard Foster Jones, *The Triumph of English: A Survey of Opinions Concerning the Vernacular from the Introduction of Printing to the Restoration* (Stanford: Stanford University Press, 1953); Arthur Quiller-Couch, "On the Lineage of English Literature (I)," in *The Art of Writing* (New York: Capricorn Books, 1961): 176–200, and "On the Lineage of English Lit-

erature (II)," in *The Art of Writing* (New York: Capricorn Books, 1961): 200–29; Veré Rubel, *Poetic Diction in the English Renaissance: From Skelton through Spenser* (New York: Modern Language Association, 1941); and T. G. Tucker, *The Foreign Debt of English Literature* (London: George Bell and Sons, 1907).

7. Thomas Warton, *The History of English Poetry, from the Eleventh to the Seventeenth Century* (London, 1778 and 1781; reprint London: Ward, Lock, 1870), p. 627.

8. Raymond Williams, *Keywords: A Vocabulary of Culture and Society,* rev. ed. (New York: Oxford University Press, 1983).

9. Williams, s.v. "literature."

10. Following Williams, several influential studies of Renaissance writing have pushed the category of literature to the margins of attention, or dispensed with it entirely. Terence Cave prefers the word "writing" to "literature" in *The Cornucopian Text* (1979), for example, "in order to avoid making a priori restrictions of material." Literature "can only be imagined in opposition to non-literary discourse: it is non-serious rather than serious, fictitious rather than true," whereas writing, Cave argues, "is indifferent to these distinctions." Terence Cave, *The Cornucopian Text: Problems of Writing in the French Renaissance* (Oxford: Oxford University Press, 1979), pp. viiii–ix. Different assumptions would appear to animate *Writing Matter,* Jonathan Goldberg's study of the theory, practice, and materiality of Renaissance handwriting. For Goldberg, writing creates and perpetuates distinction as such; does the "ideological work" of constructing the social order; and, in the specific case of italic scripts in Renaissance England, comes "to signify socially as the mark of high literariness and a full literacy." And yet literature is the one distinction that Goldberg is careful to place beyond the scope of his book, where he imagines that it may one day be retrieved by someone else; for the "path from letters and literacy to literature . . . is work that lies ahead." Jonathan Goldberg, *Writing Matter: From the Hands of the English Renaissance* (Stanford: Stanford University Press, 1990), pp. 1–2, 10. More recent practitioners of Renaissance literary studies have not been quick to hearken to this call. To the contrary: In a provocative study of the aesthetics of Renaissance inscription, much influenced by Goldberg's attention to the materiality of writing, Juliet Fleming turns decisively against the category of literature. She argues that that "literature" is wholly anachronistic in its application to the Renaissance and works to "limit . . . our understanding of the past." For unlike "poesy," the sixteenth-century word that she follows Williams in using for vernacular writing, preferring its generality and its emphasis on making, "the category of 'literature' which is the object of study of

most twentieth-century analysis" distracts us from the fact that there are "classes of 'non-literature' entirely contained by, and rendered mute within" it. In *Graffiti and the Writing Arts of Early Modern England,* the modern inflection of the word "literature" is as unmistakable as it is in *The Cornucopian Text.* In a revealing passage, Fleming derives the "determinant characteristics" of this category—"playfulness, discursivity, imagination, and self-display"—from Stephen Greenblatt's *Marvelous Possessions.* Juliet Fleming, *Graffiti and the Writing Arts of Early Modern England* (London: Reaktion, 2001), p. 114.

11. Williams, s.v. "literature."

12. *Cambridge History of Early Modern English Literature,* ed. David Loewenstein and Janel Mueller (Cambridge: Cambridge University Press, 2002), p. 6.

13. Ibid.

14. Ibid.

15. Ibid., pp. 6–7.

16. Pp. 18–19 of Louis Montrose, "Professing the Renaissance: The Poetics and Politics of Culture," in *The New Historicism,* ed. H. Aram Veeser (New York: Routledge, 1989), pp. 15–36. Montrose's essay is conceived, in part, as a response to J. Hillis Miller's 1986 Presidential Address to the Modern Language Association, in which he expressed skepticism about "the almost universal turn away from theory in the sense of an orientation toward language as such and has made a corresponding turn toward history, culture, society, politics, institutions, class and gender conditions, the social context, the material base in the sense of institutionalization, conditions of production, technology, distribution, and consumption of 'cultural products,' among other products" (283). See J. Hillis Miller, "The Triumph of Theory, the Resistance to Reading, and the Question of the Material Base," *Publications of the Modern Language Association* 102, no. 3 (1987): 281–91.

17. Montrose, p. 24.

18. Montrose, p. 19. Jonathan Crewe, *Hidden Designs: The Critical Profession and Renaissance Literature* (New York: Methuen, 1986), p. 16.

19. Montrose, p. 18.

20. See Montrose, p. 24.

21. Crewe, p. 16.

22. Friedrich Nietzsche, "The Utility and Liability of History for Life," in *Unfashionable Observations,* trans. Richard T. Gray (Stanford: Stanford University Press, 1995), p. 86.

23. Here I make a point of distinguishing my approach to Renaissance literature from the New Historicism, a critical practice that characteristically

"constitutes a continuous dialogue between a *poetics* and a *politics* of culture" (Montrose 24). My perspective, in this regard, is indebted to the arguments made by J. Hillis Miller in *On Literature* (New York: Routledge, 2002) and to the critique of contemporary historicisms that Christopher Pye offers in *The Vanishing: Shakespeare, the Subject, and Early Modern Culture* (Durham: Duke University Press, 2000).

24. Montrose, p. 23.

25. Stephen Greenblatt, *Hamlet in Purgatory* (Princeton: Princeton University Press, 2001), p. 46.

26. Jacques Derrida, "This Strange Institution Called Literature," in *Acts of Literature,* ed. David Attridge (London: Routledge, 1992), p. 73.

27. Andrea Alciato, *Emblemata* (Lyons, 1550), p. 196.

28. Erich Auerbach, *Mimesis: The Representation of Reality in Western Literature,* trans. Willard Trask (Princeton: Princeton University Press, 1953), p. 548.

29. Donald Gordon, *The Renaissance Imagination,* ed. Stephen Orgel (Berkeley: University of California Press, 1975), p. 102.

30. On the issue of kind, see Rosalie Colie, *The Resources of Kind: Genre Theory in the Renaissance* (Berkeley: University of California Press, 1973); Alastair Fowler, *Kinds of Literature: An Introduction to the Theory of Genres and Modes* (Cambridge: Harvard University Press, 1982); *Renaissance Genres: Essays on Theory, History, and Interpretation,* ed. Barbara Lewalski (Cambridge: Harvard University Press, 1986); and Tzvetan Todorov, *Genres in Discourse,* trans. Catherine Porter (Cambridge: Cambridge University Press, 1990), especially chapter 1, "The Notion of Literature," pp. 1–12, and chapter 2, "The Origins of Genres," pp. 13–26. On the theory and practice of Renaissance imitation, see Gordon Braden, *The Classics and English Renaissance Poetry: Three Case Studies* (New Haven: Yale University Press, 1978); Terence Cave, *The Cornucopian Text;* Thomas Greene, *The Light in Troy: Imitation and Discovery in Renaissance Poetry* (New Haven: Yale University Press, 1982); and Martin McLaughlin, *Literary Imitation in the Italian Renaissance: The Theory and Practice of Literary Imitation in Italy from Dante to Bembo* (Oxford: Clarendon Press, 1995).

31. Jean Colet held that students at St. Paul's should "aboue all besyly lerne & rede good latyn authors of chosen poetes and oratours, and not[e] wysely how th[e]y wrote and spake and studi alway to folowe them: desyring none other rules but their examples [since] imitacyon with tongue and penne more avalyeth shortely to gete the true eloquent speeche than al the tradicions rules and preceptes of maysters." Jean Colet, *Aeditio* (n.p., 1527), sig. D6^r–D7^r. For Ben Jonson, nearly a century later, this injunction was com-

monplace. Referring in *Timber* to "the best kind of writing," Jonson underscored the affinity of reading and writing within the process of imitation: "For a man to write well, there are required three necessaries: to read the best authors, observe the best speakers, and much exercise his own style." Ben Jonson, *Timber: or Discoveries,* in *Complete Poems,* ed. George Parfitt (London: Penguin Books, 1988), p. 425.

32. John Foxe is quoting the church father Tertulian here. The passage is quoted in Margreta de Grazia, "Spenser's Antic Disposition" (plenary lecture presented at the meeting of the International Spenser Society, Cambridge, U.K., April 2001). I am grateful to the author for sharing this unpublished manuscript with me.

33. Virgil, *Eclogues* 1.66. Cicero, *Epistolae ad Atticum* 4.16.

34. Richard Mulcaster, "The Peroration," *The First Part of the Elementarie* (London, 1582), p. 257. For Roger Ascham's response to Cicero's characterization of early Britain, see *The Scholemaster,* ed. John Mayor (London: G. Bell and Sons, 1934), pp. 219–20.

35. At 3.2.3 in Quintilian, *The Orator's Education,* trans. Donald Russell, 5 vols. (Cambridge: Harvard University Press, 2001). Earlier, at 2.17.9–12, Quintilian appears to take a more skeptical view of the claim that it is possible to achieve eloquence without the aid of the art of rhetoric: "It is sufficient to remind ourselves that everything which art makes perfect had its origin in nature. Otherwise, let us do away with medicine, which was discovered by the observation of things conducive to health and sickness and, according to some, is based entirely on experience. . . . Let us not allow building to be an art either: primitive men constructed their huts without art. Music too: singing and dancing of some sort exist in all peoples. So if any speech [*sermo*] is to be called 'rhetoric' [*rhetorice*], then I must agree that rhetoric existed before there was an art; but if it is not true that everyone who speaks is an orator, and people did not speak like orators in those days [*tanquam oratores loquebantur*], then they must admit that the orator is produced by art, and did not exist before art."

36. Roger Ascham, *The Scholemaster,* in *English Works,* ed. William Aldis Wright (Cambridge: Cambridge University Press, 1904), pp. 213, 292.

37. Mulcaster, pp. 258, 254.

38. Mulcaster, p. 253.

39. For a study of the relationship between rhetoric and conquest, in the context of European-American colonialism in the New World, see Eric Cheyfitz, *The Poetics of Imperialism: Translation and Colonization from* The Tempest *to* Tarzan (Philadelphia: University of Pennsylvania Press, 1991).

40. I take the phrase "founding stories" from Allen Grossman, "Orpheus/Philomela: Subjection and Mastery in the Founding Stories of Poetic Production and in the Logic of Our Practice," in *Poets Teaching Poets: Self and the World*, ed. Gregory Orr and Ellen Bryant Voight (Ann Arbor: University of Michigan Press, 1996), pp. 121–39. Grossman's claim that "the story about Orpheus . . . reproduces the invariant, or paradigmatic *logic* of the poet as a civilizational agent, a maker of the social order of the human community; and it presents invariably the story of the *subjection* of the maker who intends and brings to pass the structure of the human world" is an important subtext for my arguments about the way that English Renaissance poets responded to a crisis in England's historical relationship to classical Antiquity and in their own understanding of what it meant to make new writing from ancient resources (122).

41. In this respect, my arguments have some affinity with Robert Weimann's claim that "in several fields of early modern culture, [a] shift in the grounding of validity culminated in a new sense of the relations of authority and representation," though in the context of the emergence of English literature, I would adopt a more skeptical attitude toward his related argument that "authority, including the authorization of discourse itself, was no longer given, as it were, before the writing and the reading began. . . ." Robert Weimann, *Authority and Representation in Early Modern Discourse*, ed. David Hillman (Baltimore: Johns Hopkins University Press, 1996), p. 5.

42. William Camden, *Britain, or A chorographicall description of the most flourishing kingdomes, England, Scotland, and Ireland, and the ilands adioyning, out of the depth of antiquitie*, trans. Philemon Holland (London, 1610), p. 88.

43. Richard Tottel, "To the Reader," in *Songes and Sonnettes* (London, 1557).

44. Richard Hooker, *Of the Laws of Ecclesiastical Polity* 3.3.1. *OED*, s.v. "misdistinguish." I am grateful to Paula Blank for calling this passage to my attention.

45. Thomas Wilson, *The Arte of Rhetorique* (London, 1553), sig. Aii^v. For Lucian's account of Hercules Gallicus, see "Heracles," *Lucian*, trans. A. M. Harmon (Cambridge: Harvard University Press, 1913), pp. 61–72. For a catalogue of the appearance of this figure in the Renaissance emblem book, see John Steadman, "Appendix: Renaissance Emblems of Truth and Eloquence," in *The Hill and the Labyrinth: Discourse and Certitude in Milton and His Near-Contemporaries* (Berkeley: University of California Press, 1984), pp. 137–53, and the eight unnumbered pages of illustrations that immediately precede it. I am grateful to Stephen Orgel for calling fig. 3 to my atten-

tion. See his "The Example of Hercules," in *Mythographie der frühen Neuzeit: Ihre Anwedung in den Künsten,* ed. Walther Killy (Wiesbaden: Otto Harrassowitz, 1984), pp. 25–47.

46. Contrary to modern expectations, the substitution of the lyre for the club may have underscored Hercules's barbarity for Renaissance readers. It was well known then that Linus, the legendary poet who was sometimes thought to be the father, the brother, the teacher, and the friend of Orpheus, had been murdered by Hercules with a lyre after he (Linus) had criticized his playing. See, for example, Basil Kennet, *The Lives and Characters of the Ancient Grecian Poets* (London, 1697), s.v. "Linus": "his three Famous Scholars were *Hercules, Thamyris,* and *Orpheus.* Of whom, the Ingenuity of the two last, made amends for the dulness of the first; who being corrected once by his Master, took an occasion to knock out his Brains, with the Harp which he was awkwardly managing" (2).

47. Fig. 3 is taken from Vincenzo Cartari, *Vere e Nove Imagini* (Padua, 1615), p. 546. The smaller portrait in the upper-left corner is a reproduction of the reverse of a silver coin that was minted in Rome, circa 66 B.C., by Quintus Pomponia Musa, a master of the mint, as part of a series of ten coins that included reverse portraits of each of the nine muses. Presumably the images were copied from statues in the temple of Hercules Musarum, near the Circus Flaminius. See also August Friedrich von Pauly, *Real-encyclopädie der classischen Alterthumswissenschaft* (Stuttgart: J. B. Metzlersche, 1922), s.v. "Hercules Musarum." I am grateful to David Sullivan for his assistance in tracing the history of Ripa's portrait to its ancient source. See http://www .beastcoins.com/QPomponiaMusa/QPomponiusMusa.htm. Reproductions of those coins appear on the title page of Sambucus, *Emblemata* (Antwerp, 1564). For a reproduction of this page, see chapter 1, fig. 18.

48. These lines are Ovid's; see *Amores* 1.15.35–36. Shakespeare uses them as the epigraph to *Venus and Adonis* (1593). See William Shakespeare, *Venus and Adonis,* in *Narrative Poems,* ed. Jonathan Crewe (New York: Penguin Books, 1999), pp. 4–5. I use Crewe's translation.

49. See Hanna Gray, "Renaissance Humanism: The Pursuit of Eloquence," *Journal of the History of Ideas* 24, no. 4 (1963): 497–514, and the primary texts that are translated and introduced by Quirinus Breen in "Giovanni Pico della Mirandola on the Conflict of Philosophy and Rhetoric," *Journal of the History of Ideas* 13, no. 3 (1952): 384–412, and "Melancthon's Reply to G. Pico della Mirandola," *Journal of the History of Ideas* 13 , no. 3 (1952): 413–26.

50. I established this list of synonyms for "eloquence" by consulting the searchable text of sixteen Renaissance dictionaries in the online database

that has been created by Ian Lancashire at the University of Toronto. For the Early Modern English Dictionaries Database (EMEDD), see http://www.chass .utoronto.ca/english/emed/emedd.html.

51. Ascham, *Scholemaster,* p. 283.

52. Francis Clement, *The petie schole with an English orthographie, wherin by rules lately prescribed is taught a method to enable both a childe to reade perfectly within one moneth, & also the vnperfect to write English aright* (London, 1587), p. 45. I am grateful to Jennifer Waldron for calling this passage to my attention.

53. *Politeuphuia. Wits common wealth* (London, 1598), sig. H2^v.

54. Martin Elsky, *Authorizing Words: Speech, Writing, and Print in the English Renaissance* (Ithaca: Cornell University Press, 1989), p. 52.

55. William Webbe, *A Discourse of Englishe Poesie* (London, 1586), sig. Bii^r, italics mine.

56. Jonson, p. 430.

57. My interest in mythical thinking was stimulated by Jean Seznec, *Survival of the Pagan Gods: The Mythological Tradition and Its Place in Renaissance Humanism and Art,* trans. Barbara Sessions (New York: Pantheon Books, 1953), and Roberto Calasso, *Literature and the Gods,* trans. Tim Parks (New York: Alfred Knopf, 2001).

58. The phrase is Geoffrey Hartman's. See Geoffrey Hartman, "The Voice of the Shuttle: Language from the Point of View of Literature," in *Beyond Formalism: Literary Essays, 1958–1970* (New Haven: Yale University Press, 1970), p. 355.

59. On this distinction see Cicero, *De inventione* 1.19.27 and *Ad Herennium* 1.8.13.

60. John Milton, *The History of Britain, that Part especially now call'd England, from the first Traditional Beginning, continu'd to the Norman Conquest* (London, 1672), p. 7.

61. For language, dialect, and diction, see the works by Paula Blank, Richard Foster Jones, Veré Rubel, and T. G. Tucker that I list in note 4. For the literary career, see Patrick Cheney, *Spenser's Famous Flight : A Renaissance Idea of a Literary Career* (Toronto: University of Toronto Press, 1993), and Richard Helgerson, *Self-Crowned Laureates : Spenser, Jonson, Milton, and the Literary System* (Berkeley : University of California Press, 1983). For the emergence of the vernacular canon, see Jonathan Brody Kramnick, *Making the English Canon: Print Capitalism and the Cultural Past, 1700–1770* (Cambridge: Cambridge University Press, 1998); Douglas Patey, "The Eighteenth Century Invents the Canon," *Modern Language Studies* 18, no. 1 (1988): 17–37; Trevor Ross, *The Making of the English Literary Canon: From the Middle Ages*

to the Late Eighteenth Century (Montreal: McGill-Queen's University Press, 1998); and Richard Terry, *Poetry and the Making of the English Literary Past, 1660–1781* (Oxford: Oxford University Press, 2001). For the history of the material text, see Arthur Marotti, *Manuscript, Print, and the English Renaissance Lyric* (Ithaca: Cornell University Press, 1995), and Wendy Wall, *The Imprint of Gender: Authorship and Publication in the English Renaissance* (Ithaca: Cornell University Press, 1993). For ideology, politics, economics, and "the social," see Richard Halpern, *The Poetics of Primitive Accumulation: English Renaissance Culture and the Genealogy of Capital* (Ithaca: Cornell University Press, 1991), and Robert Matz, *Defending Literature in Early Modern England: Renaissance Literary Theory in Social Context* (Cambridge: Cambridge University Press, 2000). For the Reformation, see Brian Cummings, *The Literary Culture of the Reformation: Grammar and Grace* (Oxford: Oxford University Press, 2002). For premodern theories of epistemology, see Denise Albanese, *New Science, New World* (Durham: Duke University Press, 1996), and Marjorie Swann, *Curiosities and Texts: The Culture of Collecting in Early Modern England* (Philadelphia: University of Pennsylvania Press, 2001).

Chapter One: Choosing Orpheus

1. Martin Heidegger, "The Origin of the Work of Art," in *Basic Writings*, ed. David Farrell Krell (San Francisco: Harper Collins, 1993), p. 143.

2. On the figure of Orpheus, see: *Orpheus: The Metamorphoses of a Myth*, ed. John Warden (Toronto: University of Toronto Press, 1985); Kenneth R. R. Gros Louis, "The Triumph and Death of Orpheus in the English Renaissance," *Studies in English Literature, 1500–1900* 9, no. 1 (1969): 63–80; Allen Grossman, "Orpheus/Philomela," pp. 121–39; W. K. C. Guthrie, *Orpheus and Greek Religion: A Study of the Orphic Movement*, rev. ed. (London: Methuen, 1952); D. P. Walker, "Orpheus the Theologian and Renaissance Platonists," *Journal of the Warburg and Courtauld Institutes* 16 (1953): 100–20.

3. Philip Sidney, *The Defence of Poesy*, in *Sir Philip Sidney: A Critical Edition of the Major Works*, ed. Katharine Duncan-Jones (Oxford: Oxford University Press, 1989), p. 213.

4. Geffrey Whitney, *A Choice of Emblemes*, ed. Henry Green (New York: Benjamin Bloom, 1967; repr. of London, 1866), p. 186. See also Geffrey Whitney, *A Choice of Emblemes*, ed. John Manning (Aldershot: Scolar Press, 1989). For an introduction to the terminology of Renaissance emblem writing, see James Elkins, "Emblemata," in *The Domain of Images* (Ithaca: Cor-

nell University Press, 1999), pp. 195–212. For a more detailed account of the genre, see John Manning's *The Emblem* (London: Reaktion Books, 2002).

5. The relevant lines are 391–93. I take my translation from *The Epistles of Horace: A Bilingual Edition,* trans. David Ferry (New York: Farrar, Straus and Giroux, 2001), pp. 178–89.

6. For the ancient distinction between civil and savage, see Arthur Lovejoy and George Boas, *Primitivism and Related Ideas in Antiquity* (Baltimore: Johns Hopkins University Press, 1935). For an account of this distinction in the context of ancient rhetoric, see Ernst Gombrich, "The Debate on Primitivism in Ancient Rhetoric," *Journal of the Warburg and Courtauld Institutes* 29 (1966): 24–38.

7. Houghton Library MS Typ 14. On this text and its relationship to the printed *Choice,* see Mason Tung, "Whitney's *A Choice of Emblemes* Revisited: A Comparative Study of the Manuscript and the Printed Versions," *Studies in Bibliography* 29 (1976): 32–101. See also John Manning, "Geffrey Whitney's Unpublished Emblems: Further Evidence of Indebtedness to Continental Traditions," in *The English Emblem and The Continental Tradition,* ed. Peter Daly (New York: AMS Press, 1988), pp. 83–108. "Orphei Musica" does not appear in the manuscript at Harvard.

8. Pierre Coustau, *Pegma cum narrationibus philosophicis* (Lyon, 1555), p. 315.

9. Amphion is the "some other named" that Sidney identifies with Orpheus and Linus as poets of the most remote antiquity.

10. Cicero, *De oratore,* trans. E. W. Sutton and H. Rackham, 2 vols. (Cambridge: Harvard University Press, 1942). I have amended the translation. The entire passage occurs at 1.8.33: "Ut vero iam ad illa summa veniamus; quae vis alia potuit aut dispersos homines unum in locum congere, aut a fera agrestique vita ad hunc humanum cultum civilemque deducere, aut, iam constitutis civitatibus, leges, iudicia, iura describere?"

11. *Facundia,* which means fluency in speech, is synonymous with *eloquentia* in the poem. So is *disertus* (line 7), which, with its pun on *disserere* ("to scatter seed" or "to sow"), further illuminates this representation of eloquence as a genealogical narrative.

12. *The Emblems of Thomas Palmer: Two Hundred Poosees,* ed. John Manning (New York: AMS Press, 1988), p. 86.

13. See, for example, *Ars Poetica* 436–7: "si carmina condes | numquam te fallant animi sub vulpe latentes." Here, the Latin word *carmen*—meaning "poem" as well as "song"—exemplifies the same kind of tension between orality and writing that we find at work in Costalius's emblem.

14. Seneca, *De brevitate vitae, Dialogues and Letters,* trans. C. D. N. Costa (New York: Penguin Books, 1997), p. 77.

15. *OED,* s.v. "literature."

16. Pierre Coustau, *Pegme de Pierre Coustau: Avec les narrations philosophiques* (Lyon, 1560), p. 389.

17. Lactantius, *Divinae Institutiones,* in Migne, *Patrologia Latina* 6.130.

18. Friedrich Nietzsche, *The Gay Science,* trans. Walter Kaufmann (New York: VintageBooks, 1974), p. 32.

19. *Bibliographie Lyonnaise: Recherches sur les Imprimeurs, Libraires, Relieurs et Fondeurs de Lettres de Lyon au XVIe Siècles* (Paris: A. Picard et Fils, 1895–1921): 10.247–8, 262–3.

20. The first picture shows Marot kneeling in prayer as he dedicates his translation to God.

21. 1.1–33 in Ovid, *Metamorphoses,* ed. W. S. Anderson (Leipzig: K. G. Saur, 2001).

22. Here Salomon appears to read Genesis through the *Metamorphoses,* a notable departure from earlier attempts to reconcile pagan and Christian theologies of origin. Lactantius, for example, reads Hesiod's *Theogony* through Genesis, arguing that even if God created the world out of chaos, he himself must have created chaos for the purpose of making something from it. "Potuit Hesiodus, qui deorum generationem unius libri opere complexus est. Sed tamen nihil dedit, non a Deo conditore sumens exordium, sed a chao, quod est rudis inordinataeque materiae confusa congeries: cum explanare ante debuerit, chaos ipsum unde, quando, quomodo esse, aut constare coepisset. Nimirum sicut ab aliquo artifice disposita, ordinata, effecta sunt omnia: sic ipsam materiam fictam esse ab aliquo necesse est. Quis igitur hanc, nisi Deus, fecit, cujus potestati subjacent omnia?" (Hesiod could have [given truthful information about God] because he reduced the generation of the gods into a work of one book. Nevertheless, he gave us nothing, since he began not from God the composer but from chaos, which is a crude and disorderly mass of confused matter. He should have explained whence, at what time, and how chaos itself began to exist. Doubtless, all things are disposed, put in order, effectuated by some artist, and so matter itself must have been made by someone. Who, therefore, could make it but God, to whose power all things are subject?) (*PL* 6.131–32). Jean de Tournes published an edition of Lactantius's *Opera omnia* in 1553.

23. See Georges DuPlessis, *Essai bibliographique sur les différents éditions des oeuvres d'Ovide ornées des planches publiées aux XVe et XVIe siècles* (Paris: Léon Techener, 1889).

24. The passage occurs at 7.168–69. John Milton, *Paradise Lost,* ed. Alistair Fowler (London: Longman, 1998). See Milton's comparable description of Chaos at 2.891–94: "a dark | Illimitable ocean without bound, | Without dimension, where length, and breadth, and height, | And time and place are lost. . . ."

25. The analogy that Salomon draws between pagan and Judeo-Christian creation narratives influenced other illustrated editions of the *Metamorphoses* and the Bible, as it did Costalius's *Pegma.* Virgil Solis alters the appearance of Yahweh in *Biblische Figuren des Alten und Neuen Testaments* (1560), replacing the god's imperial crown with a bishop's miter, though he follows Salomon's practice of using biblical and Ovidian woodcuts interchangeably. For Johann Posthius's *Tetrasticha in Ovidii Metam. lib. XV* (1563) and Johann Spreng's *Metamorphoses Ouidii* (1563), Solis copied each of Salomon's designs but used the modified woodcuts from his Genesis sequence as illustrations for Ovid's first book; Jupiter, in distinction to the anonymous, creating *deus,* wears a crown. It is difficult to say whether the presence of this Christianized deity at the beginning of the *Metamorphoses* "corrects" the pagan text or signals a continuing, humanistic accommodation between monotheistic and polytheistic versions of origin. Possibly, it was meant to do both. Other illustrators of Ovid's poem did not imitate Solis's miter. During the 1580s and 1590s, in editions of the *Metamorphoses,* the *deus* in book 1 is identical to Jupiter. See, for example, Jakob Micyllus's *Pub. Ovidii Nasonis Metamorphoseon* (Leipzig, 1582), with woodcuts by "CM." See also *P. Ovidii Nasonis Metamorphoses* (Antwerp, 1591). For an engraved version of the sequence by Crispin de Passe, see *Metamorphoseon Ovidianarum* (Cologne, 1602). For engraved versions by Hendrik Goltzius and Antonio Tempesta, see *The Illustrated Bartsch,* 165 vols. (New York, 1978–). Goltzius's engravings may be found in volume 3, 302.031–082. Tempesta's engravings may be found in volume XXXVI, 638–737. Solis's woodcuts appear in volume 19/1, 7.0–178.

26. Sidney, p. 218.

27. *Lewis and Short,* s.v. "silva."

28. Nietzsche, p. 137.

29. See *Ben Jonson,* ed. Ian Donaldson (Oxford: Oxford University Press, 1985), p. 583: "Now . . . poesy is the habit or the art; nay, rather the queen of arts, which had her original from heaven, received thence from the Hebrews, and had in prime estimation with the Greeks, transmitted to the Latins and all nations that professed civility. The study of it . . . offers to mankind a certain rule and pattern of living well and happily, disposing us to all offices of society."

30. The *Emblemata* was published in six Latin editions between 1564 and 1599. It was also translated into French in 1567 and into Dutch in 1566. See Mario Praz, *Studies in Seventeenth-Century Imagery,* 2nd edition (Rome: *Edizioni di Storia e Letteratura,* 1964), pp. 487–88. On the influence of the *Emblemata* for Whitney's *Choice,* see Gábor Tüskés, "Imitation and Adaptation in Late Humanist Emblematic Poetry: Zsámboky (Sambucus) and Whitney," *Emblematica* 11 (2001): 261–92. For Whitney's debts to Renaissance emblem writing generally, see Tung.

31. On this point, see Jean-Jacques Rousseau, "Essay on the Origin of Languages," in *Rousseau:* The Discourses *and Other Early Political Writings,* trans. Victor Gourevitch (Cambridge: Cambridge University Press, 1997), pp. 247–99, especially pp. 261–62, "Whether It Is Likely That Homer Knew How to Write."

32. Sambucus, pp. 54–55. I am grateful to Shane Butler and Bob Perelman for their comments on my translation of this poem.

33. Francis Bacon, *The New Organon,* ed. Lisa Jardine and trans. Michael Silverthorne (Cambridge: Cambridge University Press, 2000), p. 68.

34. Michel Foucault, *The Order of Things: An Archaeology of the Human Sciences* (New York: Vintage Books, 1994), pp. 23–24.

35. For the Renaissance sense that the future "catches up" to one, while also lying in front of one, see Andrew Marvell, "To His Coy Mistress," lines 21–24: "But at my back I always hear | Time's winged chariot hurrying near: | And yonder all before us lie | Deserts of vast eternity." *Complete Poems,* ed. Elizabeth Story Donno (New York: Penguin Books, 1985), pp. 50–51.

36. Pliny, *The historie of the world: Commonly called, the naturall historie of C. Plinius Secundus,* trans. Philemon Holland (London, 1601), pp. 282, 286. As every swan has its peculiar elegy, "[singing] lamentably a little before [its] death," so each nightingale has "a speciall kind of musick by her selfe," and "there is not a pipe or instrument againe in the world (devised with all the Art and cunning of man so exquisitely as possibly might be) that can affourd more musicke than . . . that little throat of hers."

37. Pliny, p. 293. Parrots "above all other birds of the aire, . . . pass . . . for counterfeiting a mans voice," but there is "a certaine Pie" that can "pronounceth that which is taught her more plainely and distinctly than the [parrot]."

38. For this medal, see *Lexikon Iconographicum Mythologiae Classicae* 7, no. 1 (1994): 74, 96. See also B. Pick, "Thraksiche Münzbilder," *Jahrbuch des Kaiserlich Deutschen Archäologischen Instituts* 13 (1898): 134–36. I am grateful to David Sullivan for his expert assistance with this material.

39. On authority and forgery in Renaissance numismatic books, see Sean Keilen, "Exemplary Metals: Classical Numismatics and the Commerce of Humanism," *Word & Image* 18 (3) 2002: 282–94. For a wider-ranging introduction to the genre, see John Cunally, *Images of the Illustrious* (Princeton: Princeton University Press, 1999).

40. Roberto Weiss, "The Study of Ancient Numismatics during the Renaissance (1313–1517)," *The Numismatic Chronicle,* 7th series, 8 (1968): 187. See also L. Dorez, "Études Aldines I: La marque typographique d'Alde Manuce," *Revue des Bibliothèques* 6 (1896): 143–60.

41. *OED,* s.v. "counterfeit." On the etymology of "counterfeit" and its Renaissance uses with respect to the visual arts, see Peter Parshall, "*Imago Contrafacta:* Images and Facts in the Northern Renaissance," *Art History* 16, no. 4 (1993): 554–79.

42. Roland Barthes, *The Pleasure of the Text,* trans. Richard Miller (New York: Hill and Wang, 2000), p. 46. I am grateful to Leonard Barkan for calling this passage to my attention.

43. Guillaume Rouille, *Promptuaire des medalles* (Lyons, 1577), sig. a4^r. I have translated Rouille's third-person references to the reader into the second person.

44. Manning, *The Emblem,* p. 114.

45. Benedetto Varchi, *Lezzioni* (Florence, 1590), pp. 631–32; quoted in Bernard Weinberg, *A History of Literary Criticism in the Italian Renaissance,* 2 vols. (Chicago: University of Chicago Press, 1961), 1:135–36. I am grateful to Rayna Kalas for calling this passage to my attention. With respect to words and things, Michel Foucault figured the Renaissance as a "great untroubled mirror," "filled with the murmur of words," in the depths of which "things gaze at themselves and reflect their own images back to one another." Foucault, *Order,* p. 27. For an indispensable account of Renaissance language theory, particularly as it bears on the relationship between words and things, see Margreta de Grazia, "Language in Elizabethan England: The Divine Model" (unpublished dissertation, Princeton University, 1975).

46. Bacon, *Advancement,* p. 139.

47. See, for example, Thomas Sprat, *The History of the Royal Society* (London, 1667). For classic examples of Bacon's attack on philology, see Francis Bacon, *The Advancement of Learning, Francis Bacon: A Critical Edition of the Major Works,* ed. Brian Vickers (Oxford: Oxford University Press, 1966), and *New Organon.*

48. Margreta de Grazia, "The Secularization of Language in the Seventeenth Century," *Journal of the History of Ideas* 41, no. 2 (1980): 320.

49. Francis Bacon, "Preparation for a Natural and Experimental History," in *The New Organon*, ed. Lisa Jardine and trans. Michael Silverthorne (Cambridge: Cambridge University Press, 2000), p. 224.

50. Sidney, p. 224.

51. All quotations from Peacham in this section are taken from *The Compleat Gentleman* (London, 1634), pp. 123–24.

52. Karl Marx, *Capital: A Critique of Political Economy*, trans. Ben Fowkes, 3 vols. (New York: Penguin Books, 1990), 1:226.

53. See, for example, the entries for *copia* and *simulacro* in John Florio, *A worlde of wordes, or Most copious, and exact dictionarie in Italian and English* (London, 1598). "Copia" is defined as "store plentie abundance. Also a couple, or paire, or brace. Also a copie, an originall, a patterne, a transcript." "Simulacro" is defined as "an image, a figure, a statue, a picture, a counterfeit, a likeness or resemeblance or patterne of any thing."

54. Henry Peacham, *Minerva Britannia* (London, 1612). Ironically, perhaps, medals make their only appearance in this book in the emblem "Crimina gravissima," where Ganymede displays them as an image of fraud and the "false coine" of sodomy (p. 48).

55. Leonard Barkan, *Unearthing the Past: Archaeology and Aesthetics in the Making of Renaissance Culture* (New Haven: Yale University Press, 1999), p. 30.

56. John Evelyn, *Numismata, A Discourse of Medals, Antient and Modern* (London, 1697), pp. 1, 64.

57. John Pointer, *Britannia Romana, or Roman Antiquities in Britain* (London, 1724), sig. (a1)ᵛ. Joseph Addison, *Dialogues upon the Usefulness of Ancient Medals, Especially in Relation to the Latin and Greek Poets*, in *The Miscellaneous Works of Joseph Addison*, 2 vols., ed. A. C. Guthkelch (London: G. Bell and Sons, 1914), 2:284.

58. For the best account of humanism's "protoarchaeology" in this respect, see Barkan, pp. 1–63.

59. *OED*, s.v. "monument."

60. Michel Foucault, "Nietzsche, History, Genealogy," in *Language, Counter-memory, Practice*, trans. Donald Bouchard and Sherry Simon (Ithaca: Cornell University Press, 1977), p. 147.

61. All references from this emblem are taken from Whitney, p. 185.

62. The relevant lines in Horace's poem are 438–41. I take the text and translation from Ferry, pp. 182–83. "Quintilio si quid recitares, 'corrige, sodes, | hoc,' aiebat 'et hoc.' melius te posse negares | bis terque expertum frustra delere iubebat | et male tornatos incudi reddere versus" ("If Quintilius read a manuscript of yours, | He'd say, 'Please, if you will, change this, and

this,' | And if, after you'd tried and failed to make | The corrections that he'd advised you to make, he'd tell you | To tear it up and take it back to the forge | To be remade").

63. William Webbe, *A Discourse of English Poetrie* (London, 1586), sig. Ei^v. "[I]f suche regarde of our Englishe speeche, and curious verse, had been pollished and bettered by men of learning, iudgement, and authority, it would ere this, haue matched [the Greeks and Romans] in all respects. A manifest example thereof, may bee the great good grace and sweete vayne, which Eloquence hath attained in our speeche, because it hath had the helpe of such rare and singuler wits, as from time to time myght styll adde some amendment to the same."

64. Jacob Burckhardt, *The Civilization of the Renaissance in Italy,* trans. S. G. C. Middlemore (New York: Modern Library, 2002), p. 130.

65. See, for example, Juliet Fleming, *Graffiti and the Writing Arts of Early Modern England* (London: Reaktion Books, 2001).

66. Although Whitney was the first to compose and publish an emblem book in English, *A Choice of Emblemes* is the fifth such books to appear in his language. Whitney's text was preceded by three translations of foreign emblem books by Jan van der Noot (1569), Paolo Giovio (1585), and Lodovico Domenichi (1585). Thomas Palmer compiled a manuscript anthology of emblems circa 1566. See *The Emblems of Thomas Palmer: Two Hundred Poosees.* ed. John Manning (New York: AMS Press, 1988).

67. For an introduction to this vocabulary, see *Post-Colonial Studies: The Key Concepts,* ed. Bill Ashcroft, Gareth Griffiths, and Helen Tiflin (New York: Routledge, 2000).

68. William Camden, *Britannia* (London, 1586). I quote from the first English translation of the text, by Philemon Holland, which appeared in 1610, pp. 87–88 (sig. H2^{r-v}). The numismatic illustrations occur on pp. 89–96.

69. In *The History of Great Britaine under the conquests of ye Romans, Saxons, Danes and Normans* (London, 1610), John Speed justifies the insertion of blank coins in this way: "And whereas some [coins] are not yet noted by that honor to the world; I haue unto suche added only blankes, if happily be reueiled [revealed] hereafter, and the bowels of the earth deliuer to others, her treasures hid, as formerly (and in these our searchinge daies) she hath already done" (p. 172).

70. The "Coniectures as Touching the British Coines" and the "Notes vpon the Romane Coins" appear on pp. 97–106. The quoted text appears on p. 88.

71. Camden, p. 106.

72. Webbe, sig. Biii^v–Biiii^r.

73. Polydore Vergil, *On Discovery*, trans. Brian Copenhaver, *I Tatti Renaissance Library* 6 (Cambridge: Harvard University Press, 2002), I.xv.6.

Chapter Two: Shakespeare's "Wild Musick"

1. Roland Barthes, *A Lover's Discourse: Fragments*, trans. Richard Howard (New York: Hill and Wang, 1978), p. 188.

2. On the figure of the nightingale, see: A. R. Chandler, *Larks, Nightingales, and Poets* (Columbus: Ohio State University, 1937), and "The Nightingale in Greek and Latin Poetry," *Classical Journal* 30 (1930–45): 78–84; Allen Grossman, "Orpheus/Philomela," pp. 121–39; Gregory Nagy, *Poetry as Performance: Homer and Beyond* (Cambridge: Cambridge University Press, 1996); Wendy Pfeffer, *The Change of Philomel: The Nightingale Medieval Literature* (New York: Peter Lang, 1985); and Thomas Shippey, "Listening to the Nightingale," *Comparative Literature* 22, no. 1 (1970): 46–60.

3. August Friedrich von Pauly, "Das singende und weissagende Haupt des O[rpheus]," *Real-encyclopädie der classischen Alterthumswissenschaft* (Stuttgart: J. B. Metzlersche, 1922), 18:1293. I am grateful to John Connor for his assistance with the translation of this article.

4. *OED*, s.v. "commonplace."

5. See 15.4 in Seneca, *De brevitate vitae*, in *Moral Essays*, 3 vols., trans. John Basore (Cambridge: Harvard University Press, 1951), 2:286–355.

6. Pierre Bourdieu, *Language and Symbolic Power*, trans. Gino Raymond and Matthew Adamson, ed. John Thompson (Cambridge: Harvard University Press, 1991), p. 66.

7. Petrarch, "Ad Lelium suum," in *Rime, Trionfi e Poesie Latine*, ed. F. Nieri (Milan: Riccardo Ricciardi, 1951), pp. 740–43; see lines 8–9. Edmund Spenser, *The Shepheardes Calender*, in *The Shorter Poems*, ed. Richard McCabe (New York: Penguin Books, 1999), pp. 23–156; the nightingale is described thus at line 25 in the "November" eclogue.

8. For a seminal interpretation of the nightingale myth in terms of its sexual ideology, see Patricia Klindienst, "The Voice of the Shuttle is Ours," in *Rape and Representation*, ed. Lynn Higgins and Brenda Silver (New York: Columbia University Press, 1991), pp. 35–64.

9. Jonathan Bate, *Shakespeare and Ovid* (Oxford: Clarendon Press, 1993), esp. pp. 83–117.

10. See, for example, Samuel Daniel's *Defense of Rime* on the thralldom of words to Greek and Latin meters: "And even the Latins, who profess not to be so licentious as the Greeks, show us many times examples, but of

strange cruelty, in torturing and dismembering of words in the midst, or disjoining them such as naturally should be married and march together. . . ." Samuel Daniel, "Classical metres unsuitable for English poetry (*c.* 1603)," in *English Renaissance Literary Criticism,* ed. Brian Vickers (Oxford: Clarendon Press, 1999), p. 445.

11. William Shakespeare, *Cymbeline,* ed. Peter Holland (New York: Penguin Books, 2000).

12. On the productivity of rape as a cultural matter, see Stephanie Jed, *Chaste Thinking: The Rape of Lucretia and the Birth of Humanism* (Bloomington: Indiana University Press, 1989).

13. *Epode* 2.1.156–57. Horace, *Odes and Epodes,* trans. C. E. Bennett (Cambridge: Harvard University Press, 1968).

14. William Camden, *Britain, or A chorographicall description of the most flourishing kingdomes, England, Scotland, and Ireland, and the ilands adioyning, out of the depth of antiquitie* (London, 1610), p. 63.

15. Camden, *Britain,* p. 63.

16. Camden, *Remaines Concerning Britaine: But Especially of England and the Inhabitants thereof* (London, 1614), p. 20.

17. Richard Mulcaster, *The First Part of the Elementary* (London, 1582), pp. 256–57.

18. Pliny, "The Preface to the Reader," in *The historie of the world.*

19. Camden, *Britannia siue Florentissimorum regnorum, Angliæ, Scotiæ, Hiberniæ, et insularum adiacentium ex intima antiquitate chorographica descriptio, authore Guilielmo Camdeno* (London, 1586), p. 27.

20. *Lewis and Short,* s.v. "iugum."

21. Camden, sig. ✣ 4. This disclaimer is, however, very arch, since Camden is quoting Cicero. "Some there be who may obiect the silly web of my stile, and rough hewed forme of my writing. Verily I acknowledge it, neither have I waied euery word in Goldsmithe's scales, as *Varro* commanded, neither purposed I to picke flowers out of the gardens of Eloquence. But why should they obiect this, when as *Cicero* the father of Eloquence denieth that this kinde of argument can ΑΝΘΗΡΡΟΓΡΑΦΕΙΣΘΑΙ, that is, be flourished out, and as *Pomponius Mela* said, *is incapable of all Eloquent speech.*" For Camden's source, see Letter 26 (2.6) in Cicero, *Letters to Atticus,* ed. and trans. D. Shackleton Bailey (Cambridge: Harvard University Press, 1999).

22. Gilles Deleuze and Felix Guattari, *A Thousand Plateaus: Capitalism and Schizophrenia,* trans. Brian Massumi (Minneapolis: University of Minnesota Press, 1987), p. 4.

23. Robert Saltwood, *A comparyson bytwene. iiij. byrdes, the larke, the nyghtyngale, ye thrusshe [and] the cuko, for theyr syngynge who shuld be*

chauntoure of the quere (Canterbury, 1533), sig. [Aiiii^r]– Bi^r. I am grateful to Bill Sherman for bringing this text to my attention.

24. George Gascoigne, *The Complaynt of Phylomene* (London, 1576), sig. Kiiv–Kiii^r.

25. Gascoigne, sig. Qii^v.

26. Gascoigne, sig. Piiii^{r-v}.

27. Spenser, *Shepheardes Calender,* "August," ll.188, 185. For an extended meditation on the nightingale in the context of Spenser's poetry, see Patrick Cheney, *Spenser's Famous Flight: A Renaissance Idea of a Literary Career* (Toronto: University of Toronto Press, 1993).

28. Hannah Arendt, "What is Authority?," in *Between Past and Future: Eight Exercises on Political Thought* (New York: Penguin Books, 1993), pp. 121–22.

29. Spenser, *The Shepheardes Calender,* "To . . . Gabriel Harvey," pp. 26–27; "August," 184; Margreta de Grazia, "Spenser's Antic Disposition," unpublished manuscript.

30. The quotations from *The Shepheardes Calender* in this paragraph are taken from E. K.'s letter "To . . . Gabriel Harvey," pp. 25–27, and from "August," ll.173–75, 185.

31. Robert Cawdrey, "To the Reader," in *A Table Alphabeticall* (London, 1604). I am grateful to Paula Blank for calling my attention to this text.

32. Spenser, *Shepheardes Calender,* "To . . . Gabriel Harvey," pp. 26–27.

33. George Puttenham, *The Arte of English Poesie* (London, 1589), pp. 271, 268.

34. Puttenham, p. 312.

35. Puttenham, p. 270.

36. Puttenham, pp. 156–57.

37. In preferring example to rule, Puttenham's text offers a vulgar answer to the classical prescriptions of Horace's *Ars Poetica* at a time when the English language itself resisted every effort to subject it to precepts. On the other hand, precisely by appealing to context as a factor that determines the meaning and value of verbal events, Puttenham's *Arte of English Poesie* could also be described as being more Horatian than any other theoretical text that the English produced prior to Jonson. As Lawrence Manley has shown, it was Horace who introduced to ancient literary theory the idea that every verbal construct "hinges upon the intercourse of men" for its "very existence"— and therefore that the decorum of texts depends not only on their internal criteria but also on the full diversity of experience, in the sense of "public expectations and demands as to what . . . internal coherence should entail." So

we should not allow Jonson's subsequent success in establishing himself as England's Horace to obscure the fact that Puttenham had as viable a claim on that distinction at the turn of the sixteenth century; nor that it was a courtier, rather than a bricklayer's son, who first devised a neoclassicism in which the "naturall rudenesse" of his mother tongue (the phrase is Spenser's) played an incomparably valuable part.

38. Puttenham, p. 270.

39. Deleuze and Guattari, p. 3.

40. Deleuze and Guattari, p. 4.

41. *Sonnet* 55.2 in William Shakespeare, *Complete Sonnets and Poems,* ed. Colin Burrow (Oxford: Oxford University Press, 2002). All subsequent reference to the *Sonnets* will be noted parenthetically in the text.

42. *Anthologia latina* 762.3–6. *Anthologia latina,* ed. Alexander Riese (Leipzig: Teubner, 1894). I am grateful to David Sullivan for this translation.

43. *Iliad* 19.709–23 in *Chapman's Homer: the Iliad, the Odyssey, and the lesser Homerica,* 2 vols., ed. Allardyce Nicoll (New York: Pantheon Books, 1956). Other references to this edition are noted parenthetically in the text. In Homer, the passage occurs at 19.520–25; for the Greek text, see Homer, *The Odyssey,* trans. A. T. Murray, Rev. George E. Dimock (Cambridge: Harvard University Press, 1995).

44. *OED,* s.v. "mone."

45. *Lucrece* 1131–32 in William Shakespeare, *Complete Sonnets and Poems,* ed. Colin Burrow (Oxford: Oxford University Press, 2002). Other references to this edition are noted parenthetically in the text.

46. Puttenham, p. 189.

47. See 5.38 in Aelian, *On the Characteristics of Animals,* trans. A. F. Scholfield, (Cambridge: Harvard University Press, 1958).

48. 10.43.81 in Pliny, *Natural History,* trans. H. Rackham (Cambridge: Harvard University Press, 1947).

49. Pliny, *The historie of the world,* p. 286.

50. In Latin, the passage reads: "deinde in una perfecta musicae scientia: modulatus editur sonus, et nunc continuo spiritu trahitur in longum, nunc variatur inflexo, nunc distinguitur conciso, copulator intorto, promittitur revocato; infuscatur ex inopinato, interdum et secum ipse murmurat, plenus, gravis, acutus, creber, extentus, ubi visum est vibrans—summus, medius, imus; breviterque omnia tam parvulis in faucibus quae tot exquisitis tibiarum tormentis ars hominum excogitavit. . . ."

51. Pierre Belon, *L'histoire de la Nature des Oyseaux, 1555,* ed. Philippe Gardon (Geneva: Librairie Droz, 1997), pp. 336–37.

52. 2.794 in Ulisses Aldrovandi, "De luscinia," in *Ornithologiae, 3* vols. (Bologna, 1599–1603). Aldrovandi's entry on the nightingale occurs at 2.771–98.

53. Juan Luis Vives, "Vestitus, et de ambulatio matutina," *Linguae latinae exercitatio* (Milan, 1539), sigs. 27^r-31^v. In Latin, the passage reads: "Ausculta eam e salice, a qua (ut Plinius inquit) perfectae musicae scientiae modulatus editur sonus. Animadverte accurate et annotabis varietates omnium sonorum: nunc non interquiescit, sed continuo spiritu in longum aequabiliter, sine mutatione; nunc inflectitur: iam minutius et concisius canit; nunc intorquet et quasi crispat vocem; nunc extendit, iam revocat: alias longos concinit versus, quasi heroicos, alias breves, ut sapphicos, interdum brevissimos, ut adonicos" (30^r-^{v}).

54. Henry Hawkins, *Partheneia Sacra, 1633,* ed. Karl Josef Höltgen, *English Emblem Books* 10. (Menston: Scolar Press, 1971), pp. 145–46: "But hearken awhile, you Musicians, how the *Nightingal* sings; obserue her wel, and you shal note, how she pauses not, but equally sings at length with a continual breath without anie change, stil holding her wind to the ful: now she sings her dimunitions, and diuides *in infinitum;* now she wrigles and curles her voice as it were, now she lengthens it againe. now she drawes it back; one while she chants forth longer verses, as they were Heroicks; another while, more short and sudden, much like vnto Saphicks; and sometimes againe, extreme short as Adonicks."

55. Richard Niccols, *The Cuckow* (London, 1609), p. 12.

56. 4.8.18 and 2.3.241, 245 in William Shakespeare, *Antony and Cleopatra,* ed. A. R. Braunmuller (New York: Penguin Books, 1999).

57. *OED,* s.v. "warble."

58. *OED,* s.v. "whorl."

59. 3.2.202–19 passim in William Shakespeare, *A Midsummer Night's Dream,* ed. Russ McDonald. (New York: Penguin Books, 2000).

60. John Milton, "*L'Allegro,*" in *Complete Shorter Poems,* 2nd ed., ed. John Carey (New York: Longman, 1997). The passage occurs at ll.133–34.

61. John Milton, "*Il Penseroso,*" in *Complete Shorter Poems,* ed. John Carey (New York: Longman, 1997). The passage occurs at l.62.

62. Puttenham, p. 26.

63. *OED,* s.v. "wood."

64. Milton, "*L'Allegro,*" 1.132.

65. For Petrarch, it is an allusion to Virgil's *Eclogues* and Ovid's *Metamorphoses,* and its presence in *Rime sparse* is intended to enrich those vulgar compositions with the value that humanism reserved to classical Antiquity

and to Latin literature in particular. The vehicle for that enrichment is an analogy that the poet draws, time and again, between the nightingale and the lyrical complainer of his poems. In *Rime* 10, for example, a sonnet that laments the absence of Stefano Colonna from a trip that Petrarch made to the Pyrenees in 1330, "there is a nightingale" that "sweetly lamenting weeps throughout the night I and burdens every heart with thoughts of love" (10.10– 12). Arising from a wood that the poet places in-between a verdant meadow and a mountain "where we in poetry descend and climb," this song is evidently Petrarch's own text, and the nightingale a figure for the poet (10.8). For in its pivotal location between the raw materials of imitative writing (the "erba verde" of other texts) and the pinnacle of eloquence to which only a tiny minority of finished compositions may ascend (the "bel monte vicino"), the nightingale represents poetic invention as a renovation, in which the old augments its value by becoming newer than, and different from, itself (10.7).

Petrarch's allusion to the nightingale synchronizes the ancient and the modern, reconciles the human to the animal, and makes male and female the same. On the other hand, the real occasion and topical references of *Rime* 10 create a certain dissonance in the poem's ideal time, in which the lyrical complainer and the nightingale are fully present to each other and, in that sense, are one. For they point to an irreducible difference between Petrarch's vulgar writing and the classical literature in which he identifies his poetic voice: the difference of modernity, which the poet represents as loss. In *Rime* 310, difference and loss are registered as an alienation so profound that the lyrical complainer no longer recognizes the nightingale as the avatar of his vulgar eloquence. In comparison to the fact of death, "the song of birds, the flowering of meadows, I the noble, graciousness of lovely ladies I for me are deserts now, wild savage beasts" (310.12–14). In *Rime* 311, the lyrical complainer and the nightingale join their voices in a song about loss whose virtuosity the reader experiences as sympathy or pity—as a surplus of feeling in which the boundary between the past and the present, reality and fiction, self and other, momentarily collapses. Yet the loss remains, neither controverted nor transmuted by a poem that concludes with this reminder: "nothing here can please and also last" (311.14). The nightingale therefore represents Petrarch's relationship to his Latin predecessors in a notably ambivalent way. For while it harmonizes the ancient and the modern into a single strain of music, the nightingale's copious lament also points to their real and insurmountable distinction. For Petrarch's texts, see Petrarch, *The* Canzoniere *or* Rerum vulgarium fragmenta, trans. Mark Musa (Bloomington: Indiana University Press, 1996).

66. Spenser, *Shepheardes Calender*, "Januarye," 1.72; "To . . . Gabriel Harvey," p. 25.

67. *Politeuphuia. Wits common wealth* (London, 1598), p. 48ᵛ.

68. 2.3.79 in Cicero, *De partitione oratoria*, trans. H. Rackham (London: William Heinemann, 1948).

69. *Politeuphuia*, p. 50ʳ.

70. 6.574–75 in Ovid, *Metamorphoses*, ed. W. S. Anderson (Leipzig: Bibliotheca Teubneriana, 2001).

71. *Ovid's Metamorphosis Englished, Mythologiz'd, and Represented in Figures*, trans. George Sandys (Oxford, 1632), p. 122.

72. Jonson gives Shakespeare's art its due, of course, yet even art would appear to be organic in Shakespeare's case. For Jonson, Shakespeare's lines are the progeny of "Nature's family" and constitute a "race" that issues from their poetic father: "Look how the father's face | Lives in his issue, even so the race | Of Shakspeare's mind and manners brightly shines | In his well torned and true filed lines." Ben Jonson, "To the Memory of My Beloved, the Author Mr William Shakespeare: And What He Hath Left Us," in *Complete Poems*, ed. George Parfitt (New York: Penguin Books, 1988), pp. 263–65.

73. Samuel Johnson, "Preface to *The Plays of William Shakespeare*," in *Selected Poetry and Prose*, ed. Frank Brady and W. K. Wimsatt (Berkeley: University of California Press, 1977), p. 316.

74. For Shakespeare's reading, see Leonard Barkan, "What Did Shakespeare Read?," in *Cambridge Companion to Shakespeare*, ed. Margreta de Grazia and Stanley Wells (Cambridge: Cambridge University Press, 2001), pp. 31–48, and Robert Miola, *Shakespeare's Reading* (Oxford: Oxford University Press, 2000).

75. *Shakespeare's Sonnets*, ed. Stephen Booth (New Haven: Yale University Press, 1977), p. 330 n. 7.

76. 4.4, 6–7 in Philip Sidney, *Certain Sonnets, Sir Philip Sidney: A Critical Edition of the Major Works*, ed. Katharine Duncan-Jones. (Oxford: Oxford University Press, 1989).

77. Joel Fineman, "Shakespeare's Ear," in *The Subjectivity Effect in Western Literary Tradition: Essays Toward the Release of Shakespeare's Will* (Cambridge: MIT Press, 1991), pp. 22–25 passim.

78. 19.61 in Cicero, *Orator*, trans. H. M. Hubbell (London: William Heinemann, 1952).

79. 4.1 passim in William Shakespeare, *Titus Andronicus*, ed. Russ McDonald (New York: Penguin Books, 2000). Other references to this edition are noted parenthetically in the text.

80. Stephen Gosson, *The schoole of abuse, conteining a plesaunt inuec-*

tiue against poets, pipers, plaiers, iesters, and such like caterpillers of a comon-welth (London, 1579), sigs. B2^{r-v}.

81. In a recently completed doctoral dissertation, Jennifer Waldron argues that when Shakespeare deprives Lavinia of her hands as well as her tongue, reducing her to silent but expressive gestures, he means to fashion an image of a kind of eloquence that is peculiar to drama, the imaginative form that stands between speech and writing and assimilates them both: the eloquence, if you will, of the human body. Waldron's analysis of the nightingale myth in *Titus Andronicus* is therefore an important rejoinder to mine, in the sense that she specifically asks how Shakespeare's decision to write plays, as well as poems, shaped his thinking about eloquence as a category of English composition. Waldron's argument that Lavinia's expressive *silence* represents dramatic eloquence, as Shakespeare understood it during the 1590s, also raises a question about my claim that Shakespeare identifies the eloquence of *Titus Andronicus* with the nightingale's *song*. For unlike Philomela, Lavinia dies without becoming a bird, and thus without recovering her voice.

Or does she? In the play's final scene, we discover that Lucius, the founder of a new dynasty of Roman emperors, has taken on the persona of Aeneas in order to legitimate his claim to Saturninus's throne. His first order of business is to establish a distinction between Romans (human beings) and Goths (wild beasts), and thereby to impose on his devastated city the piety that Tamora earlier found so "cruel and irreligious" among the Romans she called "brethren" (1.1.133, 107). Burying Saturninus in "his father's grave," and enclosing Titus and Lavinia with "our household's monument," Lucius makes sure to throw Tamora, "that ravenous tiger," into a wilderness that is, by definition, *outside* Rome—though not long ago, Rome itself was "but a wilderness of tigers": "Her life was beastly, and devoid of pity, | And being dead, let birds on her take pity!" (5.3.191–200 passim; 3.1.54). In the first line of this couplet, "pity" means "compassion"; in the second, it evidently means the opposite. Thus it seems that *Titus Andronicus* returns to the point where it began, and that nothing has changed—except, I would submit, for Lavinia, "that changing piece" (1.1.312). For over and above the meaning that Lucius intends to convey in this passage, which concludes the play, I hear his sister's voice returning—returning as an echo of her desperate pleas to Tamora in the woods ("O, be to me, though thy hard heart say no, | Nothing so kind, but something pitiful"); and as an echo of Philomela's plaintive avian music at the end of Ovid's tale (2.3.155–56). In this context, it would appear that the moment when Shakespeare's text at last falls silent and the moment when it first projects its vulgar eloquence as birdsong are one and the same.

Chapter Three: The Ancient Neighborhood
of Milton's *Maske*

1. John Keats, "On Sitting Down to Read *King Lear* Once Again," in *Complete Poems*, ed. John Barnard (New York: Penguin Books, 1988), p. 220.

2. See 2.9 in Vitruvius, *On Architecture*, trans. Frank Granger (Cambridge: Harvard University Press, 1970).

3. John Evelyn, *Sylva, or A Discourse of Forest-Trees and the Propagation of Timber in His Majesties Dominions*, 2nd ed. (London, 1670), p. 245.

4. Pref. 5–6 in Aulus Gellius, *Noctes Atticae*, trans. John Rolfe (Cambridge: Harvard University Press, 1996).

5. See chapters 10 and 24 in Suetonius, *De grammaticis et rhetoribus*, trans. John Rolfe (Cambridge: Harvard University Press, 2001).

6. *Ben Jonson: The Complete Poems*, ed. George Parfitt (New York: Penguin, 1986), pp. 123, 373.

7. 1.7–9 in Ovid, *Metamorphoses*, ed. W. S. Anderson (Leipzig: Bibliotheca Teubneriana, 2001). 1.7–9 in *Ovid's* Metamorphoses: *The Arthur Golding Translation*, ed. John Frederick Nims (Philadelphia: Paul Dry, 2000). References to these editions are noted parenthetically in the text.

8. Isidore of Seville, *Etymologiae*, ed. W. M. Lindsay (Oxford: Oxford University Press, 1911). See 13.3, "De elementis," and 17.6, "De arboris."

9. Henry Peacham, *Minerva Britanna* (London, 1612), p. 182.

10. Tacitus, *Dialogus de oratoribus*, trans. W. Peterson and M. Winterbottom. (Cambridge: Harvard University Press, 2000). The Latin text reads: "si modo dignum aliquid elaborare et efficere velint, reliquenda conversatio amicorum et iucunditas urbis, deserenda cetera officia, utque ipsi dicunt, in nemora et lucos, id est in solitudinem secedendum est" (9.6). The translation is mine.

11. See Tacitus, *Dialogus* 12.1–2: "secedit animus in loca pura atque innocentia fruiturque sedibus sacris. Haec eloquentiae primordia, haec penetralia; hoc primum habitu cultuque commoda mortalibus in illa casta et nullis contacta vitiis pectora influxit; sic oracula loquenbantur."

12. Hannah Arendt, "What is Authority?," in *Between Past and Future* (New York: Penguin Books, 1993), p. 121.

13. Lorenzo Valla, *On Pleasure*, trans. A. Kent Hieatt and Maristella Lorch (New York: Abaris Books, 1977). In 1434, Valla gave a revised edition of *De voluptate* a new title: *De vero falsoque bono* (On the true and the false good). The relevant passage appears on pp. 320–21 of Hieatt and Lorch's edition. It was widely circulated in the sixteenth century in the pages of George Sabinus, *Fabularum Ovidii interpretatio* (see, for example, Thomas Thomas's

1584 Cambridge edition, p. 245). "Scitis poetas finixisse has aves sorores fuisse, Pandionis regis filias, credo quod videbantur in cantando pene germane, et in his significasse oratoriam atque poeticam, que prope sorores sunt; atque ut hanc similitudinem ita illam discrepantiam notasse, quod in altera inest mira libido tecta et urbes incolendi, in altera vero arbusta et silvas, voluisseque hirundinem similem esse urbane eloquentie, que intra parietes, in curia, in subellis exercetur, philomelam (quam lusciniam dicimus) eloquentie nemorali et poetarum, qui silvas in solitudines consectantur et loca non ab hominibus celebrata sed a Musis amant" (You know that the poets invented the story that these birds were sisters, daughters of King Pandion, because, I think, the birds seemed to be nearly sisters in their song; and in these the poets signified the arts of oratory and poetry, which are nearly sisters. And as they noted this likeness, they also noted the difference, for one of these birds has a remarkable proclivity for living among roofs and in cities, and the other in glades and forests. The poets meant that correspondingly the swallow was associated with urban eloquence, which is exercised between walls, in the curia, and in courts, while Philomela (which we call the nightingale) was associated with the sylvan eloquence of the poets, who seek out forests and solitudes, as well as love spots frequented by the Muses, not by men).

14. Quintilian, *The Orator's Education,* trans. Donald Russell, 5 vols. (Cambridge: Harvard University Press, 2001). References to this edition are noted parenthetically in the text.

15. Terence Cave, *The Cornucopian Text: Problems of Writing in the French Renaissance* (Oxford: Oxford University Press, 1979), p. 35.

16. *Ovid's* Metamorphoses*: The Arthur Golding Translation,* 10.93–116. References to this edition are noted parenthetically in the text.

17. See Horace, *Ars Poetica* 391–401, in Horace, *Satires, Epistles, and Ars Poetica,* trans. H. Rushton Fairclough (Cambridge: Harvard University Press, 1961).

18. John Milton, "Beatiores reddit homines ars quam ignorantia," ed. Donald Lemen Clark, trans. Bromley Smith, in *Works of John Milton,* vol. 12 (New York: Columbia University Press, 1936). References to this edition are noted parenthetically in the text.

19. John Milton, "Lycidas," in *Complete Shorter Poems,* ed. John Carey (New York: Longman, 1997), pp. 237–56. References to this edition are noted parenthetically in the text.

20. John Churton Collins, quoted in Rachel Cohen, "The Very Bad Review: Two Victorian Men of Letters, One Review from Hell," *New Yorker,* 6 October 2003, p. 54.

21. 1.12.45 in Horace, *Odes and Epodes*, trans. C. E. Bennett (Cambridge: Harvard University Press, 1968).

22. 1.1.48–67 in William Shakespeare, *Henry V*, ed. Claire McEachern (New York: Penguin Books, 1999).

23. Gilbert Murray, *The Classical Tradition in Poetry* (Cambridge: Harvard University Press, 1927), p. 7.

24. In Latin, the passage reads: "Antiquissimi quique gentium indigenae in sylvis & montibus errassse dicuntur, ferarum ritu pabuli commoditatem sequuti" (270–72).

25. Evelyn, p. 244.

26. John Milton, *A Maske Presented at Ludlow Castle*, in *Milton: The Complete Shorter Poems*, 2nd ed., ed. John Carey (New York: Longman, 1997). References to this edition are noted parenthetically in the text.

27. John Milton, *The Second Defense of the English People*, trans. Robert Fellowes, in *John Milton: Complete Poems and Major Prose*, ed. Merritt Hughes (New York: Macmillan, 1957), p. 828.

28. 4.1.52–53 in William Shakespeare, *Titus Andronicus*, ed. Russ McDonald (New York: Penguin Books, 2000).

29. John Manwood, *A Treatise and Discourse of the Lawes of the Forrest* (New York: Garland, 1978). References to this edition are noted parenthetically in the text.

30. For the question of jurisdiction, as it bears upon the relationship between literature and law in the English Renaissance, see Bradin Cormack, "A Power to Do Justice: Jurisdiction and Royal Authority in Early Modern English Literature" (Ph.D. diss., Stanford University, 2001).

31. Seneca, *Seneca: His Tenne Tragedies*, trans. Thomas Newton (Bloomington: Indiana University Press, 1966), p. 78.

32. *Ovid's Metamorphoses: The Arthur Golding Translation*, 6.806–08.

33. Cave, p. 39.

34. For my text of *Odyssey*, I use George Chapman's English translation. See *Chapman's Homer: The Iliad, the Odyssey, and the Lesser Homerica*, 2 vols., ed. Allardyce Nicoll (New York: Pantheon Books, 1956). References to this edition are noted parenthetically in the text.

35. *Natale Conti's Mythologies: A Select Translation*, trans. Anthony DiMatteo (New York: Garland, 1994), p. 321.

36. *Ovid's Metamorphosis Englished, Mythologized, and Represented in Figures*, ed. Karl Hulley and Stanley Vandersall (Lincoln: University of Nebraska Press, 1970), p. 653.

37. Virgil, *Aeneid*, trans. H. R. Fairclough (Cambridge: Harvard University Press, 1986). References to this edition are noted parenthetically in the text.

38. The Aeneid *of Thomas Phaer and Thomas Twyne: A Critical Edition Introducing Renaissance Metrical Typography,* ed. Steven Lally, The Renaissance Imagination, vol. 20 (New York: Garland, 1987). References to this edition are noted parenthetically in the text.

39. See, for example, Leonora L. Brodwin, "Milton and the Renaissance Circe," *Milton Studies* 6 (1974): 21–83. For the significance of Circe in relation to the Renaissance language arts, see Wayne Rebhorn, *The Emperor of Men's Minds: Literature and the Renaissance Discourse of Rhetoric* (Ithaca: Cornell University Press, 1995).

40. Evelyn, p. 3.

41. *Ben Jonson: The Complete Poems,* ed. George Parfitt (New York: Penguin, 1986), p. 118.

42. John Milton, *Areopagitica; For the Liberty of Unlicens'd Printing,* ed. William Haller, vol. 4, *Works of John Milton* (New York: Columbia University Press, 1931), pp. 297–98.

43. Barbara Lewalski. *The Life of John Milton* (Oxford: Blackwell, 2000), p. 68.

44. William Shakespeare, *The Tempest,* ed. Peter Holland (New York: Penguin Books, 2000). References to this edition are noted parenthetically in the text.

45. John Guillory, *Poetic Authority: Spenser, Milton, and Literary History* (New York: Columbia University Press, 1983), p. 77.

46. I take my text of Psalm 137 from *The Geneva Bible: A Facsimile of the 1560 Edition,* intro. by Lloyd E. Berry (Madison: University of Wisconsin Press, 1969). I am grateful to Kirsten Tranter for calling my attention to the relevance of this text.

47. See, for example, Samuel Taylor Coleridge, letter to William Sotheby, 10 September 1802, in *Collected Letters,* ed. E. L. Griggs (Oxford: Clarendon Press, 1956), 2:862–67; Edward S. Le Comte, "New Light on the 'Haemony' Passage in *Comus,*" *Philological Quarterly* 21, no. 4 (1942): 283–98; Don Cameron Allen, "Milton's 'Comus' as a Failure in Artistic Compromise," *English Literary History* 16 (1949): 104–19; chapter 1 in Robert Martin Adams, *Ikon: John Milton and the Modern Critics* (Ithaca: Cornell University Press, 1955); John Steadman, "'Haemony' and Christian Moly," *History of Ideas News Letter* 4 (1958): 59–60, and "Milton's *Haemony:* Etymology and Allegory," *PMLA* 77 (1962): 200–07; Charlotte Otten, "Milton's Haemony," *English Literary Renaissance* 5, no. 1 (1975): 81–95; Guillory, pp. 78–79; and Stanley Fish, *How Milton Works* (Cambridge: Harvard University Press, 2001), pp. 154–56.

48. Gilles Deleuze and Felix Guattari, *A Thousand Plateaus: Capitalism and Schizophrenia,* trans. Brian Massumi (Minneapolis: University of Minnesota Press, 1987), pp. 5–7, 20.

49. *The Rambler*, ed. Walter Jackson Bate and Albrecht B. Strauss, *The Yale Edition of the Works of Samuel Johnson* (New Haven: Yale University Press, 1969), 3:203.

50. John Milton, *Poems upon several occasions, English, Italian, and Latin, with translations. . . . With notes critical and explanatory, and other illustrations, by Thomas Warton*, 2nd ed. (London, 1791), p. xx.

51. John Milton, "Ad Patrem," in *Complete Shorter Poems*, ed. John Carey (New York: Longman, 1997), pp. 153–60.

Bibliography

Adams, Robert Martin. *Ikon: John Milton and the Modern Critics*. Ithaca: Cornell University Press, 1955.

Addison, Joseph. *Dialogues upon the Usefulness of Ancient Medals, Especially in Relation to the Latin and Greek Poets*. In *Miscellaneous Works of Joseph Addison*, 2 vols., edited by A. C. Guthkelch. London: G. Bell and Sons, 1914.

Aelian. *On the Characteristics of Animals*. Translated by A. F. Scholfield. Cambridge: Harvard University Press, 1958.

Albanese, Denise. *New Science, New World*. Durham: Duke University Press, 1996.

Alciato, Andrea. *Emblemata*. Lyons, 1550.

Aldrovandi, Ulisses. "De luscinia." In *Ornithologiae*. 3 vols. Bologna, 1599–1603.

Allen, Don Cameron. "Milton's 'Comus' as a Failure in Artistic Compromise." *English Literary History* 16 (1949): 104–19.

Arendt, Hannah. "What is Authority?" In *Between Past and Future: Eight Exercises on Political Thought*. New York: Penguin Books, 1993.

Ascham, Roger. *The Scholemaster*. Edited by John Mayor. London: G. Bell and Sons, 1934.

———. *The Scholemaster*. In *English Works*, edited by William Aldis Wright. Cambridge: Cambridge University Press, 1904.

Ashcroft, Bill, Gareth Griffiths, and Helen Tiflin, eds. *Post-Colonial Studies: The Key Concepts*. New York: Routledge, 2000.

Aston, Margaret. "English Ruins and English History: The Dissolution and the Sense of the Past." *Journal of the Warburg and Courtauld Institutes* 36 (1973): 231–55.

Auerbach, Erich. *Mimesis: The Representation of Reality in Western Literature*. Translated by Willard Trask. Princeton: Princeton University Press, 1953.

Bacon, Francis. *The Advancement of Learning.* In *Francis Bacon: A Critical Edition of the Major Works,* edited by Brian Vickers. Oxford: Oxford University Press, 1966.

―――. *The New Organon.* Edited by Lisa Jardine and translated by Michael Silverthorne. Cambridge: Cambridge University Press, 2000.

Baker, Herschel. *The Race of Time: Three Lectures on Renaissance Historiography.* Toronto: University of Toronto Press, 1967.

Barkan, Leonard. *Unearthing the Past: Archaeology and Aesthetics in the Making of Renaissance Culture.* New Haven: Yale University Press, 1999.

―――. "What Did Shakespeare Read?" In *Cambridge Companion to Shakespeare,* edited by Margreta de Grazia and Stanley Wells. Cambridge: Cambridge University Press, 2001.

Barthes, Roland. *A Lover's Discourse: Fragments.* Translated by Richard Howard. New York: Hill and Wang, 1978.

―――. *The Pleasure of the Text.* Translated by Richard Miller. New York: Hill and Wang, 2000.

Bate, Jonathan. *Shakespeare and Ovid.* Oxford: Clarendon Press, 1993.

Belon, Pierre. *L'histoire de la Nature des Oyseaux, 1555.* Edited by Philippe Gardon. Geneva: Librairie Droz, 1997.

Bibliographie Lyonnaise: Recherches sur les Imprimeurs, Libraires, Relieurs et Fondeurs de Lettres de Lyon au XVIᵉ Siècles. Paris: A. Picard et Fils, 1895–1921.

Blank, Paula. *Broken English: Dialects and the Politics of Language in Renaissance Writings.* New York: Routledge, 1996.

Booth, Stephen, ed. *Shakespeare's Sonnets.* New Haven: Yale University Press, 1977.

Bourdieu, Pierre. *Language and Symbolic Power.* Edited by John Thompson and translated by Gino Raymond and Matthew Adamson. Cambridge: Harvard University Press, 1991.

Braden, Gordon. *The Classics and English Renaissance Poetry: Three Case Studies.* New Haven: Yale University Press, 1978.

Breen, Quirinus. "Giovanni Pico della Mirandola on the Conflict of Philosophy and Rhetoric." *Journal of the History of Ideas* 13, no. 3 (1952): 384–412.

―――. "Melancthon's Reply to G. Pico della Mirandola," *Journal of the History of Ideas* 13, no. 3 (1952): 413–26.

Brodwin, Leonora L. "Milton and the Renaissance Circe." *Milton Studies* 6 (1974): 21–83.

Burckhardt, Jacob. *The Civilization of the Renaissance in Italy.* Translated by S. G. C. Middlemore. New York: Modern Library, 2002.

Calasso, Roberto. *Literature and the Gods.* Translated by Tim Parks. New York: Alfred Knopf, 2001.

Camden, William. *Britain, or A chorographicall description of the most flourishing kingdomes, England, Scotland, and Ireland, and the ilands adioyning, out of the depth of antiquitie.* Translated by Philemon Holland. London, 1610.

———. *Britannia siue Florentissimorum regnorum, Angliæ, Scotiæ, Hiberniæ, et insularum adiacentium ex intima antiquitate chorographica descriptio, authore Guilielmo Camdeno.* London, 1586.

———. *Remaines Concerning Britaine: But Especially of England and the Inhabitants thereof.* London, 1614.

Cartari, Vincenzo. *Vere e Nove Imagini.* Padua, 1615.

Cave, Terence. *The Cornucopian Text: Problems of Writing in the French Renaissance.* Oxford: Oxford University Press, 1979.

Cawdrey, Robert. "To the Reader." In *A Table Alphabeticall.* London, 1604.

Chandler, A. R. *Larks, Nightingales, and Poets.* Columbus: Ohio State University, 1937.

———. "The Nightingale in Greek and Latin Poetry." *Classical Journal* 30 (1930–45): 78–84.

Cheney, Patrick. *Spenser's Famous Flight : A Renaissance Idea of a Literary Career.* Toronto: University of Toronto Press, 1993.

Cheyfitz, Eric. *The Poetics of Imperialism: Translation and Colonization from* The Tempest *to* Tarzan. Philadelphia: University of Pennsylvania Press, 1991.

Cicero. *De oratore.* Translated by E. W. Sutton and H. Rackham. 2 vols. Cambridge: Harvard University Press, 1942.

———. *De partitione oratoria.* Translated by H. Rackham. London: William Heinemann, 1948.

———. *Letters to Atticus.* Edited and translated by D. Shackleton Bailey. Cambridge: Harvard University Press, 1999.

———. *Orator.* Translated by H. M. Hubbell. London: William Heinemann, 1952.

Clement, Francis. *The petie schole with an English orthographie, wherin by rules lately prescribed is taught a method to enable both a childe to reade perfectly within one moneth, & also the vnperfect to write English aright.* London, 1587.

Cohen, Rachel. "The Very Bad Review: Two Victorian Men of Letters, One Review from Hell." *New Yorker,* 6 October 2003, 52–67.

Coleridge, Samuel Taylor. Letter to William Sotheby, 10 September 1802. In *Collected Letters,* edited by E. L. Griggs. Oxford: Clarendon Press, 1956.

Colet, Jean. *Aeditio.* N.p., 1527.

Colie, Rosalie. *The Resources of Kind: Genre Theory in the Renaissance.* Berkeley: University of California Press, 1973.

Conti, Natale. *Natale Conti's Mythologies: A Select Translation.* Translated by Anthony DiMatteo. New York: Garland, 1994.

Cormack, Bradin. "A Power to Do Justice: Jurisdiction and Royal Authority in Early Modern English Literature." Ph.D. diss., Stanford University, 2001.

Coustau, Pierre. *Pegma cum narrationibus philosophicis.* Lyon, 1555.

———. *Pegme de Pierre Coustau: Avec les narrations philosophiques.* Lyon, 1560.

Crewe, Jonathan. *Hidden Designs: The Critical Profession and Renaissance Literature.* New York: Methuen, 1986.

Cummings, Brian. *The Literary Culture of the Reformation: Grammar and Grace.* Oxford: Oxford University Press, 2002.

Cunally, John. *Images of the Illustrious.* Princeton: Princeton University Press, 1999.

Daniel, Samuel. "Classical Metres Unsuitable for English Poetry (*c.* 1603)." In *English Renaissance Literary Criticism,* edited by Brian Vickers. Oxford: Clarendon Press, 1999.

Dean, Leonard. *Tudor Theories of History Writing.* Ann Arbor: University of Michigan Press, 1947.

de Grazia, Margreta. "Language in Elizabethan England: The Divine Model." Ph.D. diss., Princeton University, 1975.

———. "The Secularization of Language in the Seventeenth Century." *Journal of the History of Ideas* 41, no. 2 (1980): 319–29.

———. "Spenser's Antic Disposition." Plenary lecture presented at the meeting of the International Spenser Society, Cambridge, U.K., April 2001.

Deleuze, Gilles, and Felix Guattari. *A Thousand Plateaus: Capitalism and Schizophrenia.* Translated by Brian Massumi. Minneapolis: University of Minnesota Press, 1987.

Derrida, Jacques. "This Strange Institution Called Literature." In *Acts of Literature,* edited by David Attridge. London: Routledge, 1992.

Dorez, L. "Études Aldines I: La marque typographique d'Alde Manuce." *Revue des Bibliothèques* 6 (1896): 143–60.

Douglas H. Gordon Collection of French Books, Special Collections, University of Virginia Library.

DuPlessis, Georges. *Essai bibliographique sur les différents éditions des oeuvres d'Ovide ornées des planches publiées aux XVe et XVIe siècles.* Paris: Léon Techener, 1889.

The Early Modern English Dictionaries Database. Created by Ian Lancashire, University of Toronto. http://www.chass.utoronto.ca/english/emed/emedd .html.

Elkins, James. "Emblemata." In *The Domain of Images.* Ithaca: Cornell University Press, 1999.

Elsky, Martin. *Authorizing Words: Speech, Writing, and Print in the English Renaissance.* Ithaca: Cornell University Press, 1989.

Evelyn, John. *Numismata, A Discourse of Medals, Antient and Modern.* London, 1697.

———. *Sylva, or A Discourse of Forest-Trees and the Propagation of Timber in His Majesties Dominions.* 2nd ed. London, 1670.

Ferguson, Arthur. *Clio Unbound: Perception of the Social and Cultural Past in Renaissance England.* Durham: Duke University Press, 1979.

———. *Utter Antiquity: Perceptions of Prehistory in Renaissance England.* Durham: Duke University Press, 1993.

Fleming, Juliet. *Graffiti and the Writing Arts of Early Modern England.* London: Reaktion, 2001.

Fineman, Joel. "Shakespeare's Ear." In *The Subjectivity Effect in Western Literary Tradition: Essays Toward the Release of Shakespeare's Will.* Cambridge: MIT Press, 1991.

Fish, Stanley. *How Milton Works.* Cambridge: Harvard University Press, 2001.

Florio, John. *Queen Anna's new world of words, or dictionarie of the Italian and English tongues, collected, and newly much augmented.* London, 1611.

———. *A worlde of wordes, or Most copious, and exact dictionarie in Italian and English.* London, 1598.

Foucault, Michel. "Nietzsche, History, Genealogy." In *Language, Countermemory, Practice,* translated by Donald Bouchard and Sherry Simon. Ithaca: Cornell University Press, 1977.

———. *The Order of Things: An Archaeology of the Human Sciences.* New York: Vintage Books, 1994.

Fowler, Alastair. *Kinds of Literature: An Introduction to the Theory of Genres and Modes.* Cambridge: Harvard University Press, 1982.

Fussner, F. Smith. *The Historical Revolution: English Historical Writing and Thought, 1580–1640.* London: Routledge and Kegan Paul, 1962.

Gascoigne, George. *The Complaynt of Phylomene.* London, 1576.

Gellius, Aulus. *Noctes Atticae.* Translated by John Rolfe. Cambridge: Harvard University Press, 1996.

Geoffrey of Monmouth. *The History of the Kings of Britain.* Translated by Lewis Thorpe. London: Penguin Books, 1988.

Goldberg, Jonathan. *Writing Matter: From the Hands of the English Renaissance.* Stanford: Stanford University Press, 1990.

Gombrich, Ernst. "The Debate on Primitivism in Ancient Rhetoric." *Journal of the Warburg and Courtauld Institutes* 29 (1966): 24–38.

Gordon, Donald. *The Renaissance Imagination.* Edited by Stephen Orgel. Berkeley: University of California Press, 1975.

Gosson, Stephen. *The schoole of abuse, conteining a plesaunt inuectiue against poets, pipers, plaiers, iesters, and such like caterpillers of a comonwelth.* London, 1579.

Gray, Hanna. "Renaissance Humanism: The Pursuit of Eloquence." *Journal of the History of Ideas* 24, no. 4 (1963): 497–514.

Greenblatt, Stephen. *Hamlet in Purgatory.* Princeton: Princeton University Press, 2001.

Greene, Thomas. *The Light in Troy: Imitation and Discovery in Renaissance Poetry.* New Haven: Yale University Press, 1982.

Gros Louis, Kenneth R. R. "The Triumph and Death of Orpheus in the English Renaissance." *Studies in English Literature, 1500–1900* 9, no. 1 (1969): 63–80.

Grossman, Allen. "Orpheus/Philomela: Subjection and Mastery in the Founding Stories of Poetic Production and in the Logic of Our Practice." In *Poets Teaching Poets: Self and the World,* edited by Gregory Orr and Ellen Bryant Voight. Ann Arbor: University of Michigan Press, 1996.

Guillory, John. *Poetic Authority: Spenser, Milton, and Literary History.* New York: Columbia University Press, 1983.

Guthrie, W. K. C. *Orpheus and Greek Religion: A Study of the Orphic Movement.* Revised edition. London: Methuen, 1952.

Halpern, Richard. *The Poetics of Primitive Accumulation: English Renaissance Culture and the Genealogy of Capital.* Ithaca: Cornell University Press, 1991.

Hartman, Geoffrey. "The Voice of the Shuttle: Language from the Point of View of Literature." In *Beyond Formalism: Literary Essays, 1958–1970.* New Haven: Yale University Press, 1970.

Harvey, Richard. *Philadelphus, or A Defence of the Brutes, and the Brutans History.* London, 1593.

Hawkins, Henry. *Partheneia Sacra, 1633.* In *English Emblem Books* 10, series ed. Karl Josef Höltgen. Menston: Scolar Press, 1971.

Heidegger, Martin. "The Origin of the Work of Art." In *Basic Writings,* edited by David Farrell Krell. San Francisco: Harper Collins, 1993.

Helgerson, Richard. *Self-Crowned Laureates: Spenser, Jonson, Milton, and the Literary System.* Berkeley: University of California Press, 1983.

Homer. *Chapman's Homer: The Iliad, the Odyssey, and the Lesser Homerica.* 2 vols. Translated by George Chapman. Edited by Allardyce Nicoll. New York: Pantheon Books, 1956.

————. *The Odyssey.* Translated by A. T. Murray. Revised by George E. Dimock. Cambridge: Harvard University Press, 1995.

Hooker, Richard. *Of the Laws of Ecclesiastical Polity.* Edited by Arthur Stephen McGrade. Cambridge: Cambridge University Press, 1989.

Horace. *Ars Poetica.* In *Satires, Epistles, and* Ars Poetica, translated by H. Rushton Fairclough. Cambridge: Harvard University Press, 1961.

————. *The Epistles of Horace: A Bilingual Edition.* Translated by David Ferry. New York: Farrar, Straus and Giroux, 2001.

————. *Odes and Epodes.* Translated by C. E. Bennett. Cambridge: Harvard University Press, 1968.

The Illustrated Bartsch. 165 vols. New York, 1978–.

Isidore of Seville. *Etymologiae.* Edited by W. M. Lindsay. Oxford: Oxford University Press, 1911.

Jed, Stephanie. *Chaste Thinking: The Rape of Lucretia and the Birth of Humanism.* Bloomington: Indiana University Press, 1989.

Johnson, Samuel. "Preface to *The Plays of William Shakespeare.*" In *Selected Poetry and Prose,* edited by Frank Brady and W. K. Wimsatt. Berkeley: University of California Press, 1977.

————. *The Rambler.* Edited by Walter Jackson Bate and Albrecht B. Strauss. Vol. 3 of *The Yale Edition of the Works of Samuel Johnson.* New Haven: Yale University Press, 1969.

Jones, Richard Foster. *The Triumph of English: A Survey of Opinions Concerning the Vernacular from the Introduction of Printing to the Restoration.* Stanford: Stanford University Press, 1953.

Jonson, Ben. *Ben Jonson.* Edited by Ian Donaldson. Oxford: Oxford University Press, 1985.

————. *Complete Poems.* Edited by George Parfitt. New York: Penguin Books, 1988.

Keats, John. "On Sitting Down to Read *King Lear* Once Again." In *Complete Poems,* edited by John Barnard. New York: Penguin Books, 1988.

Kendrick, T. D. *British Antiquaries.* London: Methuen, 1950.

Keilen, Sean. "Exemplary Metals: Classical Numismatics and the Commerce of Humanism." *Word & Image* 18, no. 3 (2002): 282–94.

Kennet, Basil. *The Lives and Characters of the Ancient Grecian Poets.* London, 1697.

Klindienst, Patricia. "The Voice of the Shuttle is Ours." In *Rape and Representation,* edited by Lynn Higgins and Brenda Silver. New York: Columbia University Press, 1991.

Kramnick, Jonathan Brody. *Making the English Canon: Print Capitalism and the Cultural Past, 1700–1770.* Cambridge: Cambridge University Press, 1998.

Le Comte, Edward S. "New Light on the 'Haemony' Passage in *Comus.*" *Philological Quarterly* 21, no. 4 (1942): 283–98.

Leland, John. *Assertio inclytissimi Arturii.* In *The Famous Historie of Chinon of Middleton . . . to which is added* The Assertion of King Arthur, edited by Walter Mead. Early English Text Society, o.s., no. 165. London: Oxford University Press, 1925 for 1923.

Levine, Joseph. "Tudor Antiquaries," *History Today* 20 (1970): 278–85.

Lewalski, Barbara. *The Life of John Milton.* Oxford: Blackwell, 2000.

———, ed. *Renaissance Genres: Essays on Theory, History, and Interpretation.* Cambridge: Harvard University Press, 1986.

Lexikon Iconographicum Mythologiae Classicae 7, no. 1 (1994): 74, 96.

Loewenstein, David, and Janel Mueller, eds. *Cambridge History of Early Modern English Literature.* Cambridge: Cambridge University Press, 2002.

Lovejoy, Arthur, and George Boas. *Primitivism and Related Ideas in Antiquity.* Baltimore: Johns Hopkins University Press, 1935.

Lucian. "Heracles." In *Lucian,* translated by A. M. Harmon. Cambridge: Harvard University Press, 1913.

MacLean, Gerald. *Time's Witness: Historical Representations in English Poetry, 1603–1660.* Madison: University of Wisconsin Press, 1990.

Manning, John. *The Emblem.* London: Reaktion Books, 2002.

———. "Geffrey Whitney's Unpublished Emblems: Further Evidence of Indebtedness to Continental Traditions." In *The English Emblem and the Continental Tradition,* edited by Peter Daly. New York: AMS Press, 1988.

Manwood, John. *A Treatise and Discourse of the Lawes of the Forrest.* New York: Garland, 1978.

Marotti, Arthur. *Manuscript, Print, and the English Renaissance Lyric.* Ithaca: Cornell University Press, 1995.

Marvell, Andrew. "To His Coy Mistress." In *Complete Poems,* edited by Elizabeth Story Donno. New York: Penguin Books, 1985.

Marx, Karl. *Capital: A Critique of Political Economy.* Translated by Ben Fowkes. 3 vols. New York: Penguin Books, 1990.

Matz, Robert. *Defending Literature in Early Modern England: Renaissance Literary Theory in Social Context.* Cambridge: Cambridge University Press, 2000.

McKisack, May. *Medieval History in the Tudor Age.* Oxford: Oxford University Press, 1971.

McLaughlin, Martin. *Literary Imitation in the Italian Renaissance: The Theory and Practice of Literary Imitation in Italy from Dante to Bembo.* Oxford: Clarendon Press, 1995.

Mendyk, Stan. *'Speculum Britanniae': Regional Study, Antiquarianism, and Science in Britain to 1700.* Toronto: University of Toronto Press, 1989.

Miller, J. Hillis. *On Literature.* New York: Routledge, 2002.

———. "The Triumph of Theory, the Resistance to Reading, and the Question of the Material Base." *Publications of the Modern Language Association* 102, no. 3 (1987): 281–91.

Milton, John. *Areopagitica; For the Liberty of Unlicens'd Printing.* Edited by

William Haller. Vol. 4 of *Works of John Milton*. New York: Columbia University Press, 1931.

—. "Beatiores reddit homines ars quam ignorantia." Edited by Donald Lemen Clark and translated by Bromley Smith. Vol. 12 of *Works of John Milton*. New York: Columbia University Press, 1936.

—. *The History of Britain, that Part especially now call'd England, from the first Traditional Beginning, continu'd to the Norman Conquest*. London, 1672.

—. *Milton: The Complete Shorter Poems*. Edited by John Carey. 2nd ed. New York: Longman, 1997.

—. *Paradise Lost*. Edited by Alistair Fowler. London: Longman, 1998.

—. *Poems upon several occasions, English, Italian, and Latin, with translations. . . . With notes critical and explanatory, and other illustrations, by Thomas Warton*. 2nd ed. London, 1791.

—. *The Second Defense of the English People*. Translated by Robert Fellowes. In *John Milton: Complete Poems and Major Prose*, edited by Merritt Hughes. New York: Macmillan, 1957.

Miola, Robert. *Shakespeare's Reading*. Oxford: Oxford University Press, 2000.

Montrose, Louis. "Professing the Renaissance: The Poetics and Politics of Culture." In *The New Historicism*, edited by H. Aram Veeser. New York: Routledge, 1989.

Mulcaster, Richard. "The Peroration." In *The First Part of the Elementarie*. London, 1582.

Murray, Gilbert. *The Classical Tradition in Poetry*. Cambridge: Harvard University Press, 1927.

Nagy, Gregory. *Poetry as Performance: Homer and Beyond*. Cambridge: Cambridge University Press, 1996.

Niccols, Richard. *The Cuckow*. London, 1609.

Nietzsche, Friedrich. *The Gay Science*. Translated by Walter Kaufmann. New York: Vintage Books, 1974.

—. "The Utility and Liability of History for Life." In *Unfashionable Observations*, translated by Richard T. Gray. Stanford: Stanford University Press, 1995.

Orgel, Stephen. "The Example of Hercules." In *Mythographie der frühen Neuzeit: Ihre Anwedung in den Künsten*, edited by Walther Killy. Wiesbaden: Otto Harrassowitz, 1984.

Otten, Charlotte. "Milton's Haemony." *English Literary Renaissance* 5, no. 1, (1975): 81–95.

Ovid. *Metamorphoseon Ovidianarum*. Cologne, 1602.

—. *Metamorphoses*. Edited by W. S. Anderson. Leipzig: K. G. Saur, 2001.

————. *Metamorphoses Ouidii.* Translated by Johann Spreng. 1563.

————. *Ovid's* Metamorphoses: *The Arthur Golding Translation.* Edited by John Frederick Nims. Philadelphia: Paul Dry, 2000.

————. *Ovid's Metamorphosis Englished, Mythologiz'd, and Represented in Figures.* Translated by George Sandys. Oxford, 1632.

————. *Ovid's* Metamorphosis *Englished, Mythologized, and Represented in Figures.* Translated by George Sandys. Edited by Karl Hulley and Stanley Vandersall. Lincoln: University of Nebraska Press, 1970.

————. *P. Ovidii Nasonis Metamorphoses.* Antwerp, 1591.

————. *Pub. Ovidii Nasonis Metamorphoseon.* Translated by Jakob Micyllus. Leipzig, 1582.

————. *Tetrasticha in Ovidii Metam. lib. XV.* Translated by Johann Posthius. 1563.

Palmer, Thomas. *The Emblems of Thomas Palmer: Two Hundred Poosees.* Edited by John Manning. New York: AMS Press, 1988.

Parry, Graham. *The Trophies of Time: English Antiquarians of the Seventeenth Century.* Oxford: Oxford University Press, 1995.

Parshall, Peter. "*Imago Contrafacta:* Images and Facts in the Northern Renaissance." *Art History* 16, no. 4 (1993): 554–79.

Patey, Douglas. "The Eighteenth Century Invents the Canon." *Modern Language Studies* 18, no. 1 (1988): 17–37.

Patrologiae cursus completus: omnium SS. patrum, doctorum scriptorumque ecclesiasticorum. Edited by Jacques-Paul Migne. Paris: Migne, 1844–.

Peacham, Henry. *The Compleat Gentleman.* London, 1634.

————. *Minerva Britannia.* London, 1612.

Petrarch. "Ad Lelium suum." In *Rime, Trionfi e Poesie Latine,* edited by F. Nieri. Milan: Riccardo Ricciardi, 1951.

————. *The* Canzoniere *or* Rerum vulgarium fragmenta. Translated by Mark Musa. Bloomington: Indiana University Press, 1996.

Pfeffer, Wendy. *The Change of Philomel: The Nightingale Medieval Literature.* New York: Peter Lang, 1985.

Pick, B. "Thraksiche Münzbilder." *Jahrbuch des Kaiserlich Deutschen Archäologischen Instituts* 13 (1898): 134–36.

Piggot, Stuart. *Ancient Britons and the Antiquarian Imagination: Ideas from the Renaissance to the Regency.* London: Thames and Hudson, 1989.

Pliny. *The historie of the world: Commonly called, the naturall historie of C. Plinius Secundus.* Translated by Philemon Holland. London, 1601.

————. *Natural History.* Translated by H. Rackham. Cambridge: Harvard University Press, 1947.

Pocock, J. G. A. *The Ancient Constitution and the Feudal Law: English Historical Thought in the Seventeenth Century.* New York: W. W. Norton, 1967.

Pointer, John. *Britannia Romana, or Roman Antiquities in Britain.* London, 1724.

Politeuphuia. Wits common wealth. London, 1598.

Praz, Mario. *Studies in Seventeenth-Century Imagery.* 2nd ed. Rome: Edizioni di Storia e Letteratura, 1964.

Puttenham, George. *The Arte of English Poesie.* London, 1589.

Pye, Christopher. *The Vanishing: Shakespeare, the Subject, and Early Modern Culture.* Durham: Duke University Press, 2000.

Quiller-Couch, Arthur. *The Art of Writing.* New York: Capricorn Books, 1961.

Quintilian. *The Orator's Education.* Translated by Donald Russell. 5 vols. Cambridge: Harvard University Press, 2001.

Rebhorn, Wayne. *The Emperor of Men's Minds: Literature and the Renaissance Discourse of Rhetoric.* Ithaca: Cornell University Press, 1995.

Riese, Alexander, ed. *Anthologia latina.* Leipzig: Teubner, 1894.

Ross, Trevor. *The Making of the English Literary Canon: From the Middle Ages to the Late Eighteenth Century.* Montreal: McGill-Queen's University Press, 1998.

Rouille, Guillaume. *Promptuaire des medalles.* Lyons, 1577.

Rousseau, Jean-Jacques. "Essay on the Origin of Languages." In *Rousseau: The Discourses and Other Early Political Writings,* translated by Victor Gourevitch. Cambridge: Cambridge University Press, 1997.

Rubel, Veré. *Poetic Diction in the English Renaissance: From Skelton through Spenser.* New York: MLA, 1941.

Saltwood, Robert. *A comparyson bytwene. iiij. byrdes, the larke, the nyghtyngale, ye thrusshe [and] the cuko, for theyr syngynge who shuld be chauntoure of the quere.* Canterbury, 1533.

Sambucus. *Emblemata.* Antwerp, 1564.

Seneca. *De brevitate vitae.* In *Dialogues and Letters,* translated by C. D. N. Costa. New York: Penguin Books, 1997.

————. *De brevitate vitae.* Vol. 2 of *Moral Essays.* Translated by John Basore. Cambridge: Harvard University Press, 1951.

————. *Thyestes.* In *Seneca: His Tenne Tragedies,* translated by Thomas Newton. Bloomington: Indiana University Press, 1966.

Seznec, Jean. *Survival of the Pagan Gods: The Mythological Tradition and Its Place in Renaissance Humanism and Art.* Translated by Barbara Sessions. New York: Pantheon Books, 1953.

Shakespeare, William. *Antony and Cleopatra.* Edited by A. R. Braunmuller. New York: Penguin Books, 1999.

————. *Complete Sonnets and Poems.* Edited by Colin Burrow. Oxford: Oxford University Press, 2002.

————. *Cymbeline.* Edited by Peter Holland. New York: Penguin Books, 2000.

———. *Henry V.* Edited by Claire McEachern. New York: Penguin Books, 1999.

———. *A Midsummer Night's Dream.* Edited by Russ McDonald. New York: Penguin Books, 2000.

———. *The Tempest.* Edited by Peter Holland. New York: Penguin Books, 2000.

———. *Titus Andronicus.* Edited by Russ McDonald. New York: Penguin Books, 2000.

———. *Venus and Adonis.* In *Narrative Poems,* edited by Jonathan Crewe. New York: Penguin Books, 1999.

Shippey, Thomas. "Listening to the Nightingale." *Comparative Literature* 22, no. 1 (1970): 46–60.

Sidney, Philip. *Sir Philip Sidney: A Critical Edition of the Major Works.* Edited by Katharine Duncan-Jones. Oxford: Oxford University Press, 1989.

Simpson, James. "Ageism: Leland, Bale, and the Laborious Start of English Literary History, 1350–1550." *New Medieval Literatures* 1 (1997): 213–36.

Skinner, Quentin. *Reason and Rhetoric in the Philosophy of Hobbes.* Cambridge: Cambridge University Press, 1996.

Speed, John. *The History of Great Britaine under the conquests of ye Romans, Saxons, Danes and Normans.* London, 1610.

Spenser, Edmund. *The Shepheardes Calender.* In *The Shorter Poems,* edited by Richard McCabe. New York: Penguin Books, 1999.

Sprat, Thomas. *The History of the Royal Society.* London, 1667.

Steadman, John. "Appendix: Renaissance Emblems of Truth and Eloquence." In *The Hill and the Labyrinth: Discourse and Certitude in Milton and His Near-Contemporaries.* Berkeley: University of California Press, 1984.

———. "'Haemony' and Christian Moly." *History of Ideas News Letter* 4 (1958): 59–60.

———. "Milton's *Haemony*: Etymology and Allegory." *PMLA* 77 (1962): 200–07.

Suetonius. *De grammaticis et rhetoribus.* Translated by John Rolfe. Cambridge: Harvard University Press, 2001.

Swann, Marjorie. *Curiosities and Texts: The Culture of Collecting in Early Modern England.* Philadelphia: University of Pennsylvanian Press, 2001.

Tacitus. *Dialogus de oratoribus.* Translated by W. Peterson and M. Winterbottom. Cambridge: Harvard University Press, 2000.

Terry, Richard. *Poetry and the Making of the English Literary Past, 1660–1781.* Oxford: Oxford University Press, 2001.

Todorov, Tzvetan. *Genres in Discourse.* Translated by Catherine Porter. Cambridge: Cambridge University Press, 1990.

Tottel, Richard. "To the Reader." In *Songes and Sonnettes*. London, 1557.

Tucker, T. G. *The Foreign Debt of English Literature*. London: George Bell and Sons, 1907.

Tung, Mason. "Whitney's *A Choice of Emblemes* Revisited: A Comparative Study of the Manuscript and the Printed Versions." *Studies in Bibliography* 29 (1976): 32–101.

Tüskés, Gábor. "Imitation and Adaptation in Late Humanist Emblematic Poetry: Zsámboky (Sambucus) and Whitney." *Emblematica* 11 (2001): 261–92.

Valla, Lorenzo. *On Pleasure*. Translated by A. Kent Hieatt and Maristella Lorch. New York: Abaris Books, 1977.

Van Es, Bart. *Spenser's Forms of History*. Oxford: Oxford University Press, 2002.

Varchi, Benedetto. *Lezzioni*. Florence, 1590. Quoted in Bernard Weinberg, *A History of Literary Criticism in the Italian Renaissance*. Chicago: University of Chicago Press, 1961, 1:135–36.

Vergil, Polydore. *On Discovery*. Translated by Brian Copenhaver. In *I Tatti Renaissance Library* 6. Cambridge: Harvard University Press, 2002.

Virgil. *Aeneid*. Translated by H. R. Fairclough. Cambridge: Harvard University Press, 1986.

———. *The* Aeneid *of Thomas Phaer and Thomas Twyne: A Critical Edition Introducing Renaissance Metrical Typography*. Translated by Thomas Phaer and Thomas Twyne. Edited by Steven Lally. Vol. 20 of *The Renaissance Imagination*. New York: Garland, 1987.

Vitruvius. *On Architecture*. Translated by Frank Granger. Cambridge: Harvard University Press, 1970.

Vives, Juan Luis. "Vestitus, et de ambulation matutina." In *Linguae latinae exercitatio*. Milan, 1539.

von Pauly, August Friedrich. "Das singende und weissagende Haupt des O[rpheus]." Vol. 18, of *Real-encyclopädie der classischen Alterthumswissenschaft*. Stuttgart: J. B. Metzlersche, 1922.

Walker, D. P. "Orpheus the Theologian and Renaissance Platonists." *Journal of the Warburg and Courtauld Institutes* 16 (1953): 100–20.

Wall, Wendy. *The Imprint of Gender: Authorship and Publication in the English Renaissance*. Ithaca: Cornell University Press, 1993.

Warden, John, ed. *Orpheus: The Metamorphoses of a Myth*. Toronto: University of Toronto Press, 1985.

Warton, Thomas. *The History of English Poetry, from the Eleventh to the Seventeenth Century*. London, 1778 and 1781. Reprint, London: Ward, Lock, 1870.

Webbe, William. *A Discourse of Englishe Poesie.* London, 1586.

Weimann, Robert. *Authority and Representation in Early Modern Discourse.* Edited by David Hillman. Baltimore: Johns Hopkins University Press, 1996.

Weinberg, Bernard. *A History of Literary Criticism in the Italian Renaissance.* 2 vols. Chicago: University of Chicago Press, 1961.

Weiss, Roberto. "The Study of Ancient Numismatics during the Renaissance (1313–1517)." *Numismatic Chronicle,* 7th series, 8 (1968): 187.

Whitney, Geffrey. *A Choice of Emblemes.* Manuscript. MS Typ 14. Houghton Library, Harvard University.

———. *A Choice of Emblemes.* Edited by Henry Green. London, 1866. Reprint, New York: Benjamin Bloom, 1967.

———. *A Choice of Emblemes.* Edited by John Manning. Aldershot: Scolar Press, 1989.

Williams, Raymond. *Keywords: A Vocabulary of Culture and Society.* Revised edition. New York: Oxford University Press, 1983.

Wilson, Thomas. *The Arte of Rhetorique.* London, 1553.

Index

Numbers in italics refer to pages with illustrations.